'*Policing Non-Citizens* makes a landmark contribution to the study of crimmigration law. Leanne Weber masterfully connects ground-breaking empirical findings to the kind of theoretical and policy arguments about policing and migration that provide genuine guidance for contemporary governance. The book is a must-read for anyone concerned about the connections between policing, borders, and citizenship in our globalizing world.'

Juliet Stumpf, Professor of Law, Lewis & Clark Law School, Portland, Oregon, USA

'In this study Leanne Weber vigorously investigates the role of the police and other agencies in identifying unlawful non-citizens in Australia against the backdrop of key theoretical debates on borders and belonging. In a unique and timely way, this book bridges the divide between policing literature and migration studies.'

Joanne van der Leun, Professor of Criminology, Leiden Law School, the Netherlands

'Leanne Weber offers a meticulous analysis and integrative examination of how nodal governance and third party policing is used to police non-citizens. Her research exposes a wide range of street-level manifestations of state power under complex and dynamic conditions of global mobility in the 21st century. *Policing Non-Citizens* is, therefore, essential reading for scholars, practitioners and policy makers who want to better understand and respond to the global crisis that compromises a secure belonging for all.'

Lorraine Mazerolle is an ARC Laureate Fellow and Research Professor in the Institute for Social Science Research (ISSR) at the University of Queensland, Australia

'Weber's case study of immigration enforcement in New South Wales, set in rich analytical context, describes a system transformed by neoliberalism and the growing capacities of information sharing. Australia has abandoned the visibly cruel "attrition through enforcement" model in favor of a more insidious networking of social agencies to remove people "out of place" with enforcement through attrition.'

Professor Doris Marie Provine, School of Social Transformation, Arizona State University, USA

POLICING NON-CITIZENS

Policing Non-Citizens explores the intersection between policing, border control and citizenship under the transformative conditions of globalisation. This book concentrates on the policing of the internal border and the networked nature of that border policing effort. It draws on empirical research conducted in the Australian state of New South Wales which was designed to identify the means by which individuals designated as 'unlawful non-citizens' are detected by networks of public and private agencies.

Guided by a nodal governance framework, but drawing also on the literature relating to crimmigration, government-at-a-distance and third party policing, *Policing Non-Citizens* combines detailed empirical data with the identification of broader themes in contemporary governance. These include the pluralisation of migration policing partners, the reliance on new technologies and modes of identity-based surveillance, the dynamics of cooperation and resistance, points of overlap and convergence between criminal and immigration law, the reliance on risk-based and intelligence-led technologies, and the structural embedding of border control to create a potentially ubiquitous border.

This book will be of interest to academics and students from a range of disciplines: criminology, sociology, law, anthropology, social geography and policy, citizenship and migration studies.

Leanne Weber is Senior Larkins Research Fellow in the School of Political and Social Inquiry at Monash University, Melbourne, Australia. She researches border control using criminological and human rights frameworks. Her previous books include *Stop and Search: Police Power in Global Context* (2012, Routledge, with Ben Bowling) and *Globalization and Borders: Death at the Global Frontier* (2011, Palgrave, with Sharon Pickering).

Routledge Studies in Criminal Justice, Borders and Citizenship

Edited by
Katja Franko Aas, *University of Oslo*
Mary Bosworth, *University of Oxford*
Sharon Pickering, *Monash University*

Globalising forces have had a profound impact on the nature of contemporary criminal justice and law more generally. This is evident in the increasing salience of borders and mobility in the production of illegality and social exclusion. *Routledge Studies in Criminal Justice, Borders and Citizenship* showcases contemporary studies that connect criminological scholarship to migration studies and explore the intellectual resonances between the two. It provides an opportunity to reflect on the theoretical and methodological challenges posed by mass mobility and its control. By doing that, it charts an intellectual space and establishes a theoretical tradition within criminology to house scholars of immigration control, race and citizenship, including those who traditionally publish *either* in general criminological *or* in anthropological, sociological, refugee studies, human rights and other publications.

POLICING
NON-CITIZENS

Leanne Weber

Routledge
Taylor & Francis Group

LONDON AND NEW YORK

First published 2013
by Routledge
2 Park Square, Milton Park, Abingdon, Oxon OX14 4RN

Simultaneously published in the USA and Canada
by Routledge
711 Third Avenue, New York, NY 10017

Routledge is an imprint of the Taylor & Francis Group, an informa business

British Library Cataloguing in Publication Data
A catalogue record for this book is available from the British Library

Library of Congress Cataloging-in-Publication Data
Weber, Leanne.
Policing non-citizens/Leanne Weber.
pages; cm
1. Immigration enforcement. 2. Illegal aliens. 3. Emigration and immigration—
Government policy. 4. Police. 5. Border patrols. 6. Security, Internal. I. Title.
JV6038.W43 2013
363.2′3—dc23
2013003617

ISBN: 978-0-415-81128-6 (hbk)
ISBN: 978-0-415-81129-3 (pbk)
ISBN: 978-0-203-07050-5 (ebk)

Typeset in Bembo
by Book Now Ltd, London

MIX
Paper from
responsible sources
FSC   FSC® C013056
www.fsc.org

Printed and bound in Great Britain by
TJ International Ltd, Padstow, Cornwall

CONTENTS

ILLUSTRATIONS

Figures

Tables

Boxes

SERIES EDITORS' PREFACE

In this detailed account of policing in Australia, Leanne Weber explores how contemporary law enforcement practices are shifting in response to globalisation. As police around the world are increasingly required to enforce immigration law and secure the border, *Policing Non-Citizens* has implications for our understanding of security and policing more broadly. Whereas the police have typically been considered in relation to the nation state, imbricated in the rights and duties of the citizenry, Weber suggests that their role and justification is changing.

This is a qualitatively rich account of the rise and rise of 'crimmigration' based on close examination of the ways immigration processes are drawn upon by the police in regulating groups, individuals and activities deemed undesirable. Immigration powers, which fall short of the same individual protections and high standards the criminal justice system and criminal law historically demands of state agencies, Weber argues, are increasingly used to solve policing 'problems'. As such, this study reveals the precariousness of those with irregular or temporary migration status and the ways policing cultures can drive the entanglement of migration and criminal justice endeavours. It foregrounds important theoretical and empirical trajectories for criminological research focused on internal borders and the ways these are operationalized and experienced by those charged with their patrol.

Drawing on extensive empirical research, as well as theoretical debates within and beyond criminology, Weber has produced a nuanced account of state power under conditions of mobility. While building on the important body of work on racial and ethnic discrimination in policing, the book is also a significant innovation, since it is among the first to systematically address the issue of internal border controls. We are pleased to include this ground-breaking study in the *Criminal Justice, Borders and Citizenship* series. As with the other volumes, this book reveals how a consideration of migration alters the frame of understanding of quite familiar parts of the criminal justice system.

Katja Franko Aas
Mary Bosworth
Sharon Pickering
March 2013

ABOUT THIS BOOK

As with other periods of momentous and rapid change, globalisation has given rise to deep-seated problems of order. While structural changes, such as the deregulation and global reach of capitalism and associated political turmoil, are the primary sources of instability in the developed world, contemporary problems of insecurity are often attributed to the spontaneous incursions of suspect populations into zones of relative affluence and order (Weber and Bowling 2008). These unsettling developments have led to intensified efforts by developed states to reinforce and redefine boundaries of belonging and entitlement in the name of security (Bosniak 2006; Bosworth and Guild 2008; Dauvergne 2008; Watson 2009; Zedner 2010). These developments raise many questions about the policing of non-citizens and others whose claims to belong are disputed or unclear. At the external border, unwanted mobilities may be actively 'policed out' using pre-emptive technologies designed to selectively prevent border crossing. This book concentrates on the policing of the internal border and the networked nature of that border policing effort. It draws on empirical research conducted in the Australian state of New South Wales (NSW) which was designed to identify the means by which individuals designated under federal law as 'unlawful non-citizens' are detected by networks of public and private agencies ('Policing Migration in Australia: An Analysis of Onshore Migration Policing Networks', Australian Research Council Discovery Grant DP0774554, Chief Investigator Leanne Weber, Research Team Amanda Wilson, Jenny Wise and Alyce McGovern).

The aims of the migration policing study were to establish the role played by the major migration policing partners in NSW, to consider why they contribute to the policing of migration, and to contemplate the wider social and institutional implications of these governmental practices directed exclusively at the policing of non-citizens. In Australia, many actors, including the Department of Immigration and Citizenship (DIAC), state and federal police agencies, a range of regulatory and service industry organisations, private employers and individual citizens, contribute to migration policing. However, as the institution most closely aligned with the production of order, it is particularly pertinent to ask what role state police are playing in the emerging modes of ordering associated with globalisation. I have argued elsewhere that a fundamental re-evaluation of this role is needed in societies 'that are not only multi-cultural but also globally inter-connected' (Weber and Bowling 2004: 212). This book therefore pays extra attention to the role of the NSW Police Force in patrolling the boundaries of belonging, and includes a chapter dedicated to policing strategies that straddle the criminal–administrative or 'crimmigration' nexus (Stumpf 2006).

In his classic text, Waddington characterised modern policing as the policing of *citizens* who possess democratic rights and freedoms which are at one and the same time protected and potentially threatened by the rise of such a powerful state institution (Waddington 1999). Waddington sees citizenship and the police role as so closely aligned that he argues that it is 'tempting to regard the installation of Peel's professional police as itself an expression of citizenship' (Waddington 1999: 22). Loader and Walker (2007: 27) also understand modern police organisations to be 'deeply implicated in the wider cultural project of nation-formation', and align the production of security by the state with the delineation of a bounded political community. Elsewhere, Loader has argued that new strategies are needed if 'policing is to be capable of recognizing, rather than denigrating or silencing, the security claims of *all citizens*' (Loader 2006: 213, emphasis added). These authors argue for a reassertion of inclusive, social democratic traditions in which policing and order maintenance might be constructed as public goods. However, in a rapidly globalising world, fundamental questions arise about who is a member of the 'public', and thus entitled to reap the benefits of collective security. Loader and Walker acknowledge that globalisation potentially expands the boundaries within which security is to be pursued, and advocate a 'shift towards transnational sites and networks of security provision' (Loader and Walker 2007: 236). But this provides no clear answer to the question they pose themselves, namely: 'Who or what is the proper object of security – individuals, collectivities, states, humanity at large?' (Loader and Walker 2007: 9). In the absence of a 'global sovereign' who can be expected to work for the security of humanity at large, these authors recognise that border control as currently practised can sacrifice the security of others in the name of security for recognised citizens.

These dilemmas are not exclusive to the globalisation context. We do not lack historical precedents regarding the policing of non-citizens, since colonisation is effectively the policing of populations who have been stripped of citizenship rights within their own countries. Waddington recognises this link between colonialism and citizenship, and notes that colonialism marks out a 'sharp distinction … between exercising coercive authority over one's own citizens and others whose claim to citizenship [is] non-existent or rejected' (Waddington 1999: 23). Finer distinctions can also be drawn within ostensibly democratic societies in which the legal and political rights of marginalised groups are subverted in practice by inequalities in social and economic power – a phenomenon described by Young (2003: 449) as 'citizenship thwarted'. In this case, policing effectively offers 'protection to citizens from the internal threat posed by those on the margins of citizenship' (Waddington 1999: 42). A historical example of a similar form of exclusionary policing is the consigning of 'pauper-claimants' to the control of a disparate group of 'social police' whose members were variously responsible for enforcing the English 'poor laws' as well as the criminal law (Neocleous 2000). As Neocleous (2000: 82) explains: 'social police is in some sense a form of border patrol – the policing of the borders of citizenship; the borders, that is, of the categories defining those who are to come under the greater control, surveillance and administration by the state'.

In *Policing Non-Citizens* I explore this intersection between policing, border control and citizenship in the context of the transformative conditions of globalisation. While a key role of policing has been to 'keep the [socially] excluded in their place' (1998; Waddington 1999: 41, parenthesis added), this book is concerned with how the (literally) excluded are expelled from places not considered to be 'theirs'. Although the role of state police is of particular interest in this study, policing is broadly conceived as the set of institutions tasked with 'producing and administering a general condition of stability and prosperity' (Loader and Walker 2007: 27), with migration policing concerned with pursuing those objectives through the enforcement of immigration law.

While the boundary between citizens and non-citizens remains an important distinction, the divide between those with legal status and those without is the primary focus of internal border policing. However, as Van der Leun has noted, the consequences of being categorised as 'illegal' are not automatic but depend heavily on actual levels of enforcement (Van der Leun 2003). The following chapters explain what migration policing looks like in NSW, who takes part in the detection of unlawful non-citizens, why they do it and how they go about it. While a complete survey of the task of policing non-citizens would also include discussion of non-citizens or other immigrants as victims, offenders and users of police services, the present study engages with non-citizens *qua* non-citizens, and considers the everyday practices by which they are subjected to surveillance and apprehension *because* of their extant, or potential, illegal status. Although the divide between legally and illegally present non-citizens is the primary site for immigration enforcement, migration policing is also observed to patrol the boundary between citizens and non-citizens, and to sometimes encroach beyond it. This book begins with an overview of some theoretical positions on policing, immigration control and contemporary technologies for the production of security which will help to illuminate these practices.

ACKNOWLEDGEMENTS

The empirical study that underpins this book began life at the University of New South Wales (UNSW) in Sydney, then migrated across state borders to Monash University in Melbourne. The first acknowledgement that must be made is to the Australian Research Council (ARC) for financing the empirical work through the award of a Discovery Grant (Policing Migration in Australia: An Analysis of Onshore Migration Policing Networks, DP0774554). While the project resided at UNSW, Alyce McGovern, and then later Jenny Wise and Amanda Wilson, diligently collected documentary information, assisted with the fieldwork, analysed survey responses and kept track of all the disparate research materials that were collected. Their assistance was indispensible to the successful completion of the study. Once the research was located at Monash University, Rebecca Powell provided some of the crucial finishing touches in response to queries that arose while I was drafting the book.

It was Monash University that provided me with the opportunity to turn the research findings into a book through the award of a three-year research fellowship via its competitive Larkins Fellowship scheme. I am extremely grateful for the opportunity this has provided to complete this project and advance many others. The vibrant research environment within the criminology group at Monash University has offered the intellectual stimulation and encouragement critical to bringing major projects to fruition. I would like to acknowledge the close group of colleagues with whom I have worked on other ARC projects on a regular basis for the past few years – namely, Michael Grewcock and Claudia Tazretier from UNSW, and Marie Segrave and Sharon Pickering from Monash University, but especially Sharon Pickering whose seemingly boundless energy continues to be an inspiration. Helen Gibbon from UNSW and Dean Wilson from the University of Plymouth provided very helpful and considered feedback on several of the chapters.

Many of the ideas that have found their way into this book have been influenced by the writings of international scholars who are pioneers in developing a criminology of the border, and by personal discussions with many of them at international conferences and invitational workshops. Foremost among this group are Ben Bowling of King's College London, Katja Franko Aas of the University of Oslo, Mary Bosworth and Lucia Zedner of Oxford University, Dario Melossi from the University of Bologna, Nancy Wonders and Ray Michalowski from Northern Arizona University, Marie Provine and Marjorie Zatz from Arizona State University, and latterly Vanessa Barker from Stockholm University, Juliet Stumpf from Lewis and Clarke Law School and Joanne Van der Leun from the University of Leiden. The online Border Crossing Observatory (www.borderobservatory.org), founded by Sharon Pickering and hosted at Monash University, has enhanced my ongoing contact with this active community of scholars.

Finally, sincere thanks are due to the team that has helped to craft this book and launch it into the world. The editorial team at Routledge has been truly supportive and a pleasure to work with. Thanks go in particular to editorial assistant Nicola Hartley, who responded promptly and supportively to all my queries and obtained the evocative image featured on the book's cover. Commissioning Editor Tom Sutton welcomed *Policing Non-Citizens* into the new Studies in Criminal Justice, Borders and Citizenship series with an enthusiasm that encouraged me to try to make this book the best that it can be. In Melbourne, I was fortunate to be assisted by Julia Farrell, who applied her prodigious editorial skills to help finesse the manuscript with diligence, patience and flair. My partner Tony endured many nights alone in front of the television while I worked late on this book, which I suspect he didn't really mind.

Copyright permissions

The following material has been reproduced in a similar or identical format with permission of the copyright holders from the published works by the author listed below:

Table 4.2 and Figure 4.3, plus some extracts from interview data, have been reproduced from Weber, L. (2012) 'Policing a world in motion', in J. McCulloch and S. Pickering (eds) *Borders and Crime: Pre-crime, Mobility and Serious Harm in an Age of Globalization*, London: Palgrave/Macmillan.

Figure 5.1, plus some extracts from interview data, have been reproduced from Pickering, S. and Weber, L. (2013) 'Policing transversal borders', in K. Aas and M. Bosworth (eds) *The Borders of Punishment: Criminal Justice, Citizenship and Social Exclusion*, Oxford: Oxford University Press.

Tables 2.2 and 2.3, Figure 7.1, plus some extracts from interview data, have been reproduced from Weber, L., Wilson, A. and Wise, J. (2013 forthcoming) 'Cops and dobbers: a nodal cartography of onshore migration policing in New South Wales', *Australian and New Zealand Journal of Criminology*.

Table 2.3 and Figures 4.2 and 4.4, plus some extracts from interview data, have been reproduced from Weber, L. (2011) '"It sounds like they shouldn't be here": immigration checks on the streets of Sydney', *Policing and Society*, 21(4): 456–67, Special Issue on Stop and Search in Global Context (Leanne Weber and Ben Bowling, eds), also reproduced in Weber, L. and Bowling, B. (eds) (2012) *Stop and Search: Police Power in Global Context*, London: Routledge.

Cover image © Steven Greaves Photography

ACRONYMS

AAT	Administrative Appeals Tribunal
AFP	Australian Federal Police
AHRC	Australian Human Rights Commission
ARC	Australian Research Council
ATO	Australian Taxation Office
BVE	Bridging E Visa
CERT	Compliance Early Response Team
CIMU	Compliance Information Management Unit
CJS	Criminal Justice Stay
COE	Confirmation of Enrolment
COPS	Computerised Operational Policing System
DCS	Department of Corrective Services
DEEWR	Department of Employment, Education and Workplace Relations
DIAC	Department of Immigration and Citizenship
DIMIA	Department of Immigration and Multicultural and Indigenous Affairs
DoCS	Department of Community Services
DV	Domestic violence
ECLO	Ethnic Community Liaison Officer
ESOS Act	*Education Services for Overseas Students Act 2000* (Cwlth)
ETA	Electronic travel authority
EU	European Union
ISS	Immigration Status Service
IT	Information technology
LAC	Local Area Command
LEPRA	*Law Enforcement (Powers and Responsibilities) Act 2002* (NSW)
MOU	Memorandum of Understanding

MSIs	Migration Series Instructions
NLC	National Liaison Committee
NSW	New South Wales
PRISMS	Provider Registration and International Student Management System
RRT	Refugee Review Tribunal
RTA	Roads and Traffic Authority
QA	Quality Assurance
STMP	Suspect targeting management plan
TSETT	Transnational Sexual Exploitation and Trafficking Team
UK	United Kingdom
UNSW	University of New South Wales
US	United States
VEVO	Visa Entitlement Verification Online

1

POLICING INTERNAL BORDERS

Policing the boundaries of belonging

Globalisation, sovereignty and security

As Aas has observed, '[r]ather than creating "citizens of the world", the globalising process seems to be dividing the world; creating and even deepening the "us" and "them" mentality – the national from the foreign' (Aas 2007: 98). In parallel with the 'governing through crime' thesis (Simon 2007), the primacy attached to border protection under conditions of globalisation can be seen as an attempt to maintain political control over one of the key remaining aspects of national sovereignty (Sassen 1996). So important has the idea of border security become that in most developed countries, immigration control measures have spread to numerous 'sites of enforcement' other than the physical border (Weber and Bowling 2004). These include pre-emptive measures ranging from visa regimes to naval blockades, which create a virtual, offshore border; new technologies such as biometrics and computerised alert systems which manifest at geographical borders; and a plethora of post-entry strategies intended to hasten the departure of those whose continued presence is unwanted.

Critics point out that defensive border control policies are an ineffective, and often inhumane, response to the fundamental challenges of contemporary governance: 'While classical conceptions of security focused on defending the sovereignty and territorial integrity of the nation state, it is doubtful whether nations' efforts to enhance national identity and national security through exclusionary immigration policies any longer make sense' (Zedner 2009: 59, citing Dauvergne 2007). According to Bigo, however, the main source of the 'knowledge power' recruited by those who govern us is 'in their capacity to define the sources of our insecurity and to produce techniques to manage them' (Bigo 2000: 94). Thus the pervasive embrace of risk management as a governmental strategy in late modernity has ensured that borders retain their status as significant sites for risk-based governance.

In anxious times, those with disputed entitlements to remain in secured zones may find themselves 'situated at the heart of local struggles for safety and security' (Aas 2007: 82). The pursuit of national security and local safety through physical expulsion and the reinforcement of membership has been dubbed 'governing through migration control' (Bosworth and Guild 2008) – a phrase that emphasises the parallels with the criminological thesis of 'governing through crime'. Governing through migration control has several strands. First, crime control mentalities and technologies may leach into migration control strategies. These trends have been articulated in the influential 'crimmigration thesis' (Stumpf 2006) which will be discussed later in this chapter. But migration control can also operate relatively independently as a site of governance, signifying a state of contestation over conceptions of citizenship and belonging. Bosworth and Guild see these two governmental strategies as linked, and encapsulated in the 'articulation of citizenship through the criminalisation of migration' (Bosworth and Guild 2008: 715).

Citizenship, order and belonging

Zedner (2010: 380) has noted that '[o]pposing the pull of globalization stands the counterpressure to resist the influx of migrants by strengthening borders and limiting access to citizenship in the name of security'. Under these conditions citizenship becomes a 'privileged status' accorded only to the deserving, while non-citizens are categorised according to hierarchies of desert and entitlement. Bosniak has argued that alienage is an inevitable product of boundaries and that complete inclusiveness can only be a 'fantasy' within the present system of sovereignty:

> For status noncitizens – for aliens – the privilege of presence is conditional. In the case of lawfully present aliens, a variety of factors may trigger the process of territorial removal. In the case of the undocumented, it is, additionally, the very fact of their *hereness* that renders them deportable.
>
> *(Bosniak 2006: 139)*

Because of the ever-present threat of deportation, Sassen (1996) has argued that the distinction between those with legal migration status and those without it is more salient in contemporary states than that between citizens and non-citizens. For one thing, the slow creep of human rights thinking is beginning to erode the benefits once attached only to citizenship. Taking a slightly different view, Dauvergne asserts that citizenship, while somewhat 'unhinged' in the face of globalisation, still remains a 'thin but unbreakable guard rail' (Dauvergne 2008: 121, citing Macklin 2006). She argues that migration and citizenship law work together to construct the internal border, with migration law tackling the 'dirty work' of denying entry and authorising expulsion, while citizenship law 'perfects the exclusionary mechanism of migration law by cloaking it in a discourse of inclusion' (Dauvergne 2008: 124). This exclusionary symbiosis is clear in Australian law, where the term 'unlawful non-citizen' reinforces a double divide: first, between citizens and non-citizens, and then between those who are lawfully and unlawfully present.

In the face of an inability to exert complete control over geographical borders, classifying unwanted sections of the population as 'illegal' becomes a key strategy in the fabrication of order: 'Capturing the moral panic about extralegal migrants and enshrining it in law allows governments control that their borders lack. When a part of the population is labelled "illegal" it is excluded from within' (Dauvergne 2008: 17). The pursuit of order through border control forges a powerful connection between the promise of security and perceptions of belonging, so that 'citizenship law works in tandem with migration law as a legal expression of degrees of belonging', with migration law operating as the 'last bastion of sovereignty' (Dauvergne 2008: 141).

Policing 'crimmigrants'

While the combination of immigration and citizenship law exerts a powerful system of control over non-citizens, this nexus is strengthened further by resort to the criminal law. This process has been observed most keenly in the United States (US), where Stumpf (2013: 7) has coined the term 'crimmigration' to cover 'the letter and practice of laws and policies at the intersection of criminal law and immigration law'. The trend is seen as a 'two-way street', whereby an increasing range of criminal offences can lead to deportation, while previous civil violations by immigrants have crossed the boundary into the criminal sphere (Stumpf 2006: 16).

Although criminal and immigration law at first appear to be very different, Stumpf argues that they are united by their capacity to include and exclude. This is so because, unlike other spheres of law that deal with relations between individuals or corporations, both immigration and criminal law apply to relations between individuals and the state. Hence, while immigration law defines national membership explicitly, criminal law defines it implicitly through various modes of exclusion. Stumpf notes that many of the exclusions faced by ex-felons in the US resemble a state of alienage, such as the ineligibility to vote. Echoing elements of the 'governing through crime' (Simon 2007) and 'culture of control' (Garland 2001) theses, she relates the 'crimmigration crisis' to a shift in penal thinking away from rehabilitation and social incorporation and towards exclusion and risk reduction, which she calls the 'sovereign state model'. Picking up ideas also discussed by Zedner (2010) under the banner of neoliberalism, Stumpf analyses the sharpening of boundary defining through 'membership theory' in which rights entitlements can be flexibly and conditionally ascribed on the basis of desert. She concludes: 'Under the sovereign state model ex-offenders and immigrants become the "outsiders" from whom citizens need protection' (Stumpf 2006: 39).

Other authors have made similar observations without reference to the crimmigration thesis. Pratt (2005) conveys the convergence of immigration and criminal paradigms through the term 'immigration penalty', while Krasmann

(2007) describes the impetus to expel dangerous others from the social body as 'enemy penology'. Inda has analysed similar trends in governance in terms of what he calls 'anti-citizenship technologies':

> normal people must protect themselves and be protected from the hordes of anti-citizens – the criminal, the underclass, the homeless, the vagrants, the truly disadvantaged – who threaten their security and quality of life....As with the government of crime more generally, the rationale for managing illegal immigrants through police measures is that the public must be protected from the would-be criminals who threaten their well-being and contentment.
>
> *(Inda 2006: 126)*

Writing from a European perspective, Van der Leun and Van der Woude (2013) have argued that the crimmigration thesis does not easily translate to other contexts where the legal trends noted in the US have not been as pronounced. They concede that a climate exists in the Netherlands in which 'criminals and immigrants are seen and framed as potential "dangerous" others' (Van der Leun and Van der Woude 2013: 43), but argue that the convergence of the criminal and immigration spheres is more evident in 'unconscious social processes' such as racial and ethnic profiling within the criminal justice system, which they interpret as 'an *inward* sign of intersecting migration and crime control' (Van der Leun and Van der Woude 2013: 44, emphasis added). These authors propose an expanded definition of crimmigration as 'the intertwinement of crime control and migration control' (Van der Leun and Van der Woude 2013: 43) in order to establish a wider socio-legal perspective from which to research the phenomenon.

This wider socio-legal perspective is evident in the exploration of crimmigration in Europe by Katja Aas. Aas (2011) identified a growing trend across the European Union (EU) towards the intensive surveillance and social sorting of 'crimmigrant others' through a plethora of new technologies. She concluded that the 'illegalities produced through definitions of unauthorised mobility as a criminal matter are thus proving to be the major target of EU surveillance systems' (Aas 2011: 337). In fact, laws intended to criminalise illegal status directly are being, or have been, seriously entertained, inter alia, in the Netherlands (Van der Leun and Van der Woude 2013) and in some US states (Provine 2013). Approaching the question of harsh treatment for non-citizens from the other pole of the criminal–administrative nexus, Bosworth and Guild note that:

> [t]hough such examples suggest a different moral, ethical and legal framework for dealing with non-citizens, it is not a matter of identifying 'institutional racism' or individual malfeasance, though examples of both of these can be found in the literature (Shaw 2004). Rather, substantially harsher treatment of non-citizens flows naturally – some would argue inevitably – from the 'administrative' nature of immigration law.
>
> *(Bosworth and Guild 2008: 712)*

The policing of non-citizens in Australia (or more specifically of asylum seekers against whom the harshest of policing measures have been directed) has also been examined in terms both of its administrative character, and its criminalising effects. I have written about administrative detention as a 'criminal-justice-like' power exercised in relation to asylum seekers with none of the constraints applied to the use of imprisonment (Weber 2002a). And Pickering (2005) has charted the creation of the 'criminal refugee' in Australia through the adoption of a 'law and order' approach to asylum seekers accompanied by discourses of dangerousness. However, literal criminalisation in Australia has so far been targeted on large-scale and systematic activities such as 'people smuggling' and organised visa fraud, rather than on individual breaches of immigration law. The merging of the criminal and immigration domains is evidenced most powerfully in Australia in the expansion of criminal deportation (discussed in Chapter 5) and in 'inward signs' of crimmigration within operational policing (discussed in Chapter 4).

Policing, recognition and identity

Enforcing the boundaries of belonging is not only a matter of law but requires an active policing effort. Immigration controls are performed in different locations by a diversity of agencies and individuals possessing varying degrees of 'police-like' powers and characteristics (Pickering and Weber 2013; Weber and Bowling 2004). Migration policing agencies include specialist border authorities (discussed in relation to Australia in Chapter 3) and a range of other public agencies and private citizens (discussed in Chapter 6). Policing scholars have also identified many parallels between the exclusionary outcomes that can arise from mainstream policing and the more literal exclusion of non-citizens. For example, Ericson and Haggerty equate everyday police work with the construction and patrolling of 'symbolic borders' that 'make clear who is one of us and who is the other, and establish where people allowed to remain within those symbolic borders should be assigned' (Ericson and Haggerty 1997: 259). Waddington (1999) agrees that policing is 'inextricably tied' to processes of social exclusion and inclusion, adding that the act of mobilising police assistance in response to victimisation is effectively an act of claiming citizenship.

Loader and Walker (2007: 107) also assign a primary role to the state, and to police in particular, as 'mediator[s] of belonging'. They note that the historic role of the nation-state in 'identity construction work' has provided its citizens with a sense of 'social rootedness and secure belonging' (Loader and Walker 2007: 176). This security has been brokered largely through the mark of citizenship as a source of territorially based solidarity among strangers. However, these authors argue that harms of 'mis-recognition or non-recognition' can occur where governments elevate the assertion of national boundaries to levels that 'generate forms of xenophobic hostility towards those marked out *by* territorial frontiers as foreigners or *within* territorial frontiers as strangers' (Loader and Walker 2007: 108, emphasis in original). This leaves individuals who are not recognised as citizens, at best, in a state of 'precarious belonging' (Loader and Walker 2007: 112). Populations existing in such a state often find themselves subject to the control of police who thereby become the 'arbiters of their citizenship':

> [P]olice patrol the boundaries of citizenship: the citizenship of those who are 'respectable' is secured, while those who attack the state exclude themselves from citizenship. Between these extremes are those whose claim to citizenship is insecure and needs repeatedly to be negotiated. Police are the de facto arbiters of their citizenship. It is they who are 'police property' and this is a mark of their marginality.
>
> *(Waddington 1999: 41)*

Thus, policing in contemporary societies comes to be directed at groups whose citizenship is in dispute, whether they are actual non-citizens or 'pseudo-citizens' such as former (and perpetually unforgiven) felons (Stumpf 2006). Under the pressures of globalisation, those who are *actual* non-citizens join the ranks of 'police property' alongside other groups with diminished citizenship rights, such as colonised peoples, known criminals, the mentally ill and the disreputable poor. But the involvement of police in the performance of national borders is not without its risks, and poses new sets of problems for governments. Sassen notes the 'expanded use of policing as an instrument to maintain control over immigration', arguing that '[w]hen the objects of stronger police action include an ever-expanding spectrum of people – immigrant women, men and children – sooner or later the state will get caught in the expanding web of civil and human rights' (Sassen 1996: xix). In other words, the excluded will become numerous and politically significant enough to exert pressure for change. For the moment, however, governments of late modernity appear to be caught in a web of their own making, constructed not from human rights principles, but from the imperatives of risk-based governance.

Modes and mentalities of migration policing

Policing through risk and surveillance

Contemporary governance is characterised by forward-looking policies aimed at solving problems and pre-empting potential threats. Governing through risk entails the categorisation of people or activities into hierarchies of threat in order to direct resources towards the most risky people, places and situations. This produces highly information-driven strategies and has spawned a 'risk profiling' industry directed towards the anticipation and codification of danger. Castel argues that risk governance promotes suspicion to the 'dignified rank of a calculus of probabilities' (cited in Coleman and McCahill 2011: 21). Prudentialism based on assessments of risk can be distinguished from both sovereign and disciplinary power as described by Foucault by its disinterest in seeking to change behaviour, and its non-normative focus on problem-solving and containment.

The origins and wider implications of these so-called post-disciplinary developments in governance are succinctly summarised in the following passage from Ericson and Haggerty:

> This shift in orientation towards risk, surveillance, and security is fostered by a changing legal regime in risk society. As the emphasis on control diminishes, the criminal justice institution moves away from deterrence-based law enforcement and towards compliance-based law enforcement…. The emphasis shifts to acquiring the knowledge necessary to set acceptable standards of risk. This emphasis not only entails a lessening of crime control in favour of surveillance as an end in itself but also means that 'due process' protections for suspects are eroded in favour of 'system rights' to the kinds of knowledge useful for surveillance.
>
> *(Ericson and Haggerty 1997: 18)*

Lyon accords such primacy to the spread of surveillance technologies that he refers to twenty-first century societies as 'surveillance societies' which are characterised by highly developed 'information infrastructure[s]' (Lyon 2001: 28). Information technologies are deployed with particular emphasis on establishing a 'scientific basis for securing identities' (Lyon 2005: 71). Fixing identity is the key to assigning individuals to the risk categories that underpin surveillance operations. The biometrics industry, which translates bodily characteristics into electronic information, has therefore emerged as a key player in the science of 'managing identities' (Muller 2005). Aas (2011: 341, citing Muller) has noted that by creating 'docile bodies' with fixed and unambiguous identities, biometrics can be seen 'as an exemplary bio-political technique connecting the individual both to his or her own identity and to the external systems of governance'. Surveillance technologies are deployed not only as systems of identity management, but also through more general techniques of risk assessment. Coleman and McCahill (2011: 70, citing Marx) refer to a 'new surveillance' that 'monitors geographical places, time periods and categories of person rather than individual subjects', based on aggregate risk calculations. For Mattelart, these techniques of governance reflect a convergence between the logics of policing and markets: 'the ability to anticipate individual behaviour and construct categories based on statistical frequency is the common thread among the "styles" of marketing specialists, the "scores" of financiers and the "profiles" of the police' (Mattelart 2010: 184).

These technologies of risk and surveillance are readily apparent in regimes of border control. Pratt (2005) has demonstrated how Canada's 'risk-smart borders' operate through information, scanning and surveillance technologies. Rather than evoke a post-disciplinary model of power, Pratt considers that these border control programmes lie at the *intersection* of sovereignty and governmentality. In other words, the sovereign power to exclude is expressed *through* modalities of risk management which 'have no official purpose other than to confine and ultimately expel the actual bodies and undesired noncitizens' (Pratt 2005: 22). Risk-smart internal borders effectively create hierarchies of citizenship and entitlement by infusing risk categories with normative judgements:

> In the context of immigration penality and border control, the practices of classifying and filtering the high from the low risk, the undeserving and undesirable from the deserving and desirable, produce borders and 'make up' citizens. Just as the moralizing categorization of the deserving and undeserving poor legitimizes differential treatment on the basis of these categories, so too do the distinctions between the deserving and undeserving refugee and the desirable and undesirable immigrant.
>
> *(Pratt 2005: 17)*

For Lyon, the process described by Pratt is not 'an intrinsically anti-social or repressive process' but, rather, is a direct consequence of systems of entitlement supported by 'information infrastructures'. He asserts that the 'focused attention on individual lives characteristic of modernity underpins eligibility to benefits of citizenship, such as the right to vote or state support' which is mediated through highly automated systems: 'The relevant data is on file, and may be produced to prove identity and to verify claims' (Lyon 2001: 31). The normative outcomes of these processes of 'social sorting', he observes, can only be determined empirically. This means that marginalised groups can suffer both from targeted surveillance intended to exclude them, and from being unrecognised in relation to supportive forms of surveillance that might potentially benefit them. For example, lack of access to services may result for individuals who are 'invisible because of their illegality to the surveillance mechanisms of contemporary states' (Dauvergne 2008: 20). On the other hand, where surveillance mechanisms are geared towards exclusion rather than entitlement, the problem of illegality is more about the 'liberty to participate in society *without* surveillance or suspicion' (Provine 2013: 116).

Networked policing

The rise of technology-driven surveillance is closely aligned with the advent of networked forms of governance. According to Aas, technology, not geography, is now central to defining the space of governance, and enables the dissemination of knowledge-power among a range of actors:

> New technologies thus seem both to transform the traditional space of government and to disrupt territorial boundaries, as well as appearing to state and commercial organizations to be the most efficient solution for addressing the problems of governance and security.
>
> *(Aas 2005: 207)*

In turn, information technologies allow a largely invisible governance framework to be diffused throughout society. As Lyon (2001: 29) explains, the reach of these technologies 'renders everyday life more transparent than ever before to a growing number of agencies whose design is to influence it'.

The adoption of a whole-of-government approach to complex policy problems is attractive to governments from the perspective of cost effectiveness as it allows for a pooling of skills and resources. However, social theorists interpret the emergence of cross-agency cooperation as part of a broader and deeper trend associated with the fragmentation and dispersal of state authority (Braithwaite 2000; Garland 1996). This has ushered in a new era in which networks are said to be replacing bureaucracies as the preferred mode of governance. Castells (2000: 76) has argued that networks 'constitute the new social morphology of our societies', being flexible enough to accommodate rapid innovation without collapsing into instability.

Applying these theories of governance within criminology, Johnston and Shearing (2003) have characterised contemporary policing in terms of multi-nodal 'security networks'. Participants may be state actors ('first sector'), corporate or business actors ('second sector'), or non-government organisations ('third sector') (Shearing and Wood 2003). Within a nodal model of governance, no set of nodes is given conceptual priority. State agencies are considered to be just one among many possible nodes (or 'switchers', to use Castells's terminology). Nodes within security networks are conceptualised as sites of governance at which knowledge and resources are mobilised in order to 'manage a course of events' (Burris *et al.* 2005: 33). These sites do not necessarily equate to fixed physical locations, although they may do. They may be highly structured or merely loose assemblages. They can be identified according to their underlying 'mentality' (or objectives) and distinct 'institutional' forms; and they may be enduring or temporary.

Dupont (2004) identifies four ideal types of security network: local (involving information exchange between traditional and non-traditional social control agencies and local communities, mobilised against local crime concerns); institutional (relatively closed, inward-looking networks established to pool resources and improve the coordination of efforts of existing government agencies); international (which mirror the structure of the institutional model, but extend beyond borders and increasingly incorporate non-government actors); and virtual (information-based networks, as envisaged by Castells, which transcend space and time).

Another useful way of categorising networks is provided by Gelsthorpe's models of multi-agency working (Gelsthorpe 1985, cited in Johnston and Shearing 2003: 108) in which five models of inter-agency relations, are identified, defined according to their level of integration (see Figure 1.1). This form of classification emphasises the dynamics of inter-agency (or inter-nodal) functioning based on working relationships and operational practices.

Within these broad groupings, more detailed questions can be asked about the day-to-day functioning of multi-agency networks. Dupont (2004: 84) proposes that network dynamics should be analysed in terms of the uneven distribution of cultural, social, political, economic and symbolic capital, noting that 'networks are not egalitarian structures, and some members are quite powerful while others

1 Communication models (which are restricted mainly to information exchange, either full or partial)
2 Cooperation (joint action, or consent to act, where agencies maintain separate boundaries but agree to work on mutually defined problems)
3 Coordination (agencies work systematically within defined agency boundaries, but pool resources to tackle mutually agreed problems)
4 Federation models (agencies operate integrated services, while maintaining some areas of distinctiveness)
5 Merger models (where maximum integration of purpose and method is achieved, resources are pooled and functional distinctions begin to dissolve)

FIGURE 1.1 Models of inter-agency working.

Source: Gelsthorpe (1985) cited in Johnston and Shearing (2003).

are barely capable of maintaining their connections'. Burris *et al*. agree that networks need not necessarily be 'horizontal', but that a 'circuitry of power' can be discerned, which is exercised through the use of 'force, persuasion, economic pressure, norm creation and manipulation' (Burris *et al*. 2005: 31). Although critics have asserted that proponents of nodal governance make unrealistic claims about inter-agency cooperation, Wood and Shearing (2007: 28) argue that their nodal governance framework provides a 'conceptual architecture for analyzing trends in governance that is equally comfortable with the idea that governance can be contested and uncoordinated as it is with the idea that it can be cooperative and coordinated'.

The idea of 'third party policing' offers another alternative to a purely 'horizontal' conception of nodal governance. As articulated by Mazerolle and Ransley (2006), in this mode of policing, police retain the position of control while forming largely ad hoc, tactical partnerships to solve particular local crime problems. These informal partnerships are generally brokered by street-level officers who achieve their crime control objectives by deploying incentives and threats that operate 'in the shadow of the law'. For example, a shopkeeper may be encouraged to take action to prevent repeated calls for police assistance, on the basis that legal action might otherwise be taken against her for some actual or purported regulatory breach. In this case, local regulations are used as a 'legal lever' to achieve a policing outcome. The term 'third party' refers to the role of actors who 'are neither the primary authors nor beneficiaries of the misconduct they police' (Wood and Shearing 2007: 15, citing Gilboy 1998: 135). Third party relationships can be more formal than the case described above. Wood and Shearing (2007) give the example of mandatory reporting to state authorities under threat of penalties – a controversial strategy that has been attempted across a number of policy areas from the reporting of child abuse to the detection of illegal entrants.

Mazerolle and Ransley locate their empirical analysis of third party policing in Australia within broader trends in neoliberal governance. They conclude that '[t]hird party policing, as a form of regulatory-based police activity, is thus likely to become a dominant mode of police action into the twenty-first century' (Mazerolle and Ransley 2006: 64). While these authors offer no observations about trends in border control, their observation that third party policing involves the convergence of the criminal and civil domains echoes some of the features of the 'crimmigration thesis' in which enforcement practices are also seen to cross the criminal/administrative divide.

One author who has explicitly connected trends in the pluralisation of policing with the governance of borders is Anna Pratt, who notes that:

> Risk technologies and calculations are not solely a matter for the state. Communities, individuals, businesses are all expected to assume responsibility for the management of risks. The construction and mobilization of 'the community' and individuals in the risk-based policies and practices of immigration penality (e.g., through third party liability programs, border watch, community policing, informants, etc.) are thus consistent with the individualized ethos of neoliberalism and the new logics of risk that fracture the social sphere 'into a multitude of diverse pockets, zones, folds of riskiness'.
>
> *(Pratt 2005: 218, citing Rose 1999)*

The mobilisation of communities, individuals, business and a broad array of government agencies into migration policing networks in Australia is explored in Chapters 6 and 7.

'Responsibilisation' and the decentring of the state

Nodal, networked or third party policing requires the recruitment of previously uninvolved actors into a policing role. Mazerolle and Ransley (2006) explain that third parties are either enticed or coerced into performing crime control functions through the application of 'legal levers' whereby the failure to cooperate may result in adverse legal action. More formalised models of 'government-at-a-distance' rely on a variety of techniques of persuasion, as explained by Garland (2001: 126): 'The state's new strategy is not to command and control but rather to persuade and align, to organize, to ensure that other actors play their part.' Garland refers to this governmental strategy as 'responsibilisation'. Techniques of persuasion range from direct requests to the provision of information related to the risks and interests of the party concerned, and also include the threat or application of coercive sanctions. The intention is to expand the power of the state by recruiting actors with a wide range of knowledge and other resources, while accepting some loss of control: 'The intended result is an enhanced network of more or less directed, more or less informal, crime control, complementing and extending the formal controls of the criminal justice state' (Garland 2001: 124).

Other analyses of pluralism within neoliberal governance draw explicit links between devolved authority and the free market. In a marketised system, it is governments that 'steer' while market providers 'row' (Braithwaite 2000). As

with government-at-a-distance, the task of government becomes one of negotiated 'alignment' whereby

> [e]nrolled actors align the direction given by a centre with their own objec-
> tives, and in doing so change the directions. The result is that the direction
> is, and indeed must be, translated into terms that are compatible with others.
> The art of governance here is the art of alignment.
>
> *(Wood and Shearing 2007: 19, citing Deukmedjian 2002)*

A similar model, possibly envisaging a stronger role for the state, is suggested by
Loader and Walker's advocacy of 'anchored pluralism', in which the state remains
the 'anchor of collective security provision' with a view to ensuring that security
is made available to all as a public good (Loader and Walker 2007: 193).

Wood and Shearing take the notion of the decentred state much further than
the theories just discussed. They argue that there has been an observable diversifica-
tion of the steering as well as the rowing function. For these authors, '[n]odes are
sites of knowledge, capacity and resources that function as governance *auspices or
providers*' (Wood and Shearing 2007: 27, emphasis added). Nodal governance is not
merely an observation about the reliance of neoliberal governments on diverse
sources of market provision, but makes claims about the emergence of 'private
governments'. As an example, Wood and Shearing cite the activities of transnational
private militias in Iraq – a scenario in which a significant loss of control by governments might not be unexpected.

Critics of nodal governance as conceived by Johnston and Shearing (2003) and
Wood and Shearing (2007) have taken issue with these authors' methodological
decentring of state power, arguing that this conception tends to mask the continued exercise of centralised authority through indirect means. These critics note
that it is difficult to find security networks (other than in conflict zones, perhaps)
where the police (or other relevant state agencies) have relinquished their 'auspicing' role. For example, Crawford (2006) has argued that there is little empirical
evidence that nodal policing is the predominant model in Britain. He concludes
that real-world examples of plural policing are characterised by competition and
distrust (thus aligning more with a market model), rather than by a cooperative,
horizontal partnership compatible with a truly nodal model.

Whatever their views about the relationship between the state and other security actors, most commentators agree that contemporary states are expanding their
resources and powers by adopting networked approaches. Loader and Walker (2007:
20, emphasis added) argue that the diffusion of responsibility for security 'represents a shuffling of cards *within* the state rather than a diffusion of responsibility to
non-state actors'. Garland (1996: 454) suggests that '[w]here it works ... the
responsibilization strategy leaves the centralized state machine more powerful than
before, with an expanded capacity for action and influence'. For Lyon (2001), the
advent of the 'surveillance society' in which the capacity for surveillance spreads
beyond the state (with many similarities to nodal governance) does not necessarily

imply either the diminishing of state power or the inception of a 'high-tech police state'. Even the proponents of the nodal governance thesis concede that the challenge this poses to the status of governments as the 'auspices' for security provision does not necessarily assume a loss of state control in practice:

> The shift to a nodal governance perspective is not one that assumes a decline in state authority and power. Indeed, one could argue that state power is now even more diffuse and pervasive through the ways in which it governs through the knowledge, capacity and resources of others. The conceptual shift we advocate is simply one that recognizes the diversity of entities, what we term 'nodes', that function as *auspices or providers* of security goods or both.
>
> *(Wood and Shearing 2007: 33, emphasis added)*

For these authors, the relative positioning and influence of the state and other actors in security networks remains a matter for empirical observation while remaining open to all possible auspice/provider combinations.

The following chapters report the findings of the migration policing study. The study was designed to establish the role played by the major migration policing partners in the Australian state of NSW, to consider why they contribute to migration policing efforts, and to contemplate the wider social and institutional implications of these policing practices directed specifically towards non-citizens. Many of the themes outlined in this opening review of the literature emerged strongly throughout the research, including the proliferation of migration policing partners, the reliance on new technologies and modes of identity-based surveillance, the importance of understanding the dynamics of cooperation and resistance, the areas of overlap and convergence between criminal and immigration law, the reliance on risk-based and intelligence-led technologies, and the shifts away from a primary reliance on deterrence towards compliance-based systems in which deterrence still plays a role. Before proceeding to the findings, I set out in Chapter 2 the research design for the migration policing study and describe the legal and organisational context in which migration policing occurs in NSW.

2

RESEARCHING MIGRATION POLICING NETWORKS

The migration policing study

A nodal cartography of migration policing networks

This book contains original data obtained from the migration policing study.[1] The study was designed to identify the major agencies involved in the detection of 'unlawful non-citizens' in the state of NSW and map the relationships between them, using the broad idea of 'nodal cartography' (Johnston and Shearing 2003). The specific questions driving the data collection were:

- What are the *institutions* of migration policing? In other words, what agencies are involved in identifying 'unlawful non-citizens', and what role do they play as interconnected nodes in migration policing networks?
- What are the underlying *mentalities* of agencies within migration policing networks? More specifically, what are the motivations for each of the agencies to participate in migration policing networks, and what steps are taken to actively recruit them?
- What are the associated *technologies* and *practices* of the agencies within migration policing networks? What contribution does each partner make in terms of financial and legal resources, professional skills and knowledge, provision of information and assistance on the ground?
- What are the *relationships* between different nodes in these networks? Answering this question entails an analysis of the dynamics of migration policing networks, including both the productive and problematic aspects of inter-agency collaboration.
- What are the *implications* of the dispersal of authority for migration policing across a range of disparate agencies, and of the specific migration policing practices identified? The focus here will be on normative implications seen from a broad social perspective, and impacts on public perceptions of the agencies involved.

While the idea of nodal cartography was a useful framing device for the data collection, the adoption of this practical aspect of Johnston and Shearing's methodology does not imply a wholesale endorsement of their nodal governance perspective. Central to their approach to studying security networks is the assertion that the relative dominance of one or other node is solely to be established through empirical enquiry, and that state dominance should not be presumed a priori. However, it would be surprising if the role of state agencies were found to be significantly decentred within migration policing networks, given the particular salience of immigration control as a form of contemporary statecraft. The approach taken in the migration policing study therefore accorded a central role to DIAC and the NSW Police Force from the outset as key drivers of migration policing networks. It was not expected that private security or other commercial actors would play a significant role in migration policing (in contrast to the realm of immigration detention in which private security corporations dominate), but the research design was nevertheless open to identifying commercial actors through the 'fanning out' methodology described below.

Since the migration policing study was the first empirical research to be conducted on immigration enforcement practices in Australia, it could legitimately be labelled as 'exploratory'. The desire for a flexible, open-ended approach to data collection led to the adoption of a series of mixed-method case studies. One case study was built around the DIAC Compliance Office in Sydney, and five case studies were conducted in selected NSW Police Local Area Commands (LACs). The Sydney Compliance Office was chosen because it handles the vast majority of immigration enforcement workload nationally, estimated at 60 per cent by senior DIAC staff. The NSW Police Force plays an equally dominant role in immigration enforcement, accounting for more than half the immigration checks conducted by Australian police agencies (discussed in Chapter 4). Three metropolitan police stations in Sydney and two police stations in rural New South Wales were chosen as case studies. The police locations were selected using data provided by DIAC which showed that they were all actively involved in carrying out checks on immigration status. The stations were also selected to reflect different geographical locations and demographics. One urban location had a well-established multicultural community, another inner-city location was likely to host transient residents and workers, and the third urban LAC contained the Villawood Detention Centre within its boundaries.[2] The sampling rationale was purposive; that is, it was intended to identify as wide a range of migration policing practices as possible, rather than to be representative of the NSW Police Force as a whole.

Beyond these core case studies, a fanning out methodology was employed (see Figure 2.1) to identify other key players, including what Shearing and Wood (2003) describe as the second (commercial) and third (non-profit) sectors, were they to be identified as partners by any of the core agencies. Unlike the police and DIAC case studies, which were pursued in as much detail as research access agreements would allow, the approach to these 'outer layers' of the data collection

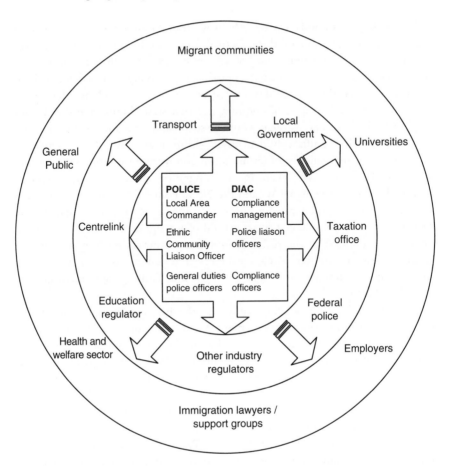

FIGURE 2.1 Fanning out methodology.

process was to achieve a broad mapping of migration policing institutions and their inter-agency connections, rather than to produce a deep examination of practice within the individual agencies. Indeed, obtaining access to this wide range of agencies proved to be extremely time-consuming, and the collection of primary data did not in fact reach the outer limits of the detection system at all (notably the health system and private individuals such as employers). Given the institutional focus of the study and the necessary limits on time and resources, no attempt was made to ascertain the views of those who are subjected to migration control processes. In contrast, a sociological study of 'processes of incorporation' of illegal immigrants in the Netherlands by Joanne Van der Leun which also examines policing practices provides detailed insights into the experiences of those who are targeted by immigration enforcement policies and practices and the communities in which they live (Van der Leun 2003). These aspects of the policing of migration in Australia remain to be explored in greater depth in future research.

Mapping migration policing using case studies

Case studies are sufficiently flexible to be tailored to specific situations, and can be fine tuned in response to emerging findings. This makes the technique ideal for exploring complex phenomena about which little prior information is available. Case studies are therefore recognised as an effective research strategy for investigating a particular phenomenon within its real-life context (Robson 1993). They are increasingly accepted as rigorous tools for social science inquiry provided there is sufficient structure and a well-articulated project logic (Yin 2009). The broad data collection plan for the migration policing study is summarised in Table 2.1. Historical and contextual information was assembled from official inquiries, departmental annual reports and other official documents. A comprehensive briefing on compliance policies, procedures and technical developments was provided by senior DIAC Compliance Office staff in Canberra at the beginning of the fieldwork period. The setting for migration policing was examined through the selected case studies and the fanning out methodology anchored to those starting points. Situated activity was explored via a series of interviews, briefings, incidental observations and a self-report questionnaire.

Mixed-methodology case studies allow for a wide variety of data collection methods to be employed, depending on the research goals and context. Because of the difficulties of conducting observational research in circumstances where the relevant activities (in this case, the detection of suspected unlawful non-citizens) may be occurring in a wide variety of locations and at unpredictable times, interviews were the favoured data collection method used in this research, supplemented by a survey of operational police officers and some incidental place-based observations. Early attempts to observe structured enforcement practices, such as 'joint operations' organised by the NSW Police Force, did not identify any instances of the detection of unlawful non-citizens and delivered less useable information than the other data collection methods. Interviews with individuals who could act as institutional spokespersons were chosen as the most efficient way to gain insights into what were

TABLE 2.1 Resource map for migration policing study

History	Research element	Research focus
Temporal dimension through which other elements move, e.g. impact of Palmer Report	Context	Australian immigration law; attitudes towards and images of unlawful non-citizens
	Setting	Agencies involved in migration policing: targeted individuals, organisations and communities
	Situated activity	Dynamics of migration policing networks, apprehension of unlawful non-citizens in action
	Self	Attitudes and perceptions of enforcement officials and targeted individuals (individual perceptions not systematically explored in this study)

Source: Adapted from Layder, D. (1993) *New Strategies in Social Research, Figure 1.1.*

expected to be difficult-to-observe practices, such as chance encounters with unlawful non-citizens, exchanges of electronic data, the development of inter-agency Memoranda of Understanding (MOUs) and meetings of inter-agency committees. Interview techniques also opened up the possibility of exploring the mentalities driving these developments, to the extent that motivation can be discerned through guided discussion.

The key informant approach assumes that a single spokesperson has the organisational knowledge, sense of authority and motivation to discuss departmental procedures openly and honestly, and that a single 'organisational perspective' exists. This, of course, is not always true. The conduct of multiple interviews within the two core organisations of the NSW Police Force and DIAC meant that specialist informants could be targeted about specific procedures and operational practices. The multiple study sites used for the NSW Police Force case studies allowed comparisons to be made among similarly placed interviewees to assess consistency or identify individual or place-based differences. Where possible, the information provided about specific procedures was checked by reference to legislation and departmental documents. In smaller or more peripheral organisations, reliance on a single informant posed more of a limitation, so the information obtained is more schematic. Despite these limitations, key informant interviewing using the fanning out methodology produced a body of especially rich data from the core agencies and at least indicative information from the more peripheral partners, commensurate with the broad and exploratory objectives of the study.

Interviews were relatively unstructured and questions were tailored to the specific function of each interviewee. Data was collected through recorded interviews conducted at the informant's place of work, which focused on identifying policies, partnerships and organisational incentives for participation in migration policing networks. Most interviews covered the broad topics indicated in the points set out below, although there was some variability between the approach taken for organisations whose primary role was immigration compliance and those whose involvement in migration policing was more sporadic or tangential:

- What is your organisational role?
- What involvement do you have with the enforcement of immigration law?
- How do you go about each of these activities?
- What legal powers do you use?
- Who do you work with – both within and outside your organisation?
- Why does your organisation take part in these activities?
- Why do you involve other agencies in these activities? (if applicable)
- What are the main challenges arising from working with other agencies on immigration enforcement?

The starting point for substantive data collection within each of the police case studies was the Ethnic Community Liaison Officer (ECLO). ECLOs in NSW are unsworn police employees with specialist knowledge of policing as it impacts on local ethnic minority communities. The testimony of these ECLOs was extremely useful in providing some insight into the community impacts of migration policing practices, albeit second-hand. Each NSW Police Force case study began with an informal discussion with the local area commander about the purpose and requirements of the study and ended with a formal interview at which the results of the survey conducted at that station were discussed. Aside from the active relationship between the NSW Police Force and DIAC, the fanning out methodology as applied within the police case studies generally led inwards to the interviewing of key officers from central agencies based at the NSW Police Force Headquarters who were responsible for specialist functions such as information exchange, diversity policies or criminal prosecutions.

The case study based at the Sydney DIAC Compliance Office began with several familiarisation visits, described by the DIAC research partners as a 'walk-through' of the various functional units. Later, more formal interviews were conducted with the managers of each functional area and with the overall state manager of the NSW Compliance division. In general these interviews were less relaxed than the discussions held with operational police, and often took place with several officers present. Permission to interview compliance field officers who carry out the practical aspects of detecting and apprehending individuals was requested but not granted. This was possibly because of continuing local sensitivities over the public criticisms discussed in the next section, although the reason given was that researchers would not 'learn anything' from such an exercise. While material obtained from such interviews would have added depth to the study overall, it is not integral to the broad inter-agency mapping process, which was the main objective of the study. Interviews with more peripheral migration policing partners were confined to one key informant per organisation. The distribution of the 67 research interviews conducted for the study is presented in Table 2.2 below. The numbers refer to the interviews completed not individuals interviewed. The majority of interviews were conducted during 2008 and 2009.

A certain bias towards the collection of information about the police role in immigration enforcement will be immediately apparent from these figures. This is due in part to the criminological background of the researcher, but also reflects the relative openness of the police organisation to participation in the study. A self-report questionnaire was also completed by operational officers in all five police case study sites. The primary purpose was to identify the nature and extent of the involvement of operational police in immigration enforcement, assess their

TABLE 2.2 Summary of interviews completed ($n = 67$)

Canberra-based DIAC staff	6	Other law enforcement agencies	3
Sydney-based DIAC staff	7	Other federal government agencies	4
NSW Police station-based personnel	30	Universities/tertiary student groups	4
NSW Police central agencies	7	Other state and local agencies	6

knowledge of their powers under the *Migration Act 1958* (Cwlth) and determine the priority they place on immigration enforcement within their everyday work. The police questionnaire is attached at Appendix 1. It was administered to general duties police officers and other front-line police, including crime investigators, intelligence analysts and highway police. The sampling processes varied across locations due to operational constraints imposed by local area commanders, and consisted of various combinations of self-selection, co-option by superior officers, and on some occasions attendance at the operational briefing of an incoming shift or an offsite training session. A profile of the 371 survey responses obtained, in terms of posting, function and rank, is provided in Table 2.3.

A reasonable spread across different ranks and functions was achieved. However, repeated attempts to obtain comparable staffing data at each of the case study locations in order to assess the representativeness of the samples proved unsuccessful. As a result, the findings have been used to supplement the interview data with additional insights into operational practices, rather than to report generalisable quantitative findings. The well-known limitations of relying on self-reported practice as a guide to actions on the ground need to be balanced against the gains in identifying a wide range of practices that extend well beyond what could have been observed given the available time and resources.

Taken together, these data collection strategies provide snapshots of migration policing practices from a number of different perspectives, including opportunistic encounters by operational police in the course of their routine activities, specialist

TABLE 2.3 Profile of responses to operational police survey (*n* = 371)

LAC:	Urban 1	Urban 2	Urban 3	Rural 1	Rural 2	Missing	Total
	72 (19%)	106 (29%)	111 (30%)	39 (11%)	43 (12%)	0	371
Rank:	Probation constable	Constable	Senior constable	Sergeant	Senior sergeant	Inspector	Missing	Total
	41 (11%)	115 (32%)	135 (38%)	57 (16%)	4 (1%)	8 (2%)	11	371
Role:		General duties	Highway patrol	Intelligence pro-active	Detectives	Other	Missing	Total
		203 (62%)	25 (8%)	16 (5%)	44 (13%)	39 (12%)	44	371
Years at station:		<1	1<2	2<5	5<10	10+	Missing	Total
		31 (9%)	80 (23%)	135 (39%)	79 (23%)	24 (7%)	22	371
Years in police:		<1	1<2	2<5	5<10	10+	Missing	Total
		16 (5%)	36 (10%)	79 (23%)	111 (32%)	108 (31%)	21	371

Notes
LAC = Local Area Command.
Percentages exclude missing values. Totals greater than 100% are due to rounding.

DIAC officers dedicated to fulfilling particular compliance and enforcement functions, and employees from a range of regulatory and service provision agencies who have become enmeshed in the increasingly complex migration policing machinery.

Legal and policy framework

Who is 'unlawful'?

The Australian approach to immigration control is notable for its requirement that every non-citizen present on Australian soil must hold a valid visa. One senior immigration official described Australian border control as 'virtually unique' in that 'Australia, New Zealand and Japan are the only three countries in the world … that have virtually universal visa systems or entry and exit systems from the country' (Interview 45, Canberra DIAC). Consistent with this universal approach to controlling the country's borders, Australian immigration law specifies a bewildering array of visa categories. A number of temporary and permanent visas are available within the broad categories of 'workers' (with clear distinctions made between blue collar, white collar and business categories), 'migrants' (which overlaps with the workers category and includes provision for family reunion and humanitarian protection visas), 'visitors' (with categorical distinctions based on nationality determining access to electronic travel authorities (ETAs) and working holiday visas), and 'students' (distinguished on the basis of their level and type of study). Risk-based thinking is apparent in the allocation of temporary visitor visas, since 'high-risk' nationalities (considered statistically more likely to overstay their visas or submit in-country asylum applications) do not have access to the electronic travel authorities available to citizens of nations identified as less risky. Intending visitors from non-ETA countries must complete paper applications which are subject to greater scrutiny and generate a more extensive stored record, including identity verification information such as a photograph.

Sub-class 457 visas were introduced to enable skilled workers to enter Australia temporarily on organised employer-sponsored programmes. The initial schemes were seen to be open to abuse by employers, and the incoming Labor government in 2007 placed a high priority on increasing workplace regulation and monitoring the use of these visas (Deegan 2008; Joint Standing Committee on Migration 2007). These temporary labour schemes have since been supplemented by flexible Enterprise Migration Agreements which have been negotiated with major mining corporations, but are arguably designed for the broader demands of a 'just-in-time' economy. Student visas have also attracted controversy due to their relationship with avenues for permanent residence and the opportunities this has created for fraudulent practices by some higher education institutions. Concerns have also been raised over the welfare of international students, some of which relate to visa conditions and their enforcement. In particular, the restriction to 20 hours of paid work per week has been criticised as creating financial hardship and employment exploitation for many tertiary students (Marginson *et al.* 2010; Senate Legal and Constitutional Affairs References Committee 2006).

Under s 14 of the Migration Act, all non-citizens who enter or remain in Australia without a valid visa are considered to be 'unlawful non-citizens'. Unlawful non-citizens can be classified into the following categories:

- those who enter Australia without authority;
- those who overstay temporary visas;
- those whose temporary visas are cancelled due to a breach of conditions, usually working without authorisation or failing to undertake the activities for which the visa was granted (for example completing a university degree);
- those who have their permanent visas cancelled on character grounds, usually after committing a serious criminal offence.

By far the majority of individuals who are subject to Australia's internal border controls fall within the second and third categories, most often as overstayers. Of these, only the small proportion who are attempting to stay in Australia for the long term are likely to be of major interest to immigration compliance authorities:

> Most overstayers only overstay in Australia for a few days. This is often in an attempt to avoid the cost and perceived inconvenience of applying for an extension of their visas prior to their departure. People who overstay for longer periods do so either to prolong their holiday, to work, to enjoy the Australian lifestyle and climate, or because of family or other links to Australia. Of the people that overstay each year, the vast majority of cases are resolved by the overstayer departing Australia of their own volition, being granted another visa or by being removed from Australia.
>
> *(Department of Immigration and Multicultural and Indigenous Affairs [DIMIA] 2005: 37)*

The universality of Australia's visa regime is matched by a plethora of strict conditions which generate considerable potential for people to become unlawful while still in possession of an unexpired visa. The main powers to cancel visas (see Appendix 2) are contained in s 109 (providing incorrect information, whether deliberate or inadvertent), s 116 (general breach of conditions) and s 501 (character grounds):

> Visas can be cancelled for a range of reasons. These include where they were obtained with false information, if the holder presents a significant health or safety risk to the Australian community, if visa conditions were breached or simply because changed circumstances no longer warrant the person continuing to hold the visa. Except in a limited number of circumstances, visa cancellation is discretionary, that is, a delegated officer makes a decision to cancel only after carefully weighing up the reasons for and against cancellation.
>
> *(DIMIA 2005: 43)*

The most common breach of a temporary visa encountered by DIAC compliance officers is working without permission. This can occur in a number of contexts. Suspicions that international students have been working in excess of their 20-hour limit have led to searches of student residences by DIAC compliance officers and subsequent detentions and deportations (Marginson *et al.* 2010; Senate Legal and Constitutional Affairs References Committee 2006). Some breaches, such as non-attendance at courses, trigger automatic visa cancellation. Those who have their *permanent* resident visas cancelled on 'character' grounds are another small but socially significant category. New provisions within the Migration Act passed in 1999 removed some of the protections that longstanding residents had previously enjoyed, paving the way for an increase in the use of this expulsion strategy (Commonwealth and Immigration Ombudsman 2006; Senate Legal and Constitutional Affairs References Committee 2006). Although no removal targets have been publicly announced in Australia, the enactment of s 501 powers reflects a political commitment to ensure the exclusion of this 'high-risk' group. The use of these discretionary powers has varied widely under different immigration ministers. Former Minister Philip Ruddock leads the field after personally cancelling 459 visas from 2000–01 to 2002–03 (Nicholls 2007). The 157 visa cancellations on character grounds reported in the latest annual report indicate that, despite less enthusiastic personal intervention by subsequent ministers, total cancellations are returning to similar levels (DIAC 2012: 174).

The legal avenues for cancellation of temporary and permanent residence visas reflect the mutability of the distinction between those who are deemed to be lawfully and unlawfully present. Beyond this source of legal insecurity for non-citizens, controversy over a series of wrongful detentions and deportations of Australian citizens which came to public attention around 2005 (discussed in Chapter 3) demonstrated that having the law on one's side did not necessarily protect against expulsion where the onus in practice was on the individual to establish their lawful status. These cases proved that the crucial boundary between lawful and unlawful presence was determined not only by immigration and nationality law but also by official practices. An individual's immigration status might be incorrectly recorded, disputed or subject to change; they may have legal avenues about which they are unaware or which they have not pursued; and their identity may be unknown to authorities or in dispute. Thus, rather than being part of a simple lawful/unlawful dichotomy, lawfulness is best understood as a dynamic, discretionary and elusive proposition.

Despite these uncertainties, Australian authorities promulgate figures about the unlawfully present population that Dauvergne (2008: 13) describes as 'precisely rendered'. The most recent estimates at 30 June 2011 reported that 58,400 people were in Australia without legal authority (DIAC 2011: 152). This confidence in the capacity of government to quantify the unlawfully present population, and the border control mentality it reflects, stands in stark contrast to the situation in Britain, where estimating the size of the country's much larger unauthorised population is considered to be a matter for expert research (Pinkerton *et al.* 2004). British immigration officials have admitted that they had not the 'faintest idea' how many people were in Britain illegally (Dauvergne 2008: 11). In the US, media reports estimate the size of the undocumented population not in units of hundreds or even thousands, but to the nearest million (Gaynor 2011; Preston 2010).

The last general amnesty for those in breach of Australian immigration law dates back to 1980 (Nicholls 2007). Once a non-citizen is identified as being without a valid visa, their departure is said to be the most likely outcome (DIMIA 2005: 54). The bland bureaucratic vocabulary of locations,[3] removals and unlawful non-citizens masks the human dimensions of these enactments of the internal border. There is no published statistical information, let alone qualitative data, that could illuminate these dimensions, most of which require detailed research which is yet to be undertaken in Australia.[4] The focus for this book remains solely on identifying the mechanisms through which unlawful non-citizens are detected, and assessing the likely social and institutional implications of those practices. Before proceeding to this task, it is important to identify the most significant legal powers available to the key agencies tasked with patrolling Australia's internal borders.

Migration Act enforcement powers

The Migration Act defines the following people as 'designated officers' who are technically authorised to enforce any of the provisions of the Act: DIAC officers, Customs officers, Protective Services Officers, Australian Federal Police (AFP), state police officers, and others authorised in writing by the Minister. In practice, non-DIAC officers exercise a very limited range of Migration Act functions, and even DIAC employees are only trained to apply powers that pertain to their particular area of responsibility, such as granting specific types of visas or, in the case of compliance personnel, cancelling particular visa classes or conducting compliance fieldwork. The powers that are most relevant to the *detection* of unlawful non-citizens are the powers to:

- require evidence from third parties about suspected unlawful non-citizens (s 18, s 336D)
- search premises and seize evidence (s 251)
- enter education provider's premises (s 268CA)
- require evidence from non-citizens to establish their lawful status (s 188)
- detain suspected unlawful non-citizens (s 189).

The power under s 18 of the Migration Act to require third parties to provide information and documents believed to be 'relevant to ascertaining the identity or whereabouts of another person whom the minister has reason to believe is an unlawful non-citizen' enables DIAC officers to request records from other government departments or private individuals. This provision is backed by criminal sanctions for failing to cooperate, although the wording (which consistently refers to 'the person' of whom the request is made) suggests that the most likely target of this coercive power may be private individuals connected to the suspected person rather than other government agencies. Section 336D of the Migration Act authorises the release of identifying information, inter alia, to allow cross-checking with other data sources. Inter-agency requests for information are also subject to the provisions of the *Privacy Act 1988* (Cwlth) and various bilateral MOUs. Alternatively, information may be sought from third parties with the consent of the suspected person. This is an aspect of compliance work that reportedly receives considerable attention in the training of DIAC compliance officers, indicating its importance as an investigative tool:

> [I]t's not a compulsory power, it is a power [where] you need to seek the person's consent to provide the information. And again we need to be quite transparent that you don't need to provide us with this information, providing this information to us is a matter of consent, you can say no and there will be no ill consequences or results of you saying no.
>
> *(Interview 47, Canberra DIAC)*

Evidence about an individual's unlawful status may also be obtained via searches of homes or other premises with or without the consent of the occupant. Section 251(6) of the Migration Act empowers authorised officers to enter and search at any time any premises where the officer has reason to believe they may locate an unlawful non-citizen or the holder of a valid visa containing work restrictions, or find any documentation relating to the entry or proposed entry of a prohibited or unlawful non-citizen. Sub-section (6)(d) authorises seizure of any such documentation found, while sub-section (8) mandates officers to 'use such reasonable force as is necessary for the exercise of his or her powers under this section'. Amendments were introduced in 2001 to authorise Migration Act officers to enter educational establishments with monitoring warrants obtained from magistrates or members of the Administrative Appeals Tribunal (AAT), reflecting the growing emphasis on monitoring the use of international student visas.

These powers are more constrained in scope than comparable police powers of search and seizure, since only the specified travel and identification documents can be seized. On the other hand, they are far less constrained in terms of access. Migration Act warrants are issued under this section by delegated authorities within DIAC rather than by an independent judicial authority. The administrative rationale underlying the use of search and seizure powers, including the desire to retain their 'flexibility', is explained in the following extract from a 2004 submission by DIAC to a Senate Standing Committee:

> The primary purpose for the Migration Act seizure provisions are [sic] to actively enable enforcement of the Migration Act, rather than for evidentiary purposes in a criminal offence context. Seizure provisions are most often used to seize travel documents and tickets, or to seize valuables to recover costs incurred to the Commonwealth. To enable these functions to work successfully in the immigration compliance environment they have been designed with the flexibility to cater for the unique demands of enforcing the Migration Act.
>
> *(DIMIA 2004: 6)*

Where criminal matters are involved, DIAC officers can also apply to magistrates for less restricted '3E' warrants (under the *Crimes Act 1914* [Cwlth]).

The power under s 188 of the Migration Act to require non-citizens to provide evidence to establish their lawful status (most usually a valid visa) enables proactive checks of legal status to be made in the presence of the individual concerned. This may occur during organised workplace operations by DIAC or joint agency teams, during visits by police and/or DIAC officers to private homes, or following street stops by police. The power is triggered by the very wide criterion that the officer 'knows or reasonably suspects' the person to be not necessarily an *unlawful* non-citizen, but merely a non-citizen. This sweeping power casts the entire non-citizen population as potential suspects and puts the onus on the suspected individuals to establish their identity and legal status. No equivalent power exists for police or other authorities to demand documentation from otherwise law-abiding citizens. The legislation therefore licenses the questioning of anyone whose 'Australianness' is considered suspect, and creates a clear demarcation in law between the levels of non-interference enjoyed by citizens and non-citizens.

Since September 1994, non-citizens without valid visas have been subject to automatic removal. As explained in departmental instructions: 'Removal of unlawful non-citizens occurs by *force of law* – that is, no specific order for removal is required, provided that all the conditions in the Act have been satisfied' (DIMIA 2001, emphasis added). Section 189 of the Migration Act requires that if a designated officer 'knows or reasonably suspects' that someone is an unlawful non-citizen, 'the officer *must* detain the person'. The current law on Migration Act detention dates from changes also introduced in 1994 (Crock *et al.* 2006) which specify that the detention of suspected unlawful non-citizens is mandatory, and should continue until the individual is either granted a visa or removed from the country. Prior to the changes, continued detention could only be authorised by a magistrate (Dickins 1995). Courts are now explicitly precluded from intervening, with the result that administrative detention is subject to less external monitoring than the detention of criminal suspects. With this comparison in mind, Nicholls has argued that the mandatory detention system has fostered a 'culture of control' whereby immigration officials have been able to exert 'complete power over non-citizens' (Nicholls 2008). In practice, many unlawful non-citizens are not detained after detection, but are granted a bridging visa pending a resolution of their situation.

The Palmer Inquiry (discussed in Chapter 3) established that s 189 of the Migration Act must be read in conjunction with s 196, which sets out the circumstances in which a detained person may be released, and concluded that a reasonable suspicion that a person *is* in fact an unlawful non-citizen must be maintained if detention is to be continued (Palmer 2005). Legal opinion sought by the Inquiry confirmed that the onus was not on the detainee to dispel the suspicion that they were illegally present, but on the detaining officer to make sufficient enquiries to establish a reasonable suspicion that they were. However, no legislative amendments have been made to limit or clarify the scope of these broad powers. Furthermore, although the Commonwealth Ombudsman (2001) recommended as early as 2001 that immigration detention should be subject to a regime of accountability at least as extensive as the safeguards accorded within the criminal justice system, detention under the Migration Act still operates entirely without external review. Clearly, some legal ambiguity remains in the minds of immigration officials, especially where the point of contention is over establishing identity:

> Our ability to question people is probably not as strong as police. We have a thing called 'Questioning Detention' but we can only detain a person to question them if they are on a current visa and we suspect that they are in breach of their visa conditions. We can't detain a person to establish what their identity is, and that poses quite a few problems for us in many respects.... We can detain them as long as we have reasonable suspicion ... so there is a lot of tension at that point with regard to the detention of that person and how we actually manage that.
>
> *(Interview 42, Canberra DIAC)*

Despite these considerable coercive powers, DIAC compliance officers do not consider themselves to be an 'enforcement agency' and have a sense of operating 'in a completely different environment' from the police (Interview 42, Canberra DIAC). However, DIAC compliance officers enjoy a level of access to intrusive enforcement procedures that is unparalleled within the criminal justice system. While the Commonwealth Ombudsman maintains a broad oversight of immigration enforcement functions, including detention, the day-to-day application of coercive Migration Act powers depends only on internal DIAC Migration Series Instructions (MSIs) and on the training and professionalism of departmental officers to ensure their legitimate use.

NSW state police powers

As designated officers under the Migration Act, NSW police are authorised to question non–citizens (under s 188) and are required to detain them under s 189 if they believe they are unlawfully present. In addition, they possess a broad range of general powers to question, investigate, arrest and detain in relation to traditional police functions of crime control and order maintenance. The general powers of operational police officers were codified relatively recently in NSW in the *Law Enforcement (Powers and Responsibilities) Act 2002* (NSW), commonly referred to as LEPRA.

Perhaps the most controversial aspects of police powers in NSW have been the provisions that enable aggressive place-based street policing, such as neighbourhood 'lockdowns', use of sniffer dogs in designated areas, 'move-on' powers and the conduct of street stops; and the summary powers of NSW police to issue criminal infringement notices with financial penalties attached. These powers that underpin policing in public areas are relevant to migration policing because they form the context in which s 188 powers are likely to be exercised in everyday policing. Of course law is not the only, or even the main, factor shaping police practice. According to the NSW Police Ombudsman, when explicit move-on powers were first enacted in the *Crimes Legislation Amendment (Police and Public Safety) Act 1998* (NSW), which authorised police to require individuals to move from public places without suspicion that they were intending to commit an offence, it transpired that police members had always assumed that they possessed these powers (NSW Ombudsman 2000). One local area commander summed up the street policing powers within LEPRA in the following terms:

> So, we have that basis, our move-on powers, someone obstructing a pedestrian, a vehicle or traffic, they are causing a nuisance and generally causing a bit of a pest of themselves, we could move them on from the area. We also have at the extreme end the powers of arrest, and there is nothing to stop us just going up and talking to someone to go and gather intelligence. So the whole basis of our proactive intervention, if you like, is that four-pronged attack of intelligence, move on, search, and at the extreme arrest.
> *(Interview 23, NSW Police Force Local Area Commander)*

Commentators have long criticised the readiness of NSW governments to enact new police powers to address any emerging area of public concern. In relation to the introduction of LEPRA, Dixon and Schimmel noted:

> Unfortunately, it appears that the government is more concerned with using the legislative process as a tool of law and order politics, promoting symbolic, instant responses to problems – 'drug houses', 'knife-carriers', dealers who conceal drugs inside their bodies, consorting gangsters – than with the hard grind of substantial statutory reform.
> *(Dixon and Schimmel 2002: 61)*

The 'substantial statutory reform' envisaged by these authors was a consolidation and simplification of police powers, coupled with real protections against their misuse. Police move-on powers have also been widely described by critical commentators as 'street-sweeping' (Brown *et al.* 2006) or 'street-cleaning' (Cunneen 2007), targeted disproportionately at already marginalised groups such as Aboriginal youths and other young people. The only restriction imposed on officers deploying the powers to search for knives or drugs, or give move-on directions, is that they must identify themselves, provide verbal reasons for deploying their powers, and explain that failure to comply is an offence. At the time of the NSW Ombudsman's Inquiry in 2000 the only information recorded about the exercise of move-on powers by police was in relation to refusals, apparently for operational rather than accountability reasons (NSW Ombudsman 2000). Even after the enactment of LEPRA, a lack of ongoing external oversight has led critical commentators to conclude that police powers in NSW are largely unregulated: '[t]here is considerable anecdotal evidence to suggest that the police regard the knife laws as "nod and a wink" legitimacy for the pro-active and unrestrained searching of young people in any situation' (Brown *et al.* 2006: 852). A national review of state move-on powers conducted in 2007 placed the NSW powers at 'the most permissive end' of the legislative spectrum, enabling a move-on order to be issued where 'a person's mere presence could cause anxiety to another person, or interference with another's "reasonable enjoyment" of the space' (Walsh and Taylor 2007: 158).

In addition to these controversial powers, s 11 of LEPRA empowers police to require disclosure of identity 'if the officer suspects on reasonable grounds that the person may be able to assist in the investigation of an alleged indictable offence'. Subsequent sections of LEPRA create offences for failing to disclose one's true identity. Section 87L contains a power to require disclosure of identity in an 'authorised area' in which special powers are being applied, referring to the police power to 'lock down' a residential area. Political concern over public safety at railway stations has provided further impetus for the proactive policing of public places. One local area commander noted that railway-related offences, including behaving in an offensive manner, riding without a ticket, smoking on a railway station, and carrying, supplying or drinking liquor on a railway station, all provided an 'opportunity for police officers to stop and prop people in a target group' (Interview 6, NSW Police Force Local Area Commander). The *Police Powers (Drug Detection Dogs) Act 2001* (NSW) defines a 'prescribed route' around train stations in central Sydney within which police are authorised to check tickets and deploy sniffer dogs without a warrant.

Vehicle stops are authorised without reason for the purposes of random breath and drug testing, or where a vehicle or a person inside is wanted in connection with an offence – after which a general power to request a driver's licence which applies to anyone driving a car can be invoked (*Road Transport (General) Act 2005* [NSW], s 173). An officer from the Commuter Crime Unit (Interview 11) explained that this legislation provides a valuable statutory basis for police to demand the production of a driver's licence. Other legislation requires only that a name and address be provided in specified circumstances. Still, he contended, the onus is generally on a person who is approached by police to satisfy an officer of their identity, even in the absence of any clearly defined power.

This loose relationship between law and practice is suggestive of the so-called 'Ways and Means Act' through which police engineer consent for policing practices which have no clear legal basis (Dixon 1997: 93). In the interviews conducted for the migration policing study, local area commanders were open about the exploitation by police of the grey area between the law, the public's knowledge of mandated police powers, and the capacity of particular groups to mobilise their own rights:

> Most law-abiding people don't have a problem with providing cops with ID. But then again it's the manner in which you are approached, if the police are aggressive and a little bit over the top, then you might be taken aback. Well, what do you want to know that for? And at the end of the day if the police don't have that reasonable suspicion, then I don't have to tell you who I am, go away.

I don't have to tell you anything. And that is your right. But then if the police believe that they have reasonable suspicion, well then they need to be able to explain their powers to the people, and in accordance with LEPRA they need to identify themselves, tell the person the powers that they are exercising, what the consequences are if the person fails to abide by police directions. They may render themselves liable to arrest, etcetera, etcetera … you know if they start to burr up or walk away or whatever, it may increase your suspicion of them as to why they are trying to avoid talking to the cops.

(Interview 23, NSW Police Force Local Area Commander)

As Dixon (1997: 95) concluded from his research on the exercise of police powers in Britain and NSW, 'the very process of trying to obtain consent allows officers to test their suspicion about a person'. Advocates for young people in NSW therefore temper their legal advice with a heavy dose of pragmatism:

Police have a right to ask you to identify yourself, but in most cases you do not have to do so. It is usually a good idea to tell the police your name and address, or show them some ID, otherwise they might make trouble for you or even arrest you.

(Shopfront Youth Legal Centre 2008)

In light of the above discussion, it is conceivable that in some circumstances, part of that potential 'trouble' might include an immigration status check.

As Van der Leun (2003: 18) has noted, the consequences for non-citizens of being categorised as illegal depend on levels of enforcement, along with other factors such as access to community support. Unlike Van der Leun's research, the migration policing study did not explore the internal dynamics of migrant communities, but concentrated on institutional practices. Having outlined the relevant powers available to the main migration policing agencies in NSW, it remains to consider how these powers translate into practice.

3

IMMIGRATION OFFICERS AS MIGRATION POLICE

DIAC as a specialist policing agency

A 'well-oiled' deportation machine

Although the DIAC staff interviewed for the migration policing study did not describe their role as 'policing', an organisation that wields the significant powers of search, arrest and indefinite detention described in the previous chapter surely qualifies as a specialist policing agency. Reiner's well-known definition of policing as 'the set of activities directed at preserving the security of a particular social order' (Reiner 1997: 718) applies as much to the activities of immigration compliance authorities as it does to the law enforcement and order maintenance efforts of generalist police. In relation to non-citizens, however, it may be their expulsion, rather than their containment or reform, which is the means by which the security of citizens is pursued. In his history of Australian deportation, Nicholls (2007: 149) likens the enforcement wing of DIAC to a 'well-oiled' machine geared towards the automatic removal of anyone who is unable to establish their right to remain and operating with scant external oversight. The implications of this approach came into full view in 2005 when the deportation machine ran off the rails and swept up a number of Australian citizens who strayed into its path. The scandals that ensued revealed the machinery to be well oiled but poorly steered and, most alarmingly of all, operating without effective brakes.

Most prominent in the media coverage was the treatment of naturalised Australian citizens Cornelia Rau and Vivian Solon. Cornelia Rau, a longstanding Australian resident of German origin who was suffering from schizophrenia, was detained by police and later transferred to immigration custody when she claimed to be a German tourist named Anna. A long and harrowing period of administrative detention ensued under harsh and degrading conditions which shocked the Australian public when Cornelia's situation was finally brought to light. Vivian Solon, also known as Vivian Alvarez, originated from the Philippines and entered Australia as the spouse of an Australian citizen. She came to the notice of immigration authorities after being hospitalised, having been found dazed and injured in a public place for reasons that were never identified. In her case, her wrongful detention culminated in removal to the Philippines, where she was abandoned for several years, wheelchair-bound and with minimal support, until the 'mistake' was discovered. The official enquiries that followed the media outcry identified shortfalls in departmental record-keeping and identity-checking procedures; criticised rigid protocols that left no room for discretion; and called for fundamental changes in departmental culture, which was found to promote an overzealous approach to enforcement and a presumption of illegality (Commonwealth Ombudsman 2005; Foreign Affairs, Defence and Trade References Committee 2005; Palmer 2005). In due course several hundred other lawfully present individuals were found to be languishing in immigration detention and their cases were referred to the Commonwealth Ombudsman for investigation (Commonwealth Ombudsman 2007b).

International students have been another controversial target group for migration policing in Australia. Marginson *et al.* (2010: 6) report that 17,134 raids were conducted by DIAC compliance officers between 2002–03 and 2004–05, resulting in the cancellation of 24,567 student visas, sometimes leading to protracted periods of detention. More than one-third of the cancellations were later set aside on appeal to the Migration Review Tribunal. Visa cancellations dropped markedly by 2009–10 when there were 811 student visa cancellation decisions, but the appeal rate was still high and 41 per cent were set aside by the Tribunal (Migration Review Tribunal 2010). The early 2000s also heralded a rapid increase in visa cancellations on 'character' grounds, leading to the deportation of many long-term residents with significant ties in Australia. These migration policing practices also provoked controversy and resulted in a referral to the Commonwealth Ombudsman and a response from the national human rights watchdog (Australian Human Rights Commission [AHRC] 2010; Commonwealth and Immigration Ombudsman 2006).

A senior DIAC official claimed that around 200 recommendations for change had been made in various Ombudsman and AHRC reports around this period (Interview 45, Canberra DIAC). While there has been considerable criticism of the narrow focus and lack of transparency of the Palmer Inquiry from academics (Grewcock 2005) and in the political arena (AAP 2005), these controversies ushered in a new era within DIAC driven by the introduction of the 'post-Palmer' reforms. One senior official described the rationale driving these reforms as a shift from an enforcement mentality towards a 'client-centred' approach:

> In the old days it was just enforcement, enforcement, enforcement, where you have a search warrant, you go in and you detain a person and you remove them. Since Palmer we have been looking at more engagement with clients, being a bit more client focused, making sure we still get the outcomes we want,

but dealing with it in a much more client-centred way. So the taking account of client circumstances better – we don't play the hard line up front.

(Interview 42, Canberra DIAC)

Although the Palmer Inquiry and other critical reports sparked major changes in training, management and operational procedures within DIAC and the introduction of new technologies to better establish identity and guide decision-making, they did not challenge in any fundamental way the underlying legislation that drives migration policing practices, nor acknowledge the harsh treatment and injustices routinely levelled at non-citizens and those without lawful immigration status. Rather than curtailing mandatory detention powers, the incoming Labor government in 2007 announced that immigration detention would thereafter be used for the shortest practicable time and as a 'last resort' (Nicholls 2008). The claim to be using detention as a 'last resort' is a familiar official framing for the use of controversial, discretionary powers. Previous research carried out by the author on detention practices in the United Kingdom (UK) demonstrated that the interpretation of this guiding concept varies widely among those tasked with making detention decisions (Weber 2003, 2005).

After Labor came to office in the 2007 federal election, the incoming Immigration Minister Chris Evans announced his vision for 'restoring integrity' to Australia's immigration system in a speech delivered at the Australian National University, in which he claimed that the system would operate on a 'new set of values – values that seek to emphasise a risk-based approach to detention and prompt resolution of cases rather than punishment', adding that '[t]he best deterrent is to ensure that people who have no right to remain in Australia are removed expeditiously' (Evans 2008). Sceptics noted that a lack of legislative underpinning for these new values meant that whatever changes in departmental practice were achieved would be resting on shaky legal ground and would be vulnerable to future shifts in the political climate (Williams 2008). A National Communications Branch was established swiftly in the wake of the Palmer Inquiry to communicate the department's 'post-Palmer' transformation. As one sceptical media commentator put it: 'The department now spends millions in marketing and public relations to tell everyone … that it has learnt all the lessons from its policy and administrative fiascos of a few years ago and now does things entirely differently' (Waterford 2008).

The possibility of transforming DIAC's entrenched culture through organisational reforms has attracted particular scepticism. A former immigration department head, John Menadue, told a national broadcaster that the Howard government had 'tipped the balance in favour of compliance, in favour of border control, in favour of policing, rather than the humanitarian aspects which are so important within the department' (Ewart 2005). Some external critics have argued that the department had colluded enthusiastically in the adoption of harsh policies by the former conservative government and was a driving force in the systematic removal of legal remedies, based on a set of organisational norms that 'regarded non-citizens as only vaguely "entitled" to any rights of due process' (Nicholls 2007; Waterford 2008). This hostility towards due process is a characteristic often attributed to police organisational cultures (Dixon 1999). Decades of research into police culture and organisational reform have established that effecting fundamental change in organisational norms within such closed environments presents a monumental challenge (Chan 1997). Indeed, the official evaluation of the post-Palmer reforms noted the relative lack of attention given to cultural change and argued that the continuing 'heavy reliance on processes, instructions and procedures, together with some aspects of the legislative framework' interfered with the 'desire to build a client focused organisation' (Proust 2008: 33).

One DIAC informant claimed that the new compliance-based approach, aimed primarily at reducing the numbers of illegal workers, did not necessarily result in high numbers of removals (Interview 45, Canberra DIAC). However, writing in November 2008, almost a year after the research briefings for the migration policing study were conducted, one prominent commentator argued that there was no discernible change in enforcement outcomes:

> The figures show no let-up in the department's zeal. In South Australia, for example, 408 individuals were detained as illegal workers in the first nine months of the 2007–08 financial year, more than the 406 detained in that state during the full year 2006–07. Of those 408,241 had been deported; the rest were held in community detention or detention centres … the department is also on track to increase the number of deportations using the character test in section 501 of the Migration Act.
>
> *(Nicholls 2008)*

The overall removal numbers shown in Figure 3.1 support this prediction. Removal figures dipped after the Cornelia Rau and associated scandals caused a brief derailment in the removal machine. But it was soon back on track – redesigned

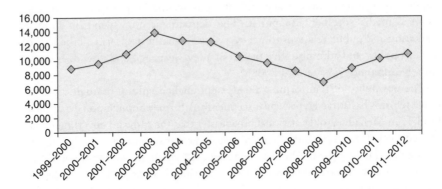

FIGURE 3.1 Removals from Australia.

Source: DIAC Annual Reports 2000–12.

for fuel efficiency rather than maximum horsepower – and removal numbers are once again on the rise. Although some further internal safeguards have been introduced under the Labor government for students and permanent residents facing visa cancellation, not even an adverse finding by the UN Human Rights Committee in relation to the forced return of convicted Australian resident Stefan Nystrom to Sweden – a country he left as a newborn baby – has quelled the government's appetite for ridding the country of those it considers to pose a risk to the Australian community (Human Rights Committee 2011).

Overview of post-Palmer reforms

The post-Palmer reforms emerged as the primary theme in the briefings provided by Canberra-based DIAC officials at the commencement of the migration policing project. Although they acknowledged the need for substantial changes to DIAC's internal procedures, referrals from other agencies were considered to have been the starting point for many of the wrongful detentions. Immigration was said to be 'at the end of a long set of failures of other systems' (Interview 45, Canberra DIAC), including the public health system, and at the 'receiving end' of problems that were passed on by other agencies, notably the police:

> We weren't being critical enough when presented with information from the police. So the police would say to us, we have this person and you know they're unlawful, we would take their word for it, and without doing anything more than perfunctory checks we would accept that.
>
> *(Interview 47, Canberra DIAC)*

In place of the former 'perfunctory checks', stricter regimes were said to have been put in place to ensure that DIAC officers would verify information before accepting referrals from other agencies as 'immigration cases'. This could mean that the 'problem might now remain with police' if DIAC determined that it had no interest in a particular individual.

Providing an improved basis for verifying identity and confirming immigration status has been a major plank of the post-Palmer reforms, beginning with the establishment of a National Identity Verification and Advice Unit in 2005. Recording information correctly from the point of application for a visa, including biometric data for applicants from high-risk countries not eligible for instantly issued ETAs, was seen to be critical, not only for the purposes of later immigration enforcement, but also in order to check entitlements to national medical care and other benefits. A document detailing the 'Strategic Plan for Identity Management in DIAC' indicates the growing importance of identity verification technologies across a range of border control strategies, including the use of biometrics to 'anchor' identity. These technologies are intended to 'establish a consistent foundation identity for non-citizens to use in the community' (DIAC 2007: 4).

As Lyon has argued:

> People have become dependent on states for an 'identity' – or, rather, identification – which both enables and inhibits movement within a given territory and across borders. The 'identity' that includes also excludes those who do not meet the criteria of citizenship.
>
> *(Lyon 2005: 74)*

To this end, an expanding data-sharing capacity has been built on this foundation of identity determination, intended to achieve this 'social sorting':

> There's virtually no one in Australia that either wasn't born here or that this department doesn't have a ... doesn't have a record of in some way. So we get community information about someone who's allegedly a non-citizen, [and] if the name that we're given is correct we've been able to verify that in our systems.... Where a name doesn't match up with anything that we have we can conduct other checks with, you know, the tax office or with other information holders. We've got power under the Act to require the information holder to give us information.
>
> *(Interview 45, Canberra DIAC)*

The Palmer Inquiry also highlighted the unreflective and, at times, inhumane way in which immigration compliance cases were being handled. The department's response has been to provide the training and information technology (IT) resources necessary for compliance officers to make sound and lawful decisions. Many key decisions that feed into compliance work, such as those around eligibility for particular visa types and entitlements, and whether grounds exist to cancel visas, are now handled by specialised centres that make particular categories of decision at a nation-wide level. The major decision made by compliance fieldwork officers, once unlawful status has been established to the required level of certainty, is whether to detain the individual concerned or grant them a bridging visa. The three basic criteria for granting a bridging visa are that the individual is making arrangements to leave, has applied for a substantive visa, or has an appeal or review outstanding. According to the research informants, further discretion may be exercised if the individual is undergoing medical treatment and/or is not fit to travel. The use of discretion by decision-makers was reported to have changed in the aftermath of the Palmer Inquiry in favour of granting bridging visas, with criminal deportees being the major exception:

> Unless a person met one of those three criteria, they ... they were going into detention. Well, that's very much changed. You know there's a lot more latitude for us to, you know, do what is ... is the fair and reasonable and appropriate thing.
>
> *(Interview 45, Canberra DIAC)*

Departmental instructions (MSIs) were undergoing a major overhaul at the time of the research briefings, with a view to encouraging DIAC compliance officers to use their judgement rather than adopt the attitude that 'this is what the instruction says and this is what we must do' (Interview 42, Canberra DIAC). A Quality Assurance (QA) process was also implemented as part of the strategy to improve the quality of decisions through internal accountability: 'We've developed a QA process that actually manages now the compliance process and oversights the high-risk areas of it. So at various points we have senior people reviewing what's actually occurred' (Interview 42, Canberra DIAC). Particular 'QA points' which trigger checking by more senior officers include the issuing of search warrants and decisions to continue detention. These checkpoints are supported by the 'Integrated Case Management' approach, which is aimed at bringing together all the material held about a 'client' that is relevant to a particular decision, in a way that will guide the decision-maker. While these innovations represent a massive investment in new bureaucratic systems,[1] research in other contexts suggests that providing guidance and internal checks and balances may still not guarantee lawful and just decisions. The author's own research with UK immigration officers established that internal reviews of detention decisions were largely ineffectual, and events tended to be swept along by a collective mentality dubbed 'removal momentum' (Weber 2003; Weber and Landman 2002).

Encouraging staff to assume higher levels of individual responsibility in making operational decisions creates a requirement for better training. DIAC has approached this aspect of its post-Palmer reforms by establishing a series of 'Immigration Colleges' representing each of the department's specialised areas. The training required for a compliance field officer was increased from only two to ten and a half weeks, and incoming compliance officers were thereafter required to complete the expanded course. Within this training particular attention was said to be given to post-Palmer policy changes, notably alternatives for detention, with the concept of 'last resort' guiding decisions:

> Detaining a person is a decision to be made as a last resort and there is now quite a strong emphasis in all the department's processes and on control points we have in place, which places a premium on identifying – have we considered all of the alternatives?
>
> *(Interview 47, Canberra DIAC)*

While this represents a major advance on an assumption in favour of detention, the author's previous research showed that individual interpretations of 'last resort' vary widely (Weber 2005).

Immigration College training also supports the QA programme more broadly. Of the ten and a half weeks of the course, it was said that eight and a half business days were spent 'on the QA points alone' (Interview 47, Canberra DIAC). According to DIAC informants, at the heart of the new training model is a 'stronger emphasis on the core values of the department, especially when we're talking about fair and reasonable dealings with clients' (Interview 47, Canberra DIAC). The training programme also focuses heavily on hands-on experience with decision-making in real-life settings, borrowing a great deal from the police model of experiential learning:

> We actually take our participants out to the AFP training site in Majura, which is a … it's a mock village if you like. But it's perfect for our training needs in that I can recreate a number of scenarios visiting upon different themes and so expose the training officers to situations and occurrences and challenges within one week which would ordinarily take them one or two years to experience otherwise.
>
> *(Interview 47, Canberra DIAC)*

Ex–police officers from various states are sometimes used as training partners to impart greater inter-agency knowledge, particularly those who have worked for other government departments such as the Department of Defence, the AFP, Centrelink or Veteran's Affairs, further cementing the training links between the police and immigration functions. Given the complexity of the relationships with other agencies, considerable attention is placed on negotiating these migration policing networks, particularly in relation to arrangements for information-exchange at local levels:

> We cover off, I suppose, at the higher levels … more generalised levels such as what the lawful basis is for our interactions with those agencies – whether it's a Memorandum of Understanding, what a Memorandum of Understanding, you know, actually allows us to do on a legal basis. And how we actually need to cover off and lawfully exchange the information, whether it be under a privacy principle that we're requesting information, whether it's under a compulsory power that we can exercise in circumstances, such as section 18 of our Act. Or whether it's freely available public information, which any member of the public could go out there and obtain immediately by looking and knowing where to look.
>
> *(Interview 47, Canberra DIAC)*

The years since the Palmer Inquiry have also seen rapid changes in departmental demographics, with a high staff turnover, both in senior ranks and at operational levels. One informant noted that 'in the seven or eight years I've been an investigator here, I probably had almost as many directors or acting directors' (Interview 44, Canberra DIAC). This was said to relate to a number of factors, not least of which were a series of staffing cuts associated with successive federal budgets.[2] But deliberate changes in the desired profile for compliance officers were also reported, apparently in an attempt to transform the discredited 'police-like' culture:

> We used to be getting some police come into the compliance environment. That's not always appropriate because they come from an enforcement mindset

and ours is not enforcement.... At one stage it was regarded as the 'black side' of the department. These days we are trying to change that view. We probably have the most highly trained people in the network currently.

(Interview 42, Canberra DIAC)

Regardless of the quality of staff training provided, the delegation of coercive powers to specialised sections of the department raises the possibility that organisational subcultures will develop around these functional differences. On the other hand, the Palmer Report noted that compliance officers tended to be drawn from other sections of the department, suggesting that there was longstanding mobility between enforcement and non-enforcement sectors. In any case, fundamental changes to organisational culture require more than mere changes in personnel. The research informants reported that significant shifts had also occurred in management style, including changes in organisational incentives which reflected new government expectations:

The number of locations used to be the measure and a few years ago we had something like over 20,000 locations. I think last year we had about eleven thousand and five locations, so we've changed the way we're operating.

(Interview 42, Canberra DIAC)

Politically determined performance indicators which previously linked funding to the numbers of detections had reportedly been replaced with measures of effectiveness that were considered to be more 'client-centred':[3]

Where we really are focusing these days is on the options for clients in terms of their personal situations to make sure that we can deal with that appropriately. Because some of these people we locate as overstayers have been in refuge for maybe 10 or 15 years, they've got tied to the country, they have an Australian citizen spouse and children often. And what is the caring, reasonable way of dealing with those? It depends what the new government will say about it. The previous government had a particular view about it.

(Interview 42, Canberra DIAC)

Reliance on new technologies

Ericson and Haggerty (1997: 18) have observed with respect to criminal justice agencies that transitions from deterrence towards compliance-based law enforcement have been accompanied by 'shifts to acquiring the knowledge necessary to set acceptable standards of risk'. Efforts to improve data management and decision-making within DIAC have indeed been underpinned by the introduction of significant new technologies. In particular, the focus on determining identity has led to the introduction of facial recognition software across a range of departmental functions, particularly the management of detainees, and the 2006 establishment of the Immigration Status Service (ISS) to provide accurate information about immigration status to external agencies. Police are by far the most frequent users of this 24-hour system. The mode of operation of the system is explained in the following statement by a senior DIAC officer:

> If the policeman has located someone, their training is to ring the Immigration Status Service – ISS. The ISS will determine whether they are of interest to DIAC or not – that is, if they are an unlawful non-citizen or not. Only about 10 per cent of cases they refer to us are unlawful and 90 per cent are not. We've dealt with 8000–10,000 cases since we've started, so that gives you an idea of the proportion that we are interested in out of those cases.
>
> *(Interview 42, Canberra DIAC)*

The outcomes of more than 10,000 queries referred to the ISS during its first 20 months of operation are shown in Figure 3.2, which is generated from data supplied by DIAC. Only 13 per cent of the queries identified an unlawful non-citizen, not all of whom were ultimately removed. Although identification rates are low, one advantage of this system for DIAC is the early screening out of cases that might otherwise have been referred to them by police. On the other hand, it is possible – although difficult to establish – that the introduction of the system has increased the likelihood that immigration avenues will be pursued by police in the first place. An additional benefit to DIAC of the ISS is in dealing with Migration

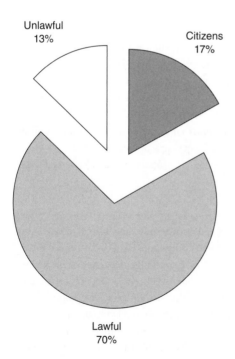

FIGURE 3.2 Outcome of ISS checks 20 February 2006 to 31 October 2007.

Act detainees held by police in remote areas, where it may be difficult to meet the Ombudsman's Office rules stipulating that interviews by a DIAC compliance officer must be conducted within four hours of apprehension.

The new Integrated Case Management model and QA system is supported by an IT interface that has the benevolent title of 'Systems for People'. The system will present departmental officers with a 'single view of the full client record', along with any operating instructions and role descriptions needed to support their decisions. This technology underpins the new intelligence-led way of working and is designed to overcome the fragmentation of information in which separate sections of the department 'all have our own little windows' (Interview 44, Canberra DIAC).

In response to the increasing complexity of the Australian visa system, separate DIAC units have been set up to perform specialist functions at a national level. For example, s 501 visa cancellations are dealt with in Melbourne by the ominously named National Character Consideration Centre, while decisions concerning the issue and cancellation of student visas are handled in Brisbane, and matters related to skilled work visas are managed in Adelaide. Each of the larger states also has a specific investigations unit designated to investigate major Migration Act offences such as people smuggling or fraud, coordinated by a national investigations unit in Canberra. These specialisations necessitate a dense network of internal connectivity throughout the organisation, which Systems for People is designed to facilitate. The intention is that the system will provide procedural consistency across states and ensure data quality from a client-centred perspective, thereby eliminating 'mistakes'.

Supporting the new emphasis on the exercise of discretion, the expectation is that '[t]his system actually makes you manage clients, it makes you think proactive' (Interview 43, Canberra DIAC). Confirmation of identity remains central to realising a client-centred approach: 'as long as you've got the right identity of someone you can pull the information together' (Interview 43, Canberra DIAC). Systems for People is expected to guide DIAC staff along the 'immigration pathway' for a particular individual towards achieving a well-documented and legally justifiable outcome:

> Now we have what we call Integrated Business Guidelines, which I can't show you, but what they are is a clear set of instructions setting out what the person needs to do, what their role is – it could be the role of a compliance officer. It then passes them over to the detention officer whose roles are defined, and the removal officer, and their roles are defined, and a case manager's roles are defined. So actually defining it down to every step that a person has to take.
>
> *(Interview 43, Canberra DIAC)*

Under the Integrated Business Model, case managers assigned to complex cases involving recalcitrant or vulnerable 'clients' play a key role in coordinating progress towards timely outcomes:

> There used to be a time when Compliance would have a plan, and Detentions would have a plan, Removals would have a plan. That's not going to happen

anymore, there's one plan. And that's where the case manager will be integral in all those links because they're driving that plan, they're the broker of it, they can actually escalate it.

(Interview 43, Canberra DIAC)

This recalibration of the system to achieve timely outcomes while injecting opportunities for discretion at specified decision-points is a direct enactment of the Palmer recommendations which highlighted the department's responsibility to 'keep prodding away and keep seeking more information until the end of the process' which 'isn't until that person is either granted a substantive visa, their immigration status is regularised, or they're removed or depart from the country' (Interview 47, Canberra DIAC).

From enforcement to risk management

Post-Palmer DIAC shows all the hallmarks of neoliberal forms of governance, including an emphasis on promoting 'voluntary' compliance while targeting more coercive measures towards 'high-risk' groups, a reliance on information technologies, and the dispersal of the policing effort across a wide range of agencies. At a forum for risk management executives held in 2007, then DIAC Secretary Andrew Metcalfe explained his efforts to create a 'risk management culture' through training courses, intranet resources, an online Risk Toolkit, a Risk Helpdesk and, for good measure, a 'network of risk advocates across DIAC' (Metcalfe 2007). From discussions held with senior DIAC officials, it seems that this risk-based approach was imported from other federal departments such as the Australian Taxation Office (ATO) and Centrelink that were already focused on promoting compliance, managing risk and detecting fraud. In fact, the strategy for organisational change within DIAC has included recruiting experienced senior staff from these federal agencies to oversee the post-Palmer reforms.

The Priorities Matrix is the flagship of DIAC's new risk-based approach. This document guides decisions across all levels of the compliance process, based on intelligence-led but politically determined risk categories. A simplified version of the Priorities Matrix for 2007–08, which was operative throughout the period of the migration policing research, is shown in Appendix 3. The matrix includes relatively stable categories of 'mandatory' and 'high-risk' work, plus a series of 'hot spots' which are presumably more responsive to ongoing intelligence analysis.[4] Although the details may change, the highest priority has always been attached to the detection of exploitation or serious immigration offences, such as trafficking, smuggling and fraud, and on effecting character-based deportations. Referrals from police and any other cases involving criminality are considered 'mandatory' work. The introduction of the Priorities Matrix signals a shift in organisational focus towards dealing with systemic problems such as institutional fraud and organised illegal working, and, by implication, away from actively identifying individual unlawful non-citizens. However, the continued emphasis on criminal deportation runs somewhat counter to this trend. As Pratt (2005: 179) has argued in relation to the 'Criminals First' programme introduced in Canada in 1994, such an approach entrenches an 'enforcement mentality' and risks creating a 'tight culture ... around front-line enforcers who tend towards a good guys/bad guys view'. The use of the 'hot spots' jargon, which seems linguistically inappropriate for risk categories that are thematically rather than geographically defined, suggests an identification with risk-based approaches adopted in crime prevention contexts that reinforces this emphasis on 'immigration penality'.

The hot spots for 2007–08 included a focus on identity management, student non-compliance and the pursuit of immigration outcomes for unresolved cases. Interviewees reported that asylum seekers account for a very minor proportion of the department's compliance work but could come to notice, for example, where individuals are initially refused refugee status and subsequently work illegally while on a bridging visa (Interview 42, Canberra DIAC). On the other hand, the removal of failed protection visa applicants is identified as an ongoing high priority in the Priorities Matrix, probably referring mainly to those who remain in detention after their applications have been rejected. Systematic strategies to remove certain groups of unsuccessful asylum claimants, such as the involuntary returns of Hazaras to Afghanistan (Neighbour 2011), could also identify the removal of failed asylum seekers as a specific, short-term hot spot.

The research team was not able to observe the activities of DIAC field officers to examine how the Priorities Matrix is translated into action, but an idealised example of how the matrix might be applied in practice was provided in one of the research briefings:

> If they've worked in a brothel and they are on a student visa they are really not of interest to us. We are really looking at trafficking issues in a brothel environment, so we would concentrate on that, or people who don't have a visa or who are working in breach of their visa conditions.... Basically what we are looking at is the mandatory and the high priorities, after that the medium and low, we rarely get down to that level. We've got limited resources and we need to put them at the higher end of our priorities, obviously.
>
> *(Interview 42, Canberra DIAC)*

Ad hoc ministerial instructions can further divert limited compliance resources in response to short-term pressures. According to media reports, critical overcrowding in detention centres during 2010, following a resurgence of 'unauthorised' boat arrivals, resulted in compliance officers being ordered to 'back off all non-essential visa checking, such as raids on brothels and illegal fruit pickers' (Maley and Taylor 2010). This flexible way of working differs markedly from the more reactive approach taken previously, which was largely driven by external referrals from police and other agencies. However, the risk-based model also serves to concentrate greater control of the immigration compliance system in the hands of government through direct ministerial determination of enforcement priorities.

Reports from external sources are likely to remain the foundation for migration policing, and considerable efforts have been made to ensure that information is sifted and shaped according to departmental and ministerial priorities, notably the establishment of special units at the state level to act as clearing houses for incoming information: 'Well, certainly one of the big changes has been state and territory offices – that they've got what we call information management units … we've got these established units where they assess all the information and assess it against the Priorities Matrix' (Interview 45, Canberra DIAC).

The formation of Compliance Early Response Teams (CERTs) at the state level has been the clearest structural indication of a 'softer' approach emphasising case resolution and the promotion of compliance: 'It's a team that deals with low-risk cases where they go to a house, knock on the door, they try and identify a person and say, "Oh look you're unlawful, you need to come in, we'll give you a bridging visa to come in. This is what you need to do." And that's working quite well' (Interview 42, Canberra DIAC).

The success of this new focus on compliance was said to be reflected in increased levels of 'voluntary' self-referrals by individuals who are, or believe themselves to be, in breach of immigration laws:

> The biggest source is now people walking in themselves…. The second-biggest source is police and other law enforcement referrals and then the third … the third and you know by far the smallest is where we actually send the field operation team out to … to try and locate someone.
>
> *(Interview 45, Canberra DIAC)*

Alongside this 'client-centred' approach, the incentives to promote voluntary compliance are reinforced by the threat of more coercive treatment:

> People tend to forget that compliance is about deterrence – persuading people to comply with the legislation and then if they don't comply, then they'll be sent letters or detained and then possibly removed. But then you also have the deterrence factor: that is, that people that blatantly and systemically offend against the Migration Act, or [commit] serious offences such as organised fraud, fraudulent applications, people smuggling, things like that, and that is then the enforcement side of it. And that's the big stick end of compliance, in other words, that if people are investigated and hopefully found guilty, then serious sanctions come into it then.
>
> *(Interview 46, Canberra DIAC)*

One effect of the risk-based approach has reportedly been to separate the 'big stick' investigative and enforcement functions from routine, more 'client-focused' compliance work. While the term 'enforcement' is reserved for serious and systematic breaches of immigration law dealt with by specialist units that have had police-like training in investigations, the more benign label of 'compliance' is applied to the day-to-day dealings with individual visa violators by compliance fieldwork teams. A senior DIAC officer involved in investigation of systemic breaches noted that these functions were now distinct in practice:

> So if we're in the field today and we were to come across an unlawful non-citizen we wouldn't be able to act on that. We wouldn't be able to detain them, we'd have to actually refer that information to Compliance, even if we're on the spot, which is different to how it used to be.
>
> *(Interview 44, Canberra DIAC)*

The actions of compliance officers in the field in detecting and apprehending unlawful non-citizens were said to be the subject of very few complaints, and research participants believed that the most legitimate grounds for criticism of the department stem from the management of cases from the point of detention (Interview 45, Canberra DIAC). The migration policing study did not set out to evaluate the outcomes of the post-Palmer reforms (see Proust 2008 for a limited review). However, they form the inescapable backdrop to this study. With the number of 'locations' of unlawful non-citizens once again increasing, and ongoing pressure on detention spaces, DIAC officials reported a rising case-load of 'clients' being managed in the community without substantive visas. The task of identifying and managing this caseload falls on the state compliance offices in each of the major cities. The remainder of this chapter examines practices at the Sydney DIAC Compliance Office as reported in interviews with key staff members.

Immigration compliance in action

Overview of Sydney Compliance Office

The DIAC Compliance Office in Sydney is the busiest and most structurally complex in Australia. At the time the fieldwork was conducted in 2008–09, the office consisted of a Client Services section, including a public access counter and numerous casework officers, and a separate set of offices in a nearby building housing a range of specialist compliance teams and a short-term detention suite. Within the general guidelines of the Priorities Matrix, state and territory DIAC offices function somewhat independently. Prior to the post-Palmer restructuring, there were three compliance fieldwork teams operating from the Parramatta DIAC office and three teams in central Sydney. This decentralisation was believed to have allowed the development of 'different cultures', whereas the smaller, centrally managed teams now operating from the central office were said to be 'more consistent' (Interview 48, Sydney DIAC). The Sydney office accounts for around 50–60 per cent of national enforcement activity (Interviews 44 and 47, Canberra DIAC). At the time the study was conducted, there were only around 35 compliance officers based there. This low staffing level highlights the reliance placed on risk-based approaches in order to target resources, and on inter-agency partnerships aimed at enhancing the detection of unlawful non-citizens.

Client Services offices provide a public interface where visa holders can make enquiries about their visa status and entitlements. The Client Services counter in the Sydney office deals with issues relating to student visas, sponsored visitor visas, applications for permanent residence and extensions to visitor visas and resident return visas (Interview 54, Sydney DIAC). The compliance staff assigned to the Client Services area deal with individuals who are identified as unlawful and assist them to regularise their status, arrange their 'voluntary' departure, or refer them to field teams for enforcement action. Within the compliance function, staff are organised into highly specialised roles and functional groups. Some roles – primarily compliance field officers – are directly focused on the detection and apprehension of unlawful non-citizens. Other compliance staff members are more involved in intelligence gathering and risk analysis, the exchange of operational information and public education. The Compliance Information Management Unit (CIMU) set up in 2003 is the engine driver of the new information-driven approach. The task of CIMU staff is to 'work up jobs' and 'look at trends and profiles in specific industries' (Interview 49, Sydney DIAC). The Remand Team works closely with the CIMU to identify individuals convicted of criminal offences who may be liable for deportation.

Whereas the fieldwork teams had previously been organised along industry lines – dealing exclusively with retail businesses or construction sites, for example – at the time the research was carried out they were organised functionally into the CERT, the Compliance Field Teams, and the Sex Team, since renamed the Trafficking Liaison Team. The Business Management Unit, also within the compliance function, was established in 2007, consisting of an Employer Awareness Team and a Student Compliance Team. Their roles, respectively, are to educate employers about the conditions attached to short-term work visas and to promote compliance with student visas, while also performing an enforcement function where needed. At the time of the interviews the CERT had 5.5 full-time equivalent staff, and the field teams had a full contingent of 24, with only 17 active officers.

Compliance officers working across these teams dealt with all visa types and were authorised to execute warrants under s 251 of the Migration Act, cancel temporary (but not permanent) visas under s 116, detain under s 189, and grant bridging visas in the field under s 65. In contrast to the view expressed by senior staff in Canberra one year earlier, the highest priority work for these teams at the time of the interviews was said to be identifying failed applicants for refugee protection visas (Interview 48, Sydney DIAC). The interviews established that unlawful non-citizens were detected through 'voluntary' presentation at DIAC counters, as a result of internal data analysis processes, following referrals from other agencies or public 'dob-ins', and via proactive operations conducted by Compliance Field Teams alone or in partnership with other agencies.

Constructing 'voluntary' reporting

Compliance officers interviewed for the study were resistant to the idea that visa compliance was 'monitored' in any way. Rather, the identification of unlawful non-citizens was characterised as an ad hoc affair, mostly involving 'voluntary' presentations to Client Services counters. In any one year, so-called voluntary presentations at public counters constitute around 80 per cent of locations of unlawful non-citizens.[5] These people may approach a DIAC counter of their own volition to make enquiries about their visa options, may be required to report to a DIAC office after being detected by Compliance Field Teams and granted a bridging visa, or may receive a notice requiring them to report to the department. The categorisation of these cases as voluntary within both departmental reporting systems and organisational discourse clearly masks the monitoring functions performed by other agencies, and the various means by which voluntary reporting is produced. A common example is that of international students referred to DIAC by education providers under statutory requirements which are discussed later in this chapter:

> Usually the student receives a letter from the education provider giving them 28 days in which to present at a DIAC office. If they present within the 28 days then the clock stops ... so they still remain on their student visa and they're set up for an interview. They're also given a notice of intent to consider cancellation. And then they come in to an interview later, a scheduled interview, and they speak with a DIAC officer who talks to them about the consideration of the cancellation.
>
> *(Interview 48, Sydney DIAC)*

People coming in to the Sydney office to enquire about their visa status are referred to compliance caseworkers if they do not hold a valid visa, with a view to either regularising their stay or initiating the removal process. Interviewees said that their role was to encourage status resolution rather than opting immediately for detention and removal. These compliance staff did not associate their work with the concept of 'enforcement' as put to them frequently by the research team:

> If the person on that counter again looks up the shared system and sees that that person doesn't hold a visa they will refer them to us. That's it.... It happens all the time. [Interviewer: *Would that necessarily end up with enforcement action being taken?*] What do you mean enforcement action? [Interviewer: *Well, being asked to leave the country or being removed?*] It really depends on what their intention is. We are there to resolve the status and basically there's several different outcomes.... It really depends on what options are available and that is what our officers do.
>
> *(Interview 54, Sydney DIAC)*

Although the migration policing project was designed to ascertain the means by which unlawful non-citizens are identified, it became apparent that the line between lawful and unlawful status is a dynamic and often indistinct one, which can involve protracted periods of case management. Therefore the status resolution function could not be dissociated from the task of identification and removal. The QA process was said to encourage greater engagement between visa holders and various specialist DIAC teams:

> Let's say they are unlawful but they have lodged a ministerial intervention request, they would go straight to our Status Resolution Team. The Status Resolution Team would talk them through the process of the ministerial intervention. They would talk through the process in regards to their other options available to them. We are now expanding that service in the long run to cover all of the Bridging E Visas but it is a new service so we are gradually introducing it. But basically we will be engaging quite thoroughly and intensively with everyone.
>
> *(Interview 52, Sydney DIAC)*

Cases can be passed to other specialist areas such as fraud investigations, police referrals and ministerial interventions. Compliance staff working in the Client Services area claimed that they canvassed all possibilities to regularise legal status immediately, and placing an individual on a bridging visa pending further applications or arrangements for departure was described as the 'last option' (Interview 54, Sydney DIAC). The third tier of intervention in the QA process is referral to the Complex Case Management Teams of all cases involving detention, or other indicators of 'vulnerability', including unaccompanied minors, the elderly and individuals with serious physical and mental health issues (Interview 54, Sydney DIAC).

Despite resisting the idea that visa holders were monitored in general, respondents conceded that individuals on bridging visas who had already come to the department's notice and those in other high-risk categories were subject to a higher level of scrutiny and formed the basis for intelligence gathering:

> Once people come to us we do identify what visa they first entered Australia on, and visa subclasses are monitored in general. You know it is publicly available that we have monitored rates for certain visa classes and certain citizenships and there is ministerial directions on risk profiles and things like that.
>
> *(Interview 52, Sydney DIAC)*

Further insight into the management of people on bridging visas was provided by a senior official interviewed in Canberra:

> Generally with a bridging visa they're ... there'll be an obligation for them to stay in touch with the department either through reporting in, you

know, on a weekly or monthly basis, or staying in touch .... It's just to allow the person to stay in the community while something happens in relation to their immigration outcome.

(Interview 45, Canberra DIAC)

Respondents claimed that referring cases for intensive case management was not based on the presupposition that the individual was on a pathway to removal: 'We don't have any view about what the outcome will be. They go into case management because they need support' (Interview 54, Sydney DIAC). Overall, interviewees presented an image of the work they do as being mainly about promoting compliance with immigration law and far less about detaining and removing, although the final resolution of cases is not always known to them:

> [Officer 1] What the outcomes are – it is really none of our business, if you understand me. The outcomes are departure, granted a visa onshore through the minister intervening, or we find another option. As I said, applying off-shore and applying to come back in, and in some cases it could be detaining and removal because they don't wish to comply. So there is several different outcomes, the same could go for case management. Compliance just doesn't deal with detaining and removing I suppose is what I am trying to say. [Officer 2] No the vast majority of what we do is nothing to do with detaining and removing.
>
> *(Interview 54, Sydney DIAC)*

This apparent disinterest in outcomes does not seem to hold in general. The department recently published a consultant's report detailing strategies to encourage 'entrenched' clients who had been in long-term case management to make 'voluntary' departures, indicating the importance attached to bringing cases to speedy resolution (Hall and Partners 2012). It was evident from the interviews held in Canberra that some individuals remain in the community on bridging visas for a considerable time until their status is resolved:

> We also have a project going currently where we are monitoring people on Bridging Visa E and what's happened to them, and if they are overstayers there is a major project trying to locate them. There is also another project to work towards immigration outcomes for all those on bridging visas who have had maybe 20 or 30 bridging visas. Some have very good reasons. For example, they are an aged and invalid person and they can't travel because of health reasons.
>
> *(Interview 42, Canberra DIAC)*

Even if this apparent restraint was, in fact, typical of compliance practices at the time the research was conducted, the tone of the Hall and Partners report suggests that the department's patience with 'entrenched clients' may be wearing thin. One decidedly pre-emptive recommendation from that report is that 'at-risk clients' be required to submit a 'Plan B' at the beginning of the appeal phase indicating what action they would take if they were refused a visa (Hall and Partners 2012).

Only about 3 per cent of unlawful non-citizens located in the community were said to be detained, but it was not possible to verify this figure independently. The deliberate restraint on the use of detention was said to pre-date the instructions issued by former minister Chris Evans:

> Look, we have for a long time used detention as a last resort.... The minister's announcement about the new directions in detention has I think shifted the focus perhaps of what we do, so that instead of thinking, Well, why should I grant a bridging visa to this person?, my expectation now is that staff will ask the question, Why shouldn't I?
>
> *(Interview 54, Sydney DIAC)*

Informants described the department's new approach based on the promotion of compliance, avoidance of detention, and minimisation of detention length as a process of 'building up trust again':

> So we are in the process of going out to community groups and talking to them about the new directions in detention and encouraging people to engage with us, and saying to them if you are unlawful, you haven't had a visa for 15 years and you have remained underground, if you come into the office and engage with us you are not going to be disadvantaged in any way. You will be provided with advice, you won't be detained unless you are a 501 [character] case, and it is really to your advantage.
>
> *(Interview 53, Sydney DIAC)*

This strategy to build up trust is seen as a necessary precondition for the voluntary reporting that is the ultimate goal. However, given the strictures of Australian immigration law, this message of reassurance cannot guarantee status regularisation, so voluntary reporting remains a high-risk proposition to those who are uncertain of their legal options. The last general amnesty for people unlawfully present in Australia reportedly took place in 1980 (Nicholls 2007). Even so, DIAC staff seemed convinced that those who present themselves voluntarily were unlikely to be removed, although they might mysteriously decide to 'just go':

> [Officer 1] Most of the people who come to light on a voluntary basis aren't removed because there is usually probably a reason, they may be eligible for something. [Officer 3] Or their status is resolved and they go voluntarily. [Officer 2] Yeah they just go. [Officer 3] It is unusual to be detained and removed. [Interviewer: *OK, so the term 'removed' – I probably should have just said something like 'are required to leave the country'.*] [Officer 3] That is the right term but I think the stress needs to be put more on the majority of – the majority

of outcomes are voluntary departures, and in some cases they will return because they have to put in a spouse visa, I am sure it is something like that.

(Interview 54, Sydney DIAC)

Examples of voluntary presentation and departure peppered the interviews to support this picture of the non-coercive application of immigration rules: 'Often we'll get people coming in with – they'll just bring their passport and their ticket and say, look, I know I'm unlawful, but I want – I'm ready to go home' (Interview 48, Sydney DIAC). Such cases might include monitored departures for individuals originally placed on a bridging visa that was conditional on their departing within a specified time. Failure to comply could then trigger further action such as detention, referral for case management or even assistance from the International Organization for Migration if the individual lacks the funds to purchase tickets. Ultimately, the ever-present threat of detention and forced removal renders the dividing line between voluntary and non-voluntary contested and unclear:

[Interviewer: *And do you ever deal with non-voluntary cases at all?*] Non-voluntary cases? So people that – no we don't. I mean we do detain here, so at some stage the person is going to be non-voluntary I suppose, but they have approached voluntarily.

(Interview 52, Sydney DIAC)

Data mining and referrals

The picture painted so far depicts migration policing primarily as the ad hoc identification of individuals without valid visas, largely through voluntary reporting. However, because Australia operates both entry and exit border checks, and maintains extensive – if not always accurate – databases of cross-border movements and visa status, it is possible to identify non-citizens who remain in the country following the expiry of their visa. Serious attempts have been made in recent years to improve the quality of data on the so-called Overstayers File. Regular reports from this centrally managed system are produced from DIAC headquarters and sent to specialist information management units within state offices. This process was explained most clearly by the DIAC personnel interviewed in Canberra:

We will get weekly what we call the Overstayers List which indicates those people who have become an overstayer during that week. They do some cleansing of the data and we get that a week later, then what we try and do is locate the individuals off that list. So that's the first port of call. The thing with overstayer data is that it is quite dynamic because people can become an overstayer for a day and then it becomes lawful tomorrow, as they can go in and get a bridging visa and be lawful tomorrow.

(Interview 42, Canberra DIAC)

However, the compliance staff interviewed in Sydney still resisted the idea that this amounted to a process of visa monitoring – apparently interpreting this term to mean constant knowledge of the whereabouts of individual visa holders – and explained that they only targeted non-compliant individuals:

> There is no active monitoring of the movements of visitors to Australia as I am sure you know.… But at the same time we also actively try to seek information about people who have become unlawful. We don't monitor their visa. The trigger for our interest is that they overstay and become unlawful. And in fact the legislation prevents us from investigating clients unless they are unlawful. So we can't conduct investigative checks of a person who is lawful.
> *(Interview 54, Sydney DIAC)*

It was unclear from these discussions how actively the names on the Overstayers List are pursued in the absence of events that would bring an individual to the department's attention, such as lodging an application for another visa. The approach was reported to be low-key:

> We don't actually go out and look for them. We would send them a letter and say, look, you need to actually, it's part of the legislation that for your first bridging visa if you are unlawful you need to be seen by a compliance officer, you need to approach the counter.
> *(Interview 52, Sydney DIAC)*

Information about suspected unlawful non-citizens can also come from other sources including allegations received by mail, email or phone, including notifications through the public 'Dob-in Service'; information provided by inter-agency committees or partner agencies; cases 'escalated' from Client Services following non-compliance with departure arrangements; or 'locations' arising from aggregate data-matching processes. It is the role of the CIMU to prioritise all available information about suspected unlawful non-citizens in accordance with the Priorities Matrix. At the time of the interviews, CIMU staff reported receiving about 350 allegations per month by phone alone, the majority from the general public. Interviewees explained that it is up to them to 'work up' jobs until there is enough information to pass them on to field teams. Prior to the introduction of this risk-based approach, local compliance teams were said to be 'self-generating a lot of their work and relying on the allegations that came in' (Interview 49, Sydney DIAC).

CIMU staff saw their role in the first instance as filtering and then 'value adding' to information received by interviewing complainants and obtaining documentary information where possible. Additional information could be obtained from other agencies using s 18 Migration Act powers which require the release of information about suspected unlawful non-citizens. Up to 75 per cent of allegations were said to be followed up in some way (Interview 49, Sydney DIAC), but many were 'archived' due to a lack of reliable information. Cases judged to require further action can be referred to Compliance Field Teams (often regarding workplace issues) or the Early Response Team in low-risk cases (generally where residential premises are concerned), or sometimes to specialist teams such as the Employer Awareness Team, the Fraud Team or the Complex Case Team.

The CIMU also generates information periodically through the aggregate matching of the Overstayers File with client data from the ATO. The privacy protections that would normally prevent such a large-scale cross-agency exchange are not applicable in this case, since all the names on the Overstayers File are suspected unlawful non-citizens by definition, and thereby fall under DIAC's s 18 powers. Despite possessing this powerful cross-agency identification tool, verification and follow-up of the matches were said to be far from straightforward:

> We get a weekly Overstayers List and we also get a quarterly one. We've just had ATO matches done against it…. First thing we do is double-check and see who's probably become – who's become lawful in the meantime…. Normally, you know, we're not heavy-handed about it. With some of the people … we'll write them a letter or give them a call and say, come on in. Or if they've been unlawful for a long time, they've lost contact with the department, then we'll probably conduct s 18 checks and then refer it. The thing is, if the person's only been here for a short time, like, and they've just overstayed their tourist visa … then usually they're … they'd be difficult to locate 'cause they don't leave a footprint.
>
> *(Interview 49, Sydney DIAC)*

In cases where individuals who have exhausted all legal avenues to remain in Australia lose contact with the department, field officers and CIMU staff might be called upon to determine their whereabouts:

> Often the information they give on their Passenger Card doesn't give us an address where we can locate them. They've already moved on after three months and consequently it's very difficult to locate them. So until they actually start to put down roots, start to rent places, gain electricity, gas, water, that sort of stuff, then they maybe get a mobile or whatever and then they will find work. The ones that are here longer we have a better chance of locating.
>
> *(Interview 42, Canberra DIAC)*

Individuals who were required to submit paper applications for visas because of the classification of their nationality as high risk were said to be much easier to trace than those on ETAs because of the greater amount of personal detail recorded. This disparity was said to be 'about managing the risk' because 'the percentage of overstayers who are ETA holders is so miniscule' (Interview 49, Sydney DIAC). This assessment is not supported by objective data. According to Crock and Berg (2011: 323), the US and China had the highest recorded rate of overstaying at June 2008, followed by the UK, Malaysia and the Philippines – a list which includes both low- and high-risk nationalities in terms of visa categories. There may be differences between nationalities, perhaps, in the average length of time spent in Australia without a valid visa and, in turn, these differential patterns, if they exist, may give rise to different imputed risks to the system of immigration control. In any case, it is apparent that the perception of these DIAC officers concerning the substantive risk associated with overstaying by particular nationalities does not align with the objective probability that some overstaying will occur.

As well as filtering and prioritising compliance work in relation to individual visa violators, CIMU staff also play a significant role in building and analysing intelligence profiles to guide wider compliance strategies:

> We could see what kind of dobs[6] – where they were coming from, what industries they were coming in for, and we were able to be more proactive in deterrence and prevention as well through interaction with our stakeholders. It also helped us to develop profiles of particular, say, businesses that were the ongoing culprits so we – it also allowed us to get consistency, more consistency into our processes.
>
> *(Interview 49, Sydney DIAC)*

Although the ATO is the only agency for which regular aggregate data matching was reported, CIMU staff said that they regularly receive notifications about suspected unlawful non-citizens from the NSW Police Force, Corrective Services, the former Roads and Traffic Authority (or RTA, now part of Roads and Maritime Services), the AFP, Workcover and Centrelink – through information voluntarily supplied by those agencies, and through the application of their s 18 powers. Section 18 is the major Migration Act power exercised by this unit:

> We've got to have reasonable belief that a person's an unlawful non-citizen, which is fairly easy from our point of view. We also have to have reasonable belief that the agency that we're asking to provide the information can provide it to us. That means we can't go fishing.
>
> *(Interview 49, Sydney DIAC)*

In some cases, processes for cross-agency information exchange about particular individuals are even more streamlined. CIMU staff reported having direct online access to selected RTA and ATO systems, although privacy requirements 'means that we can't get as many data-matching agencies to come on board as we would like' (Interview 49, Sydney DIAC).

Information is required from criminal justice agencies in order to identify lawfully present non-citizens who are liable to cancellation of their permanent visas due to criminal convictions. These 'section 501' cases have been identified as high priority within the Priorities Matrix, and this is reflected in the creation of specialist teams and procedures to proactively identify them. The Remand Team is a specialist group within the CIMU with a brief to liaise with courts, while the Prisons Removals Team based at Parramatta monitors sentenced populations to identify potentially deportable prisoners. The officers responsible for these specialised functions had no difficulty conceptualising their work in terms of monitoring. Courts-based compliance officers refer names to the Prisons Removals Team of defendants sentenced to a period of imprisonment that could trigger s 501 visa cancellation, and refer other convicted individuals known to be non-citizens to Compliance Field Teams, presumably in order to build an intelligence record. Monitoring may even start from the point at which a non-citizen is taken into police custody for a criminal matter, although early intervention still appeared to be ad hoc at the time the research was conducted.

DIAC compliance officers can send requests to police or courts asking them to hold criminal suspects who are granted bail until such time as they can be taken into immigration custody. The reported procedure was for field officers to visit each potential deportee and conduct an identity interview. Prison Removals Teams may also visit prisons and interview persons of interest, and could reportedly instigate removal procedures at times before the completion of sentences. Information is also provided regularly from Corrective Services, although no formal MOU was in place at the time the fieldwork was conducted. Specialist DIAC teams that grant Criminal Justice Stay (CJS) visas in cases where unlawful non-citizens are required to remain in Australia as criminal suspects or witnesses are another source of information about potential deportees. The Parole Board provides another potential information source, since deportable individuals might only come to light after their release from prison – for example, when defaulting on parole. There was no direct contact with federal or state prosecution authorities at the time, but it was reported that the Remand Team was looking at ways to obtain more systematic information about individuals on remand, as opposed to those already convicted.

Despite this far-reaching network of informants, early warning notification systems were said to operate on a sporadic basis, since there is no legal obligation for other agencies to notify immigration authorities of potential deportees. An investigation into the use of s 501 by the Commonwealth Ombudsman conducted in 2006 confirmed that methods of detection used at that time were ad hoc, varied between states, and depended on local relationships between immigration and criminal justice authorities (Commonwealth and Immigration Ombudsman 2006: 20). However, the ongoing status of criminal deportees as a high-priority category in the Priorities Matrix suggests that further efforts will be made to systematise their detection.

Detection in the field

As the main interface with suspected unlawful non-citizens in the community, compliance officers working in field teams are relied upon to obtain information that is crucial to determining an individual's legal status and guiding the administrative process. Information-gathering interviews were standardised as part of the post-Palmer reforms, so that field officers conduct field interviews, identity interviews (where needed), and post-location detention interviews using a pro-forma. DIAC officers reported that under the previous conservative government questions had been included in the field interview concerning the services accessed by unlawfully present individuals – apparently with a view to assessing the extent of fraudulent welfare claims and other unauthorised access to services. This information was said to have been excluded from the interview schedules in the post-Palmer reforms, for reasons that remain unknown.

The CERT was established to deal with 'low-risk' cases or 'non-warranted' jobs identified through any of the detection methods described in the previous section. This can mean visiting or telephoning families, the elderly or individuals who may have just 'inadvertently forgotten' to go home, or had left and then returned on inappropriate visas. More generally, individuals with no record of repeated non-compliance tend to be considered low risk. As with a good deal of investigative activity conducted by police, visits might proceed on a 'voluntary' basis without a warrant:

> So our preference is for people to use warrants. But there are certain circum-
> stances where we don't have enough information … but we'll think that the
> information we've got is strong enough for us to go onto the property and
> ask for the owner of the property or the senior person whether they give us
> permission to enter to do what we need to do. If they say 'no', we depart. If
> they say 'yes' we are there to do it until they say 'no' basically.
>
> *(Interview 42, Canberra DIAC)*

Respondents described the remit of the CERTs as primarily information gathering and status resolution, and it was suggested that '[t]hey have no scope to detain people' (Interview 54, Sydney DIAC). Interviewees explained that granting a bridging visa and encouraging reporting to the DIAC Client Services counter is the standard modus operandi for these teams:

> That's their job basically: to go out, detect people, give them short-term
> BVEs [Bridging E Visas] so we can actually engage with the person in a
> controlled environment with officers that are skilled in talking to them
> about what options are available.
>
> *(Interview 52, Sydney DIAC)*

If individuals subsequently 'disengage' with status resolution processes they could be referred to the Compliance Field Teams. These teams specialise in 'high risk' visits, often involving individuals who are considered to be of 'character concern' due to criminal convictions. At the time the fieldwork was conducted, only one industry-specific team remained – the Sex Team that works with the AFP to identify instances of sex trafficking, although the remit has since been widened to incorporate other instances of workplace exploitation beyond the sex industry. This was also considered to be mandatory work occupying the highest rung on the Priorities Matrix.

Compliance field operations are generally conducted under DIAC-issued warrants, often with the assistance of state police. Under the Priorities Matrix, notifications from police (discussed in Chapter 5) and cases referred from the Remand Team are considered to be mandatory work, since they involve criminal matters. In the case of unlawful non-citizens who are detected and held by police, but not necessarily charged with criminal offences (discussed in Chapter 4), there is considerable time pressure to respond to the referral either by taking the individual into immigration custody or issuing them with a bridging visa. Compliance officers are aware that the changes in detention practices which favour status resolution have caused frustration among NSW state police, who had previously come to expect the detention and immediate removal of individuals they referred to DIAC:

> I think it is safe to say that the police would like us to use our powers more judiciously, or sometimes in more circumstances if we could. But the issue is that we are not a law enforcement agency, so we need to follow our policies. And the current view is that our minister has expressed the view that we do need to detain as a last resort, and so we are following that policy.
>
> *(Interview 51, Sydney DIAC)*

Just as there was resistance to the idea of visa holders being monitored, interviewees objected to the notion that DIAC field officers 'apprehend' anybody or 'enforce' immigration law. In fact, finding terminology that was acceptable to the research informants proved to be an ongoing challenge:

> [Officer 1] Apprehending, what – suspected UNCs?[7] What do you mean by apprehending? [Officer 2] Locating is a better word. [Interviewer: *Oh, okay. So who actually apprehends them?*] [Officer 2] Nobody. [Interviewer: *Nobody?*] [Officer 2] Well, that's a bad – not a very good word. [Officer 1] It's very police orientated and we don't do that. [Officer 2] We're not police. [Interviewer: *Okay.*] [Officer 2] We locate.
>
> *(Interview 48, Sydney DIAC)*

These efforts to distance compliance fieldwork conceptually and linguistically from any form of policing surfaced frequently in the interviews. Staff in the Sydney office echoed the view expressed by senior officers interviewed at DIAC headquarters that the emphasis had shifted away from maximising removals towards the 'quality' of compliance work:

> [Officer 1] I think they focus more on quality now than quantity. [Officer 2] Yeah. There's been a distinct shift, yeah. We used to have very high targets we used to have to meet ... both for the voluntary locations and for field locations. And basically that's been scrapped. We still have locations, but it's not

linked to funding at all now. And basically this financial year, for this year, with the new minister, they've taken away the numbers completely. [Officer 3] And the focus is on working with other stakeholders to get our … our work done.… We had a very strong enforcement focus. And now we've got a – there's been a distinct shift towards prevention and deterrence. And we use enforcement as a last resort.

(Interview 48, Sydney DIAC)

However, political pressure to control unlawfully present populations had not diminished. The same informants denied that these changes had made their jobs less stressful, as the goal of maintaining the 'integrity' of Australia's migration programme also created an imperative to locate unlawful non-citizens:

We still get the question, why are the locations … [Officer 1] Down. [Officer 2] And we've still got to answer to that, because it's all caught up with the integrity angle of, you know, if we're not going out and locating people and managing that caseload, then numbers are growing of people unlawfully in the community.

(Interview 48, Sydney DIAC)

The new system of QA 'mandatory controls points' requires that key procedures such as obtaining and executing warrants have to be 'signed off'. This parallels the requirement on police to report back to courts, although through an entirely internal system. Nevertheless, the system was considered by those managing the operational officers to be 'quite strict'. In turn, these layers of procedural safeguards were thought to have contributed to some reductions in efficiency:

[Officer 2] There's a lot … a lot of layers in the process … [Officer 3] Yeah. And as a consequence, [it's] decreased the amount of work that we do in terms of fieldwork, the actual visits to premises and things, so those numbers have gone down because of all the extra structure.

(Interview 48, Sydney DIAC)

Whereas Compliance Field Teams are generalists working across a range of visa categories, most compliance issues relating to students or illegal workers are handled initially by specialist teams. This reflects both the volume of this type of work and the specific legal frameworks surrounding these visa categories. Because of the responsibilities placed on employers and education providers to ensure compliance, these visa holders are subject to a much higher level of ongoing monitoring than those in possession of other visa types. The Employer Awareness Team, as the name suggests, has a strong focus on promoting compliance through visits to employers. Statistics are also produced on an industry-wide basis to determine high- and low-risk workplaces for use when considering future requests for temporary labour, and also to inform enforcement actions. Referrals to this team were said to come primarily from the CIMU, often based on data matching against taxation records. Like other field officers, members of the Employer Awareness Team have delegated powers to cancel visas and issue bridging visas. But, as with the CERT in relation to home visits, it was reported that the team takes a 'soft' approach. Although visits are generally initiated because of a specific person of interest, informants said that they were more likely to focus their attention on employers and may refer serious cases of labour exploitation to the federal police.

Thousands of employers are registered to use the Visa Entitlement Verification Online (VEVO) system to check the work entitlements of prospective employees. The system is not a source of definitive information about an individual's immigration status, but may advise employers to contact DIAC if there is any doubt. Employers are only required to do an initial check. They will receive an 'education' visit initially if an employee is found to be working unlawfully, and officers from the Employer Awareness Team can issue an Illegal Working Warning Notice. The team was said to rely on the threat of prosecution of employers to promote compliance, although the likelihood of prosecution is actually low. Withholding future employer-sponsored visas was considered to be a more powerful sanction. Since the research interviews were conducted, a review of employer sanctions has recommended increasing the deterrent power of these criminal sanctions (Howells 2011).

Section 457 skilled worker visas, which at the time of the interviews were closely tied to nominated employers, appear to receive particular attention within DIAC. The reported approach seems to deviate from the stated focus on employers, with visa cancellation for employees a substantial possibility:

> The sponsor, if they make that person redundant – which is a sort of topical issue – reports that to the department … and [employees] have a certain period in which to find a new sponsor. But if they can't, we then need to cancel their 457 visa because they are not meeting the conditions.
>
> *(Interview 54, Sydney DIAC)*

Following complaints about the hardship created by the strict observance of this requirement (Moore and Knox 2007), a 2008 review of the operation of s 457 visas recommended an increased grace period and the provision of assistance to link workers to new employers before cancelling their visas (Deegan 2008).

Research participants claimed that DIAC offices in other states deal with breaches of student visas as a general part of compliance fieldwork, but that the numbers were high enough in Sydney to warrant specialised attention. An elaborate and highly automated reporting system is in place which requires universities and other education providers to monitor certain conditions of international student visas such as academic progress and attendance. Described as an 'automated referral system', the Provider Registration and International Student Management System (PRISMS) leaves little space for discretionary intervention. The Student Compliance Unit cancels visas if students are found to be non-compliant with their attendance or study requirements. However, PRISMS is not able to identify breaches of the 20-hour work limit, which can only be detected through the same mechanisms used to identify other forms of illegal working. It is generally the Compliance Field Teams who cancel visas if they detect students working in breach of their employment conditions. Special outreach teams operating from Client Services perform the educative and preventive role with education providers that is carried out by the Employer Awareness Team in relation to employer responsibilities, with a stated focus on preventing minors from becoming unlawful.

Because immigration officers are authorised under s 188 of the Migration Act to check the immigration status of anyone they reasonably believe to be a non-citizen, compliance fieldwork need not always be based on information received about particular individuals. Compliance Fieldwork Teams therefore engage in planned operations in high-risk locations identified through intelligence analysis to proactively identify unlawful non-citizens. Popular television programmes such as *Border Security* sometimes feature footage of DIAC Compliance Field Teams conducting place-based raids on farms, restaurants or other businesses, rather than targeting specific, named individuals. In discussions with compliance managers, 'warranted' jobs involving searches for named individuals were described as 'easy', whereas 'non-warranted' jobs that were based on more speculative information were considered less straightforward. Regular departmental press releases about workplace raids, in which unlawful non-citizens are identified, and occasional television coverage raise the profile of this otherwise invisible work, signalling its value as a deterrent to illegal working and conveying a message to the wider community that immigration laws are being enforced. These public 'risk communications' (Ericson and Haggerty 1997) invariably attribute successful raids to community tip-offs, note that any unlawful non-citizens detected are being held in immigration custody and affirm that they will be deported, as required by law. Other press releases stress the obligation on employers to check their workers' immigration status and advertise the online visa verification system and the community dob-in line.

Because the researchers were not granted permission to speak with field officers, no further detail was obtained about how or why these operations are carried out. In fact, most of the first-hand information gathered about these operations came from discussions with partner agencies (reported in Chapter 6). Sydney compliance staff confirmed that MOUs relating to the conduct of joint operations exist with Centrelink, the ATO, NSW Police Force and the former RTA, and that agreements with local councils were being negotiated. Many operations were said to be organised on a bilateral, ad hoc basis, while others are initiated by the multi-agency Cash Economy Working Group that has a specific brief to prevent illegal working (discussed in Chapter 7). Despite the post-Palmer attempts to create more distance between the DIAC compliance function and police, the Sydney Compliance Office works particularly closely with NSW police, and is the only state office within DIAC to have liaison officers posted at police headquarters. Compliance field officers were said to participate in one or two police-initiated operations per month, generally involving checks on taxi operators (reported in Chapter 4).

State police also accompany Compliance Field Teams in DIAC-led operations that are considered high risk. In July 2004, a South Korean national, Seong Ho Kang, died after being struck by a vehicle while running from a workplace raid in Sydney. The death was investigated by the Commonwealth Ombudsman who found serious shortcomings in the execution of DIAC warrants (Commonwealth Ombudsman 2007a). This event seems to have reinforced the department's reliance on police to take responsibility for high-risk activities such as pursuits:

> If they seek to abscond from the premises, it is our department's policy that we do not pursue people and part of the reason for that is if a person is running they tend to run somewhat blindly and we don't want to chase them into a situation of danger where they are a danger to themselves and to others. So, for example, we won't chase – the police generally may.
>
> *(Interview 47, Canberra DIAC)*

The interview material reported here has established that DIAC officials cloak their professional identity and activities in administrative terminology such as 'locations' and the promotion of 'compliance' and 'voluntarism', while distancing themselves from terms like 'monitoring', 'apprehension' or 'enforcement' which they associate with law enforcement bodies. They nevertheless depend on state police to exercise the coercive force that is needed when efforts at constructing 'voluntarism' fail, and also to act as their 'eyes and ears' on the ground. The question of the extent to which immigration officers can be considered to be a quasi police force will be addressed in the concluding chapter. The next chapter considers the comprehensive role played by state police operating as quasi immigration officers.

4

POLICE AS IMMIGRATION OFFICERS

DIAC's 'eyes and ears on the ground'

According to the most recent annual report for the NSW Police Force, there are just under 16,000 sworn police officers in the state (NSW Police Force 2012: 61). Given the modest size of DIAC's compliance fieldwork operation, it is not surprising that immigration authorities rely on largely opportunistic encounters between unlawful non-citizens and police to supplement their more targeted detection efforts. As one DIAC official explained:

> I think that there is probably a perception there that we have this huge workforce that is just dedicated to compliance ... and that is why we are getting out there educating [police], because they are really our eyes and ears on the ground.
>
> *(Interview 51, Sydney DIAC)*

About 18 per cent of the 15,477 'locations' of unlawful non-citizens during 2011–12 were detected either by DIAC field operations or by referrals from police, with the remainder reporting 'voluntarily', as discussed in the previous chapter (DIAC 2012). If police are assumed to contribute around the same number of locations as DIAC – an assumption that is consistent with previously reported figures – this would amount to around 1,400 unlawful non-citizens identified nationally by police in a year.

Australian police perform a taken-for-granted role in immigration enforcement. As designated officers under the Migration Act, NSW police officers are authorised under s 188 of the Act to question anyone suspected of being a non-citizen and are required to detain them under s 189 if they believe they may be unlawfully present. Although these matters do not involve any hint of criminality, state police have historically performed administrative functions in Australia and hold wide-ranging powers which are a legacy of their colonial origins, as explained by police historian Mark Finnane:

> The police in Australia were founded in a specific colonial context which gave them an important *political and administrative* role: guaranteeing the success of settler dispossession of Aboriginal land, sustaining the boundaries of urban order, acting as agents of the state in the collection of taxes, conducting elections, and counting the population.
>
> *(Finnane 1994: 34, emphasis in original)*

Fears of disorder were central to the formation of Australian police forces, particularly in NSW where the first colony was established at Sydney Cove in 1788. In addition to their significant role in supporting the colonisation process, NSW police were also deployed to create 'the illusion that something was being done to stem the threat of "immigrating hordes" [of ex-convicts] from Van Diemen's Land' (Brown *et al.* 2006: 836). Since the convict era, a changing array of groups constructed as internal threats have attracted the suspicions of police, including Irish and Chinese minorities, Bolsheviks and anarchists influenced by 'foreign' political ideologies, along with Aboriginal Australians who have been consistently identified as 'police property'. From the time of federation in 1901, and in the absence of a national law enforcement agency, state police remained the only resource available to enforce the new federal mandate to control immigration and manage 'aliens' (Finnane 2009).[1]

One might expect that the rise of a specialised bureaucracy to deal with immigration would have diminished the police role in migration policing. But Finnane's archival research established that Australian police maintained an ongoing, at times heightened, involvement in the identification of 'aliens' throughout the twentieth century, normalising the idea that migration control was the business of police. Moreover, there are some signs of an increasing demand for police involvement in migration policing in recent times. A record of a national conference on multicultural policing held in Melbourne in August 1990 reports that there was a 'firm position that police should not be involved in the enforcement of laws dealing with illegal immigrants' (Victoria Police 1990). This statement may not have been the officially endorsed view, but the fact that it was made at all suggests that there was growing pressure at the time for police agencies to take on a more significant role in migration policing. A decade later, the Police Federation of Australia (2002) was citing pressures associated with immigration detention centres to support its arguments for increased state and federal police funding. Apart from these sporadic debates there is not much evidence to suggest that the role of police in immigration enforcement has been subjected to fundamental questioning in Australia.

There appears to have been more open debate about the nexus of policing and border control elsewhere in the English-speaking world. During the 1980s the Institute of Race Relations documented many instances of British police checking immigration status during traffic stops, criminal investigations, individuals reporting crimes, and even during unannounced visits to private homes (Bowling and Phillips 2002; Institute of Race Relations 1987). While the disproportionate use of 'stop and search' in relation to ethnic minorities (both citizens and non-citizens) has continued over the ensuing decades (Bowling and Phillips 2007; Weber and Bowling 2012), the involvement of British police in the enforcement of immigration controls has been more variable (Webber 2004; Weber and Bowling 2004). During the 1990s, pressure to hold deportees in police cells was resisted by the London Metropolitan Police, who were concerned that it might damage their fragile relations with ethnic minority communities (Weber and Bowling 2004). The role of London police as both trainers and participants in special deportation squads – dubbed 'snatch squads' by their critics – has been even more controversial, particularly since their surprise tactics became associated with a number of tragic 'balcony deaths' (Weber and Bowling 2004). More recently, British police have joined the UK Border Agency in operations aimed at identifying deportable foreign nationals taken into police custody on criminal matters (Hamilton-Smith and Patel 2005; Muir 2012).

In the US, from the mid-1990s, state police and jail officials began to be enticed into the previously federal mandate of immigration control under the so-called 287(g) programme (Provine 2013). This strategy to devolve federal responsibility for border control sparked an outcry from civil liberties groups who saw the programme as a licence for racial profiling by local police (Immigration Policy Centre 2012; US Department of Justice Civil Rights Division 2011). In any case, Provine (2013: 118) explains that take-up of the programme has been slow, since:

> [s]tates and localities had grown accustomed to the idea that they had power only to assist in the integration of immigrants into local communities and that they were under a constitutional obligation not to discriminate on the basis of ethnicity or national origin or, presumably, legal status.
>
> *(Provine 2013: 118)*

Although this jurisdictional distinction also applies in Australia, both federal and state police are designated officers under the Migration Act, and therefore have a formally recognised and historically entrenched role in the enforcement of immigration law. These brief comparisons demonstrate an unusually high degree of co-option of state police within the Australian system of border control.

In a survey of 371 of the state's police officers conducted for the migration policing study, NSW state police reported taking part in a wide range of migration-related activities including detaining under s 189 of the Migration Act; working with immigration authorities on joint field operations; accompanying DIAC officers in the execution of high-risk warrants; escorting deportees on international flights (when off duty); and conducting immigration status checks in response to reports arising from criminal investigations, or in the course of day-to-day street policing (see Table 4.1). Conducting immigration checks and detaining under the Migration Act were the most frequently reported immigration enforcement activities. Around one-third of the officers who

TABLE 4.1 Number and percentage of surveyed NSW police officers reporting involvement in particular immigration enforcement activities

Conducting immigration checks	274	74%
Detaining on immigration-related matters	269	73%
Execution of DIAC warrants	130	35%
Joint police–DIAC operations	114	31%
Escorting deportees	10	3%

completed the survey also reported accompanying DIAC officers to execute warrants and/or taking part in joint operations with DIAC to identify unlawful non-citizens. Although only 3 per cent of the officers surveyed reported accompanying deportees when off duty (a task often assigned to private security companies in other countries), this extra-curricular activity was said to be the most significant source of secondary employment for NSW police officers, with between 15 and 20 off-duty officers escorting deportees on flights each day at the time the interviews were conducted (Interview 40, NSW Police Force Headquarters).

Policing migration on the streets

Street policing in NSW

Immigration checks conducted by police in NSW are embedded within operational policing practice and predicated on their access to a wide repertoire of general policing powers (Weber 2011). The foundational role played by police as all-purpose colonial administrators is still apparent in their close involvement with the legislative process and their capacity to garner significant resources and powers wherever their arguments can be linked to the preservation of public order and security. When charting the development of public order legislation in the state (key aspects of which are summarised in Chapter 2), Brown *et al.* (2006) noted that, following the introduction of uncharacteristically liberal policies in 1979, the Police Association lobbied furiously against the reform, using advertisements depicting police losing control of the streets. Those authors date the development of a broadly based 'tough on street crime' approach in NSW from around 1988.

Like many other contemporary police agencies, the NSW Police Force relies on intelligence-led approaches to identify risky people and places in order to target its proactive policing tactics. The use of geographical 'hot spots' defined through intelligence analysis as grounds for 'reasonable suspicion' to authorise street stops has attracted particular criticism from the NSW Ombudsman, who said that it 'effectively establishes a random or arbitrary search power' (NSW Ombudsman 2000: 163). Considerable evidence is now accumulating that the intelligence-based targeting of high-risk individuals, such as known criminals, suspected drug addicts and people on bail or parole, leads to the 'racialisation' of police surveillance practices (Coleman and McCahill 2011). In NSW, move-on powers and powers to search for knives that were introduced in 1998 were applied overwhelmingly against young people and were used 184 times more frequently per head of population in Bourke and Brewarrina (with large Aboriginal populations) than in the affluent Sydney suburb of Rose Bay (NSW Ombudsman 2000). Overall, move-on powers in NSW were found to be used against Aboriginal people at a rate 11 times the expected level in the 12 months following their introduction (Walsh and Taylor 2007). Despite these early warnings, the use of these powers, supposedly guided by intelligence-led analysis, is now firmly entrenched and widely endorsed in the NSW Police Force.

As Ericson and Haggerty (1997: 18) have noted, while policing is still directed towards maintaining order 'within a predictable spatial environment', in 'risk societies' the 'traditional police focus on deviance, control and order is displaced in favour of a focus on risk, surveillance, and security' predicated on the sorting of 'individuals, organizations, and institutions in their respective risk categories'. In addition to the sustained targeting of risky people and places, police in NSW rely on closed-circuit television (CCTV) and other imaging technology to drive the day-to-day prioritising of risks:

> Just about every crime committed in the city is captured on CCTV somewhere. We have lots and lots in various parts of the station, particularly in our intelligence office – pictures of people who are wanted for robberies, serious assaults, sexual assaults, thefts, exploded up all over the place. So it is very likely that every time a police officer goes out onto [the main street][2] they are going to say, 'I know that person, their picture is up in the police station'. So that gives them the cause to at least go up and speak to them.
>
> *(Interview 23, NSW Police Force Local Area Commander)*

Risk-based thinking has defined a wide range of people as suspect, often through categories as broad as 'young people hanging around'. Local police commanders explained that, within the overall intelligence-led approach, operational officers are expected to use their own judgement to target known troublemakers or direct their attention to the identified policing priorities in the area:

> We run here a number of operations on a weekly basis targeting some of our primary areas. What that involves is police in cars and police on foot in targeted areas, geographically targeted areas … it would almost be a stop-and-prop type situation where a police officer identifies somebody, for instance sake, hanging around [the railway station] with a group of males, which are sort of the target group – 9.30, 10 o'clock at night, hours of darkness, train just about to arrive – stop-and-prop type situation. What are you guys doing here? And then go through that process.
>
> *(Interview 6, NSW Police Force Local Area Commander)*

All of the senior police officers interviewed expressed their unstinting support for intelligence-led approaches. One commander claimed that the significant drops across the main crime types in his command recorded in the past 12 months could be attributed largely to 'targeting specific criminals and being suspicious about the activity of people within our environment' (Interview 18, NSW Police Force Local Area Commander). Confronted with the suggestion that these risks are very loosely defined, senior police were keen to refute any implication that intelligence-led targeting encouraged stereotyping or racial profiling. One commander commented:

> In terms of what we want them to do, they are not going out stopping and propping and dealing with people who aren't causing a ruckus. They are interfering with people who are making a nuisance of themselves on the [street] swearing, yelling out, obviously intoxicated, assaulting other people, acting in an anti-social manner.... They are the types of things that they are directed to come down on hard, and not so much because a person's heritage is other than white Caucasian.
>
> *(Interview 23, NSW Police Force Local Area Commander)*

In a formulation familiar within policing research, another local area commander claimed to 'encourage them to learn how to identify crooks', adding:

> It is all part of them learning their trade, so to speak, and that is something that can't be taught at the academy. So it's actually teaching them about how to look at who is actually acting in a suspicious manner.
>
> *(Interview 18, NSW Police Force Local Area Commander)*

This faith in intuitive, on-the-job learning was noted in a study of English police in which suspicions were considered by police to be 'skilful taken-for-granted accomplishments that could not be taught' (Quinton 2011: 360). Quinton found that officers were not able to articulate what reasonable suspicion meant in practice, that thresholds of suspicion varied widely among individual officers, and that suspicion therefore retained a 'contradictory and elastic' character:

> I suppose it is not the right way of saying it – but they have a really good gut instinct for who they should approach, and who is up to mischief. And invariably the good ones are rarely wrong. They can go up there and speak to someone, like, 'What have you got in your pockets?', and they will put out some drugs or stolen property or they will be wanted online, or they will be an unlawful non-citizen. So it is something that the good ones develop over a period of time.
>
> *(Interview 23, NSW Police Force Local Area Commander)*

In fact, nothing satisfies the criterion for what Chan (1997) describes as 'dictionary' (that is, categorical) knowledge so well as the formation of 'appropriate suspicions' about who is deserving of police attention. As with other research on the application of stereotypes by police, Quinton identified that 'signals that marked people out into broad social categories were found to have the strongest influence on suspicions, and were often symbolically associated with notions of respectability and order' (Quinton 2011: 364).

Section 188 of the Migration Act, which requires individuals who are believed to be non-citizens to provide evidence of their identity and/or legal status, effectively identifies non-citizens as a suspect group. There is no general power for police to demand proof of identity of Australian citizens in a way that equates to s 188, other than when they are lawfully stopped while driving a vehicle or where police form the view that an individual can assist with an investigation into an offence (see overview of these powers in Chapter 2). Of course law is not the only, or even the main, factor shaping police practice. Quinton (2011) found that permissive legislation in the UK allowing stops without reasonable cause in designated locations had the effect of dropping the level of suspicion considered necessary in *other* contexts. Moreover, he observed that legal powers were rarely applied for the specific purpose for which they were enacted, but tended to be applied in response to 'general signals of disorder and demeanour' (Quinton 2011: 360; see also Van der Leun 2003). Studies on discretionary decision-making consistently show that law is only one of a number of factors that guide decisions in the field and that both formal guidelines and informal practice rules may be interpreted and applied by individuals in different ways (see, for example, Weber 2003, on detention decisions made by UK immigration officers).

How and where do police check immigration status?

The establishment of the ISS in 2006 provided a capacity for police to make on-the-spot immigration checks, 24 hours a day. Awareness-raising about the availability of the system, and associated training in the interpretation of visa labels and the exercise of Migration Act powers, was being rolled out to police members at the time of the migration policing study.

Since the inception of the ISS, NSW police have been by far its most frequent users, generating more than 50 per cent of calls made to the system in the first 20 months of its operation, according to figures supplied by DIAC (see Figure 4.1). This corresponds to 6,099 of the 11,672 calls made to the operators over this period.[3] Some of these checks will have been made in the course of criminal investigations, which will be discussed later in this chapter. According to one senior DIAC official, the predominance of NSW police queries to the ISS is not surprising:

> Well, it's my guesstimation that, you know, 60 per cent of our immigration business takes place in NSW, or thereabouts. And bearing [in mind] that NSW is very ethnically diverse and it's the place of choice for newly arrived people, so it stands to reason that police as first-line community officers come in contact with [unlawful non-citizens] more so than their own [DIAC] compliance officers would.

> *(Interview 46, Canberra DIAC)*

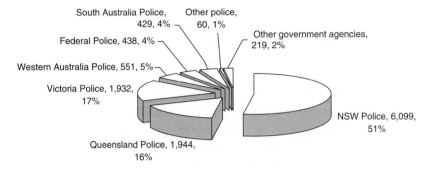

FIGURE 4.1 Calls made to the Immigration Status System 20 February 2006 to 31 October 2007 by agency (number and percentage).

Operational police officers who completed the migration policing survey reported an average of 3.6 immigration checks per officer over the 12 months prior to completing the survey, although there was considerable variation among officers in the number of checks reported (see Figure 4.2).[4] This variability might indicate a particular propensity among some officers to initiate checks, or may simply reflect variations in opportunities to conduct immigration checks due to differing operational roles.

Local area commanders from urban locations believed that most immigration checks would be conducted at the station – either by detectives during protracted investigations, or when suspects are brought into custody on other grounds. One commander saw an immigration status check as simply part of a 'thorough' investigation, whereas patrol officers were thought to be too busy to instigate checks while carrying out 'stop-and-prop' activities on the street (Interview 6, NSW Police Force

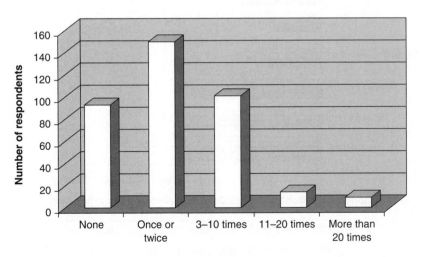

FIGURE 4.2 Reported frequency of immigration checks by operational police in previous 12 months ($n = 371$).

Local Area Commander). However, the most commonly reported method for requesting immigration checks was via the radio dispatch system (185 officers), suggesting that on-the-spot checks during street patrols featured prominently in the experience of these officers. Among those who identified as general duties officers, 78 per cent reported having conducted an immigration check at least once in the previous 12 months. Among highway patrol officers and detectives the percentages were 87 per cent and 84 per cent, respectively. This supports the view that the practice of checking immigration status occurs across a wide range of contexts. Direct queries to the ISS number were the second most frequently mentioned mode of checking (124 responses). Finally, some officers had also contacted DIAC themselves, via the local Sydney office (40 responses) or DIAC headquarters in Canberra (25 responses), or through DIAC liaison officers located at the NSW Police Force Headquarters (26 responses). These direct communication options are more suggestive of methods used by detectives or in follow-up investigations conducted by operational police after an arrest. Although only around 33 per cent of the officers surveyed had knowingly used the ISS, 58 per cent said that they had heard about it.

Figure 4.3 depicts the situations in which the officers reported conducting immigration status checks. There were variations among the study sites in the relative

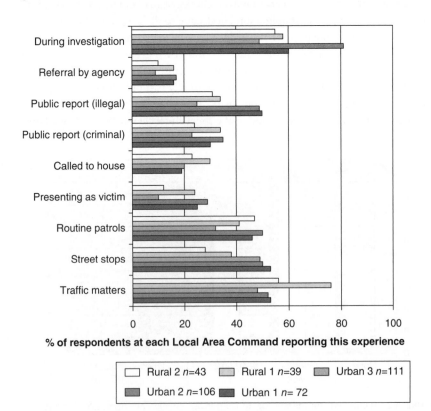

% of respondents at each Local Area Command reporting this experience

| ☐ Rural 2 n=43 | ▨ Rural 1 n=39 | ▨ Urban 3 n=111 |
| ■ Urban 2 n=106 | ■ Urban 1 n= 72 | |

FIGURE 4.3 Reported circumstances in which NSW police officers check immigration status (n = 371).

frequency with which each of the situations was nominated – some of which might be attributable to different sample profiles obtained at each site, and some to differences in demographics and policing styles.[5] It is apparent across all sites that checks of immigration status can arise through police-initiated actions such as stopping drivers or pedestrians, behind-the-scenes checks made in the course of investigations, and in response to reports from the public or other agencies.

When asked about the practice of checking the immigration status of individuals presenting as victims of crime, one local area commander suggested that this might occur where 'something has arisen to raise the doubt of someone's validity' and claimed that people make false reports about victimisation 'all the time' (Interview 18, NSW Police Force Local Area Commander). Immigration status checking in this context was said to be particularly likely to occur in relation to allegations such as trafficking and labour exploitation where the victim's immigration status would be relevant:[6]

> The only reason that we would be checking a victim is if we were doubting the victim's version. We would not initially be checking the victim because they had been sexually assaulted, and there was no dispute about that. If perhaps they were working in a brothel that was known to have illegals we would probably contact and do a check on that person, but that was mainly to ensure that they were provided with every service that they needed to be provided with.
>
> *(Interview 40, NSW Police Force Headquarters)*

It was clear from the interviews that the checking of victims' immigration status alongside checks for criminal matters such as outstanding warrants was just considered standard procedure: '[I]f we put their name in the system and nothing came up, if we still had that suspicion that they were potentially an unlawful non-citizen, yeah that would then be a separate enquiry' (Interview 23, NSW Police Force Local Area Commander). Even the senior officer cited above in relation to trafficking victims contended that immigration checking might be reasonable in other circumstances 'because victim or offender, when we load them into our systems their status has to be accurate' (Interview 40, NSW Police Force Headquarters). This suggests that immigration status is considered to be a salient factor in categorising, and gathering intelligence about, policed populations in NSW. Indeed, another local area commander depicted immigration checking as simply part of routine information gathering about anyone with whom police come into contact: 'We like to know who we are dealing with, so anyone – whether they are a victim, a witness, a complainant, a suspect – everyone gets run through the mincer – the machine – so that we know who we are dealing with' (Interview 23, NSW Police Force Local Area Commander). In this case, 'everything' probably refers to information readily available on the internal police Computerised Operational Policing System (COPS), which may record previous police contact with an individual in relation to immigration enforcement, but does not contain up-to-date information on immigration status.[7] Regardless, both the survey and interview responses revealed that immigration checks – whether made through the COPS system, the ISS or directly with DIAC – were considered to be just another tool in the process of intelligence gathering about individuals with whom police have dealings, whether as suspects or alleged victims.

As reported in Chapter 3, only around 13 per cent of queries made to the ISS across all states in the first 20 months of its operation resulted in the iden- tification of an unlawful non-citizen. The remaining targets of ISS checks were found to be Australian citizens or lawfully present non-citizens. By way of comparison, Dixon (2005) suggests that a 'generous' estimate of the *criminal* arrest rate from stop-and-search practices in Australia is around 10 per cent. More accurate data on general stop-and-search practices in England and Wales indicates an 8.5 per cent arrest rate for the London Metropolitan Police and 10.8 per cent elsewhere (Ministry of Justice 2010) – figures that have attracted sustained criticism because of the unnecessary intrusions they represent in the majority of cases which result in no law enforcement action (Bowling and Phillips 2007). In NSW, a relatively high detection rate of 20 per cent was reported in the first 12 months after the introduction of new powers to search for prohibited implements in 1998 (Fitzgerald 2000); however, the figure was much lower for young people, indicating greater numbers of unproductive searches. A 2008 review by the NSW Ombudsman of drug detection trials involving vehicle stops criticised as unacceptably low the 23 per cent success rate in discovering drugs even after positive indications by sniffer dogs, and described the many unsuccessful searches as 'usually very public and potentially embarrassing' (NSW Ombudsman 2008: iv).

The above discussion has revealed that the practice of checking immigration status on the streets of NSW seems to be routinely embedded within everyday policing tactics aimed at crime control and order maintenance, which are pursued within a very permissive legal framework. This interpretation is reinforced by the observation that 177 of the operational police survey respondents (49 per cent) claimed to have never exercised their Migration Act powers, despite 274 (74 per cent of them) reporting having made an immigration status check in the past 12 months. Only 31 per cent (111 officers) said that they had exercised Migration Act powers, while 20 per cent (72) said that they did not know. Further confirma- tion that migration policing is seamlessly embedded within everyday police practice came from local area commanders, one of whom stated: 'The cops would be far less knowledgeable in the Migration Act than what they would for the nuts and bolts proactive policing legislation' (Interview 18, NSW Police Force Local Area Commander).

Who is checked and why?

In the survey, respondents were asked to indicate their reasons for conducting the immigration checks they had reported by choosing as many options as applied to them from a predetermined list (see Figure 4.4).

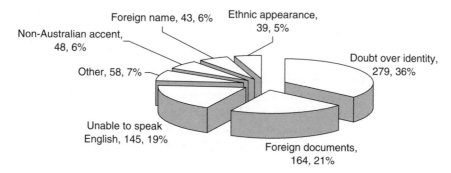

FIGURE 4.4 Reported reasons for checking immigration status showing number and percentage of responses (total 776 responses).

By far the most frequently cited reason for conducting an immigration check was uncertainty over identity. Yet the logic underpinning this practice seems circular, since the ISS was designed to provide information on immigration status, and requires a name in order to make that check. Senior officers explained that information provided through the ISS could help police judge whether the person before them matched the profile recorded by DIAC. This usage could be likened to a low-tech version of biometric data matching. Using immigration checks as a way of verifying identity opens up possibilities beyond the identification of unlawful non-citizens, such as making warrant checks and achieving other high-value policing outcomes. Police powers to issue on-the-spot fines for traffic and public order offences in NSW also create a strong incentive to check identity using whatever means are available in order to maximise cost recovery:

> I would be very disappointed with one of my officers if they stopped a motor vehicle for a person who was speeding … and they couldn't produce a driver's licence, not to then do checks. Because, you know, if they say they're Humphrey Bear, what proof have you got? And Humphrey Bear ends up getting a ticket.
>
> *(Interview 24, NSW Police Force Local Area Commander)*[8]

If ISS checks are indeed being made whenever an individual who may be a non-citizen is unable to produce a document verifying their identity, or in order to confirm the authenticity of the documents provided, this would contribute to the high number of immigration checks on individuals who prove to be lawfully present. The use of the ISS by police raised questions in the mind of one senior DIAC official interviewed for the study:

> [The police] will have a case and a client who they think may be of immigration interest. How they determine that sometimes, considering

that 90 per cent of the cases are lawful or could be Australian citizens, leaves some questions unanswered.

(Interview 42, Canberra DIAC)

One answer is that the possibility that the person is of 'immigration interest' is usually a secondary concern for police, who are more motivated by general policing objectives. On the other hand, DIAC compliance staff who worked in liaison roles with NSW state police said they encouraged police to make ISS checks, even when visas were presented, because of the growing complexity of the visa system:

> If, for example, it was a highway patrol man who picked somebody up, we would encourage them to contact ISS, because we have an increasing use of electronic visas, so we don't have labels. And that is part of the message that we are spreading so that police are aware that labels might be old, or out of date, or superseded. There is any number of things that can affect a person's status.
>
> *(Interview 51, Sydney DIAC)*

Other reasons reported by police officers for making immigration checks concerned indicators of 'foreignness' – ranging from the possession of foreign documents, to lack of proficiency in English, and ethnic appearance. Clearly, none of these cues aligns substantively with the legal category of 'non-citizen', particularly ethnic appearance. One might expect a certain reluctance on the part of police to volunteer this type of information, and it is in this area more than any other where the shortcomings of survey-based approaches are most evident. Even so, significant numbers of officers who completed the survey were prepared to acknowledge their use of these indicators as at least part of their rationale for conducting an immigration check. Of the list of options that were provided in the questionnaire, ethnic appearance is the only characteristic that would be ascertainable by police prior to questioning the individual. It is therefore likely that ethnic appearance is used as the basis for initiating encounters more frequently than was reported by survey respondents and/or that encounters are often initiated on other bases as part of general street policing practice. One specialist officer who deals with crime on trains supported the latter view:

> Police need to detect something else before they check a passport. If there are minor offences we need to validate who they are. Without any real reason we may use an immigration check to verify what they are saying. It may support whether they are honest or not. [Interviewer: *What about if you suspect he or she is an unlawful non-citizen? Is there a power to require ID?*] Yes.... But you can't look at people and suspect he or she is illegal in our society. Normally something else comes first.
>
> *(Interview 11, NSW Police Force Commuter Crime Unit)*

Intensive research such as observational studies of operational officers, examination of documentary evidence about police stops (if available) and in-depth interviews with operational police would be needed to provide a detailed understanding of the circumstances that lead to immigration status checks. Training modules that are provided for the police by DIAC inform officers that their suspicions about unlawful status must be 'based on objective evidence and not on assumption', and must be 'reasonable, maintained, documented'.[9] DIAC instructors' notes provided to the researchers explain that factors such as language proficiency or ethnicity fall under the category of 'assumptions'. However, on the one occasion when a researcher observed a training session this level of detail was not explored. In his review of the police use of sniffer dogs to detect prohibited drugs during vehicle stops, the NSW Ombudsman concluded that the interpretation of 'reasonable suspicion' applied by police in that context was too broad. He reported that searches had been made on the basis of the person having previously been in possession of drugs or in the company of others who possessed drugs, which fell short of the legal requirement that suspicion should be based on beliefs about current drug possession (NSW Ombudsman 2008: iv). In addition, NSW case law has established that 'reasonable suspicion involves less than a reasonable belief but more than a possibility' and that 'some factual basis for the suspicion must be shown' (*R v Rondo* [2001] NSWCCA 540: para 53 of Smart AJ). These authoritative pronouncements support a more general argument against profiling based either on an individual's past history or, by extension, on aggregate risk categories. However, even if officers are aware of this guidance, there is reason to believe that factors other than the law are more determinative of operational practice, as discussed in a previous section.

In addition to persons 'known to police', individuals and events that are considered to be 'out of place' are a well-documented trigger for police suspicion (see, for example, Dunham *et al.* 2005; Quinton 2011). These perceptions are often articulated in terms of individuals who 'do not belong' to their surroundings, usually with reference to a particular neighbourhood and time of day. From discussions with senior NSW police it was apparent that processes ostensibly intended to verify 'identity' are often heavily infused with judgements about who should or shouldn't 'be here':

> It is not about the name or the circumstance, it is about their observations of the individual, that they doubt that they are a resident. So by the discussion that they are having with them it sounds like they are not here – that they shouldn't be here.... I actually think that they are not answering my questions quickly enough or responding to my expectations.
>
> *(Interview 40, NSW Police Force Headquarters)*

In such cases, 'here' refers to Australia as a whole, although the signals of non-belonging might differ from place to place. In rural areas, signs of 'non-belonging' could depend on the presence or absence of 'community ties', which might then prompt further enquiries, as described by one local area commander:

> I wouldn't say a gut feeling, but you know you just get an inference that should this person be here? – whether they have any community ties, and so forth.... So it signals an alarm bell, so to speak, and people make a few more enquiries.
>
> *(Interview 29, NSW Police Force Local Area Commander)*

With many avenues available to police to require the production of identification, the failure to provide adequate ID was often cited as a basis for suspicion in itself. This initial suspicion could, in turn, generate speculation about immigration status, particularly when coupled with ethnic appearance or other purported signifiers of incongruity.

> Again, just experience tells us that people who carry no identification don't want to be identified.... So we try to drill down and find out who they are. [Interviewer: *So an immigration check would be a way to try and resolve that?*] Yeah, and again to people who shouldn't be here, generally they may have a driver's licence, Medicare cards, that kind of stuff.... The biggest giveaway, a Black African gentleman, someone from Sudan or Uganda or something like that, and they have got a credit card on them in the name of John Smith. I am sorry, but you don't look like John Smith.
>
> *(Interview 26, NSW Police Force Local Area Commander)*

In one rural area which has relatively low levels of ethnic diversity, the local commander was prepared to concede that members of particular ethnic minority groups could be readily constructed as suspected unlawful non-citizens:

> I must admit ... most of our detections are very obvious detections. Asians ... obvious Asian people, who ... really do stand out because they're not ... you know, we don't have that many Asians around. And our police being mindful that most of the itinerant workers on the ... within the grape industry especially, generally speaking, are Asians.
>
> *(Interview 24, NSW Police Force Local Area Commander)*

The systemic production of racialised policing practices has been widely observed through empirical research. Categorised suspicion is often understood as a product of the nature of police work, as argued, for example, by Reiner (2000: 91, citing Banton 1983): 'Stereotyping is an inevitable tool of the suspiciousness endemic to police work. The crucial issue is not its existence but the degree to which it is reality-based and helpful, as opposed to categorically discriminatory in a prejudiced way'. Moreover, specific policing styles adopted in particular places can either mitigate or exacerbate these inherent categorising tendencies. In some urban commands in NSW, proactive units have been formed to conduct stop-and-prop activities in specified locations, often railway stations. Their role was explained by one local area commander as being 'preventive', aimed at interacting with 'different target groups' in order to deter crime (Interview 6, NSW Police Force Local Area Commander). Another commander suggested that specialist proactive teams were more likely than general patrols to carry out immigration checks because 'they are potentially working with the type of person who you would stereotype … you would suggest is an illegal immigrant' (Interview 18, NSW Police Force Local Area Commander). The proactive targeting of particular hot spots was another widely reported tactic in which checking of immigration status could arise:

> We've advanced ourselves dramatically in the last 12 months regarding just finding out who people are, and we have some legislative powers to actually target suspects in what we classify hot spot areas…. So really, I drive the police to ensure that people are feeling safe in their environment and by doing that they are really targeting people who they believe look a bit suspicious who are in suspicious areas. And if they come to the point if they are not satisfied with that person's background or their story or their documentation and they can't actually prove who they are, then they might tap down the track of an immigration check.
>
> *(Interview 18, NSW Police Force Local Area Commander)*

Even where police stops are ostensibly directed towards the identification of a *particular* suspect, hypothetical examples given by local area commanders illustrated how much broader categories of suspicion could be mobilised:

> For example, the Pizza Hut at [location] has been robbed three times by a South-East Asian identified male, or suspected male who looks five foot nine and [of] South-East Asian appearance. So we have got a police patrol in [location] and they see three – during the day – people who fit that description. They have got reasonable cause to actually go and speak to those people. So it is all about the information that is given to them.
>
> *(Interview 18, NSW Police Force Local Area Commander)*

This account aligns with Quinton's finding in relation to English police, that anyone meeting a radio description would be stopped, while 'descriptions were often vague and lacking in detail which meant, in practice, officers had considerable discretion to stop whoever they liked' (Quinton 2011: 365). Moreover, Dunham *et al.* (2005), in their study of police stops in the US state of Georgia, found that individuals stopped on the basis of suspect descriptions, rather than an apparent misdemeanour on their part, were more likely to resent and resist police intrusions. While she observes that various kinds of aggregate profiling are routinely denied both by police and border authorities, Pratt has argued that:

> [t]here is a fine and much disputed line that distinguishes target profiling from racial profiling … Whether used as the sole factor, or one factor among many, profiling allows race, religion or ethnicity to play a determinative factor in investigative decisions.
>
> *(Pratt 2005: 208, citing Roach and Choudry 2003)*

The statements by senior NSW police reported in this section link intelligence-led strategies directly to the mobilisation of ethnically based stereotypes and other indicators of non-belonging. In relation to the question posed in this section of 'Who is checked (for immigration status) and why?', the answer as indicated by ISS statistics is 'generally, people who are lawfully present in Australia'. This finding must have far-reaching implications both for individual feelings of belonging and in relation to perceptions of police legitimacy.

Other migration policing functions

Immigration information as an investigative tool

Immigration checks also arise in the context of behind-the-scenes criminal investigations. As with checks following street stops, the motivation may not always be a desire to contribute to border control. In addition to current immigration status, the ISS provides other information that may be useful in an investigation. This includes movement records that can be used to determine whether a named individual (whether citizen or non-citizen) is recorded as being in Australia or overseas on a given date. This information might provide an alibi for a criminal suspect, or build incriminating evidence for a prosecution. The ISS might also help police detect identity fraud – for example, when the rightful holder of a document that has been presented to police is recorded as having departed Australia. As reported above, 84 per cent of the detectives who completed the survey said that they had checked someone's immigration status in the previous 12 months. Senior police reported that detectives might check immigration status as a matter of course during an investigation 'just so that they know what they are up against' (Interview 23, NSW Police Force Local Area Commander). Indeed, checking immigration status was considered to be part of a 'thorough investigative process' likely to involve a range of background checks: 'You actually do checks before you go and talk to your suspect. So it is that thoroughness of that investigative process, as opposed to the stop-and-prop situation' (Interview 6, NSW Police Force Local Area Commander).

Serious crime within NSW is investigated by the State Crime Command, which includes specific squads organised by crime type (such as firearms, drugs and organised crime), ethnicity (for example, Asian or Middle Eastern) and other status categories (such as 'bikies'). A senior officer from this command explained that immigration status is highly relevant when dealing with ethnically defined crime committed by individuals who are newly arrived and on temporary visas, but is less relevant where the main groups of interest are second- or third-generation citizens. Even so, this officer explained that accessing DIAC information is a routine aspect of building a profile about a suspect:

> So it is basic profiling. We will develop a profile on that person and a whole lot of checks are done. You know taxation, crime commission holdings, immigration, AUSTRAC,[10] so it is a package that is put together … Before we even take a step moving in any direction the profile is prepared.
>
> *(Interview 36, NSW Police Force Headquarters)*

These information sources help to build a background, not only of immigration status but also of an individual's movements and activities before arriving in Australia. Unlike the AFP, no NSW Police Force employees had direct access to DIAC databases at the time the interviews were conducted. Investigating officers can make use of an internal police enquiry system called iAsk to request information from other departments with which police have an MOU. This system is said to be used heavily by State Crime Command officers but also by detectives located in Local Area Commands (Interview 51, Sydney DIAC). The Law Enforcement Liaison Unit based at DIAC headquarters in Canberra can also provide more detailed information than the ISS if needed for a criminal investigation. Police using the iAsk system are required to show reasonable cause as to why specific information held by another agency should be made available to them. An MOU governing information exchange with DIAC in accordance with privacy legislation has reportedly been in existence since around 2000 (Interview 35, NSW Police Force Headquarters).

Individual detectives may also have personal contacts within DIAC that they use to check immigration status and seek other information. The existence of these informal links might depend to a significant extent on the personnel involved, as with the following example provided by a senior DIAC official:

> NSW [Police] has had extensive ad hoc contact via our compliance officers up until about, say, halfway through this year [2007] when that person went on leave. He's an ex–NSW police officer so he had a lot of contacts in the field.
>
> *(Interview 46, Canberra DIAC)*

Although these personal contacts are no doubt highly valued by police investigators, the close relationship between police and DIAC officers, sometimes mediated by ex–police officers who had shifted to a DIAC compliance role, was at the centre of many of the 'overzealous' immigration enforcement practices that were criticised in the Palmer Inquiry.

In relation to police investigations, DIAC information is used primarily as a resource for pursuing law enforcement goals, rather than as a tool for detecting and removing unlawful non-citizens. In fact, police who are trying to build a case for criminal prosecution sometimes complain that suspects or witnesses who are unlawfully present may be summarily removed by DIAC without their knowledge. The formal process required to prevent these removals and other connections between the enforcement of immigration and criminal law are discussed in Chapter 5. DIAC liaison officers posted within NSW Police Force Headquarters reported that they often act as brokers to ensure that criminal proceedings are not impeded by immigration enforcement processes:

> We wouldn't want to remove someone, you know, if that person was a key witness, for example, rather than an alleged perpetrator, we wouldn't want to be removing them and ruining a potential court case. We would want to liaise closely with the police and facilitate their stay if that was required.... It would depend on the case and the information that they provided, you know they don't always do it as a routine of course.
>
> *(Interview 51, Sydney DIAC)*

DIAC liaison officers said that they carried out this function by liaising with DIAC Prison Removal teams to enquire whether there was permission to remove individuals known to be involved in ongoing court cases, and would flag them as a 'client of interest' if necessary on DIAC systems. The distinction made between witnesses and suspects, although probably not a formal distinction within DIAC procedures, hints at the possibility that removal of a criminal suspect might on occasion be considered a suitable result by police and/or immigration officials (as discussed in Chapter 5).

'Crime, crime, crime' – police-generated joint operations

NSW police reported running joint operations from time to time which could identify unlawful non-citizens. However, their motivation for conducting these operations is invariably driven by crime concerns, as attested by this local area commander, with immigration enforcement a secondary matter:

> We have got lots and lots of karaoke bars; that causes a lot of grief. So from time to time we will engage DIAC and we will put together a team of police and some DIAC people and we will go through the karaoke bars and around some of the other haunts in the city checking for unlawful non-citizens. [Interviewer: *What would be the policing-related concerns?*] Crime, crime, crime.
>
> *(Interview 23, NSW Police Force Local Area Commander)*

Similar activities were reported by an informant from a major crime unit, who explained how DIAC could operate as a tool for police:

> If, for example, we were doing what we would call a sweep operation, we would go in – and we do them now around the karaoke bars or whatever,

or whether it's brothels. We would take [DIAC] with us and they would do those checks for us. And they take them away on the spot.

(Interview 36, NSW Police Force Headquarters)

Police informants repeatedly confirmed that DIAC's presence could be beneficial in operations that are driven by crime control objectives, so that police were not diverted into dealing with unlawful non-citizens:

> We've run some major operations over the last few years that have included Immigration from the outset.... We actually got Immigration involved in our last one because we were inadvertently ... we were looking for drugs, but ... we would be coming across non-lawful citizens. So we actually had Immigration on the ground for our last one in ... in case we did come across people.
>
> *(Interview 24, NSW Police Force Local Area Commander)*

One officer from a specialist Commuter Crime Unit claimed not to engage in joint operations with DIAC (Interview 11, NSW Police Force Commuter Crime Unit). But another unit which operates closer to the centre of Sydney reported conducting organised operations, sometimes involving other agencies, in which a variety of checks are carried out on taxi drivers:

> In the course of our operation obviously we are checking on the licensing requirements of the taxi, the drivers, the condition of the cab, the status of the driver in relation to his licence and possible criminal activity or his status as a citizen.... Police do their checks in relation to vehicle safety and the status of the driver and the licensing requirements, and then there are certain Memorandums of Understanding between each agency in relation to the checks that they conduct with the Ministry of Transport, Immigration and also Centrelink.
>
> *(Interview 22, NSW Police Force Commuter Crime Unit)*

DIAC officers interviewed for the study confirmed that their presence is sometimes requested by police, particularly in rural areas during roadblock operations, which might require that any unlawful non-citizens identified be transported across long distances to immigration detention centres:

> It may happen out and about in rural areas where they are checking registration and they ask us to come and join them, particularly in areas where we have high risks of unlawful immigrants.... They are pulling people over for a particular purpose and they want us to assist that because they know that they will identify people who may be unlawful during that sort of operation.
>
> *(Interview 42, Canberra DIAC)*

The least enthusiastic view of joint operations was expressed by a local area commander with responsibility for a very ethnically diverse area. He considered that joint operations did not contribute to his organisational objectives, although they could have some general value in forging relationships across state–federal boundaries:

> I can't tell you whether there is linkages between non-citizens and crime. I don't actually know whether that analysis has ever been done. So, in so far as reducing our crime rates, or crime prevention, that type of strategy really doesn't have a massive impact upon localised priorities. What it does do, however … it increases the working relationship between us and the federal government, and it removes a number of people that the government obviously wants removed. But from a policing point of view, no there is no actual motivator that would then drive police to actually do that type of work on a continuous basis.
>
> *(Interview 6, NSW Police Force Local Area Commander)*

DIAC requests for police assistance

Just as DIAC officers can be a useful resource on police-led operations, police are also called upon to assist in DIAC-led operations, primarily the execution of Migration Act warrants to apprehend named individuals. Police described a number of ways in which they assist in these contexts, from providing intelligence to assess risks, to effecting forced entry if necessary, protecting DIAC staff, keeping the peace or merely providing a uniformed presence to promote compliance:

> Whilst immigration officials will have a warrant to apprehend a person, we will actually do the entry, we will actually take the person into custody, execute the warrant and virtually hand them over…. And the reason behind that is that – it has been touted to me is that, because we are trained at doing that sort of stuff that we should do it.
>
> *(Interview 6, NSW Police Force Local Area Commander)*

Police presence would only be requested in immigration cases that have already been assessed by DIAC to be 'high risk', for reasons explained here by a senior DIAC official:

> With those high-risk cases where we need some support, we will ask the police to come. It's not unusual with some of these more difficult ones to bring in their Tactical Unit to assist us, and sometimes they will assist by providing a monitoring policeman to escort a person overseas as well…. Our compliance staff doesn't carry guns, we don't carry truncheons, we don't carry pepper spray – any of those protective mechanisms that the police have. We are very concerned about the Occupational Health and Safety issues for

our staff and we don't like our staff going into any situations where they don't have any weapons to protect themselves, so we use the police as a way of assisting us in those situations. We can actually use reasonable force under the legislation to enact our powers; we don't actually provide a lot of training.... These situations are very few and far between, but where they do turn up we ask the police for assistance.

(Interview 42, Canberra DIAC)

Most of the time, however, even high-risk warrants were said to be executed without major confrontations, and the mere presence of uniformed police is believed to promote compliance – both on the part of the targeted person, and in relation to compliance with the law by DIAC officers: '[Police] will only just see that there is compliance and once there is compliance we leave ... our main aim at these is to prevent a breach of the peace or ensure the protection of property etcetera' (Interview 40, NSW Police Force Headquarters). A senior DIAC official confirmed that promoting compliance is the major objective from their organisational perspective as well:

If you have a client who, there may be some information to suggest, may become belligerent or even possibly violent it's a precautionary ... it's a matter of risk management and risk mitigation strategy that we would take police. And more often than not the mere presence of the police there is enough to ensure compliance of the client and really that's what we're hoping for.

(Interview 47, Canberra DIAC)

In addition to assisting in the execution of Migration Act warrants, police also participate in place-based raids, in cases where DIAC either expects to locate unlawful non-citizens or has a warrant to search for documentation. Examples were provided during the interviews of operations in which DIAC questioned people present while police provided security and assistance with any resulting custodies:

One we did last year, I think I had maybe ... maybe 15 or so police involved. I arranged a prison van as well for transport. And then there was probably half a dozen or so immigration officers.... We have a briefing as per a normal operation. Our guys are in there to secure the premises and assist with the security of any detained persons, but pretty much to hold the premises.

(Interview 24, NSW Police Force Local Area Commander)

The markets near Flemington train station in Sydney were identified as the location for a lot of 'cash work' that attracts DIAC's attention. Compliance field officers would reportedly cordon off a whole section of the market and police would sometimes support them, primarily to ensure safety but also to prevent 'runners' from straying onto the railway line (Interview 11, NSW Police Force Commuter Crime Unit). This division of responsibility for coercion was confirmed by a senior DIAC official quoted in Chapter 3, who noted that it was not DIAC policy to pursue people.

Senior police did sometimes question the return on their involvement in DIAC operations, in the same way that DIAC managers noted the low success rate from ISS checks conducted by police:

> We did an operation, I think it was last year, and we assisted the Immigration Department with a warrant on a particular property that they had concerns about. And out of the 40-odd people we checked, there was only three unlawful citizens. And I think they may have been only a technicality too.
>
> *(Interview 24, NSW Police Force Local Area Commander)*

No systematic information is available from the NSW Police Force on the number of requests it receives from DIAC for assistance with the execution of Migration Act warrants. Police advised that nothing would be recorded in the COPS database unless there was a breach of the peace that was considered to be a police matter (Interview 40, NSW Police Force Headquarters). Attendance while DIAC officers execute warrants was considered by the respondents to present 'no legislative basis' for recording the matter on COPS, since no mandated police powers are being used in these activities. However, a senior DIAC official took the view that police are acting as designated officers under the Migration Act in these situations, with the implication that police are restricted to operating within the limits of the DIAC warrants (Interview 47, Canberra DIAC). However, this does not negate the capacity of police to draw on wider police powers as necessary (Interview 48, Sydney DIAC Compliance). Informants from the NSW Police Force agreed that, as representatives of a state agency, police could also bring additional powers into play in these operations:

> We not only do this work with immigration officers, we do it with DoCS [Department of Community Services], we do it with Customs, we do it with a whole range of Commonwealth agencies, we even do it with the federal police. And I think it's more a matter of us having the state-based jurisdiction, and we have certain state-based powers in terms of entry, arrest, those sorts of things that these officers don't have. So we are essentially, I would suggest, a tool for them.
>
> *(Interview 23, NSW Police Force Local Area Commander)*

The practice of supporting the execution of warrants for other agencies inevitably raises issues for police over established protocols. Police interviewed for this study took the view that they are subject to far greater levels of external scrutiny than other agencies, including DIAC, and that their participation adds a level of experience and accountability to the process, particularly with respect to search and seizure warrants where practices might later be required to withstand scrutiny in court:

> A lot of the time they will use us to be the independent officers in search warrants, not because they have to, because it is not in their policy, but because it ensures transparency within that particular operation.… Yeah, they still do the bash and barge through the door, we do the stop, videotape. A lot of other agencies don't have the scrutiny. Because of past indiscretions we went from no scrutiny to significant scrutiny, and search warrants, for obvious reasons of the past, has caused that higher level of scrutiny … you know you need to have a clear plan in place, you need to have a risk assessment in place.
>
> *(Interview 18, NSW Police Force Local Area Commander)*

One senior officer suggested that police presence acted as an external check for DIAC in ensuring warrants were executed in accordance with 'lawful process' (Interview 40, NSW Police Force Headquarters). However, actual practice may at times fall well short of this ideal. A first-hand report from a local council officer with experience on joint operations with police painted a far less flattering picture of police practice in that case (to be discussed in Chapter 6). In the wake of the Cornelia Rau affair and other scandals in which DIAC was criticised, not only for its own conduct, but for its over-reliance on state police, significant questions arise about who is in a position to provide credible, independent scrutiny of migration policing.

Migration policing and the police role

Importance of immigration enforcement for the NSW Police Force

On the basis of the interviews with police managers, it is clear that the apprehension of unlawful non-citizens is not a major organisational incentive for the NSW Police Force. As one senior officer put it, 'I still think we do only perform it in participation, it is still not our primary role' (Interview 40, NSW Police Force Headquarters). One senior officer considered that the present Labor government was placing less emphasis on immigration enforcement than the previous conservative administration (Interview 18, NSW Police Force Local Area Commander). In her study of immigration enforcement by Dutch police, Van der Leun (2003: 167) also concluded that the surveillance of illegal immigrants had a low priority: 'Many police officers claim that in practice there is no such a thing as an active search for undocumented immigrants. They rarely ask immigrants for documents, and seldom check their legal status.' She attributed this disinterest to lack of manpower, to the perception that illegality was not an urgent problem or a crime problem at all, to frustrations over difficulties in expelling illegal immigrants, and to the wish to protect relationships with minority communities. Van der Leun therefore concluded that local police performed a 'passive control' in migration policing, compared with the 'active control' displayed by national Aliens Police (comparable to the DIAC compliance function) who were nevertheless dependent on local police for identification.

Despite a reportedly low-key approach, intelligence-led policing tactics in NSW ensure that police play a significant role in locating unlawful non-citizens through opportunistic checks of immigration status that arise in the context of routine street policing, special or joint operations, and criminal investigations. One police commander explained the importance of immigration enforcement from the police perspective in the following terms:

> The way that I see it is that the police do not, per se, prioritise looking for illegal immigrants as part of their work patterns. They identify them as part of ad hoc, normal policing operations.... There is a reliance placed upon police to be the identifiers, and for [DIAC] to come in and then take the body away. I would like to actually see it switched the other way, where there is some level of proactivity in targeting areas that need to be targeted – with police assistance or however that wants to be dealt with ... because I don't necessarily see it as a screaming priority for the command.
> *(Interview 6, NSW Police Force Local Area Commander)*

Other local area commanders agreed that locating unlawful non-citizens is not a major goal in their busy metropolitan commands, but recognised that 'bringing cultures brings immigration issues with it' (Interview 18, NSW Police Force Local Area Commander) that police are then obliged to deal with:

> We have daily contact with large numbers of people from overseas, either visitors or people who now reside in Australia but were born overseas.... It's not stressed that we need to rigorously enforce the immigration laws. I'd suggest it's more a by-product of our day-to-day operational activities.
> *(Interview 23, NSW Police Force Local Area Commander)*

Commanders in rural areas often linked immigration enforcement to factors specific to local economies and demographics:

> I don't see it as a huge issue in this command, and I don't see it as that the community thinks it's a huge issue either ... we don't have large numbers of non-lawful citizens, living within our command.... It's more a seasonal issue and people who live in other areas who have come through our command.
> *(Interview 24, NSW Police Force Local Area Commander)*

While local commanders may be preoccupied with other policing priorities, a senior officer with policy responsibilities for cultural diversity endorsed the widely held view that social harmony is best served by diligently sorting the legal from the illegal population.

> [Immigration enforcement] is something that we should be aware of, familiar with, and it is something that is part of the investigation. It could actually provide you with a course of action … it provides safety in the community. People need to know that you can't overstay your visas, you have got to do it properly. If you want to stay here you apply. I do think it is an important issue.
>
> *(Interview 40, NSW Police Force Headquarters)*

The vast majority of police officers who took part in the migration policing survey identified the enforcement of immigration law as being important to the police role (see Figure 4.5). However, this result was explained quite plausibly by local area commanders in terms of a general tendency for operational officers to consider the enforcement of all laws to be important:

> A lot of our police here are young, both in age and experience, and enforcing the law is what they are paid to do. And you can't be selective when you are enforcing the law, you either enforce it or you don't; you enforce all laws not just some … it doesn't matter what sort of law you are talking about enforcing. I would suggest that that would be a fairly general response.
>
> *(Interview 23, NSW Police Force Local Area Commander)*

When presented with this survey finding, another local area commander suggested that there was probably 'no underlying basis … for that stat', but that the

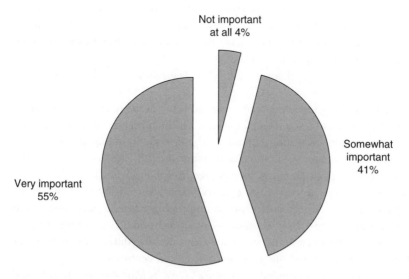

FIGURE 4.5 Importance of immigration enforcement to police role.

process of focusing the attention of these officers on the issue of immigration enforcement through the survey process would have made it seem more important (Interview 6, NSW Police Force Local Area Commander). Another commander agreed that '[i]f we think it's important [it's] because probably they have been asked whether it's important' (Interview 18, NSW Police Force Local Area Commander). While these are plausible interpretations of the survey findings, other patterns of responses (such as the mistaken belief, reported earlier, that immigration checking does not occur in street policing settings) suggest that senior managers may not always be aware of the perspectives and practices of operational police.

Officers who completed the survey were also asked whether they believed they needed more training in the use of their Migration Act powers, and in dealing with ethnically diverse communities. Their answers to these questions provide an indication of the relative importance attached to each of these functions, although they will also be influenced by the amount of training they have already received. At each study location, survey respondents were much more likely to indicate that they needed further training in the use of their Migration Act powers than in dealing with cultural diversity. This result was interpreted by local area commanders as reflecting a preference among rank-and-file police for engaging in law enforcement activities, in line with an orientation towards 'action' that has been widely documented by police researchers (for example, Reiner 2000):

> Look, personally I think the community issue ... that is the more important. But again, I am operating at a different level to the people who actually go out and do the work day to day. They think more in terms of the black and white of policing, as someone has either broken the law or they haven't. They are either here legitimately or they are not. But in terms of dealing with ethnic minority communities, that is more about developing relationships and building trust, all that sort of stuff which is important at my level, because if we don't have that within our communities then we don't get their support.
>
> *(Interview 23, NSW Police Force Local Area Commander)*

The training being rolled out across selected LACs at the time of the migration policing study was said to be focused not only on the mechanics of Migration Act powers, but also on correcting common misconceptions among police officers about the summary nature of immigration enforcement: 'I have been to one of the lectures and the cops sit there and they go, Really, I didn't know that! How come we can't just toss people out of the country?' (Interview 35, NSW Police Force Headquarters). This officer reported that an internet interface to guide police into relevant sections of the DIAC website was about to be launched in order to provide police with information on visa status, custody procedures, requirements for s 501 visa cancellations, and the policing of detention centres.

The resources being expended on training police in Migration Act powers and improving the availability of immigration-related information suggest that police in NSW are expected to play a continuing, if not enhanced, role in detecting unlawful non-citizens. When operational officers were asked in the migration policing survey whether the time they spent on immigration enforcement was increasing, decreasing or about the same, responses were spread across all categories. However, when the responses were broken down by years of service (see Table 4.2), different patterns were discernible. Officers with more than 20 years of service were far more likely to say that their time spent on immigration matters had increased. Newly appointed officers with fewer than five years of service were the most likely to indicate that it had stayed the same. The group most likely to respond that they had perceived a decrease in immigration-related work had begun their policing careers between 1998 and 2003, the years in which political pressure from the former conservative government to effect removals was at its peak.

It is difficult to make an accurate judgement about whether the police are becoming more or less involved in immigration enforcement in the absence of detailed workload statistics. As noted by Mazerolle and Ransley (2006: 97): 'police knowledge of legal tools, options and alternatives shape and prioritize police action'. But it is not clear whether the effect of increased training in Migration Act powers and the introduction of the ISS and other interfaces to data held by DIAC will decrease police referrals to DIAC through early clarification of legal status, increase the overall number of unlawful non-citizens detected, or be used primarily as a resource for advancing policing objectives that are only obliquely related to immigration enforcement. However, some senior managers were prepared to speculate that migration policing is likely to become more prevalent:

> I think it is changing. I think it is becoming more prevalent. I think people are more aware of the vast range of things open to them. I think police are more aware of immigration offences. I think people are more aware of visa violations – all of which are federal law. However, they may well have a huge impact on state policing.
>
> *(Interview 40, NSW Police Force Headquarters)*

This prospect was not yet apparent in the rural areas included in the study, where one local area commander noted 'that's why we have these federal

TABLE 4.2 Has time spent on immigration enforcement increased or decreased since you became a police officer?

Years in police	No. of officers	Increased (%)	Decreased (%)	Neither (%)
Less than 5 yrs	152	12.5	8.6	78.9
5.5 to 10 yrs	97	16.5	32.0	51.5
10.5 to 15 yrs	36	25.0	25.0	50.0
15.5 to 20 yrs	35	28.6	25.7	45.7
More than 20 yrs	24	54.2	12.5	33.3

departments looking at immigration and people overstaying' (Interview 29, NSW Police Force Local Area Commander). However, for police managers who are more exposed to rapid social changes associated with greater regional and global interconnectivity, an increasing emphasis on migration policing seems inevitable:

> I believe that, not just in this LAC, but Australia generally, immigration work will become more important as events occur overseas, whether they be man-made events such as war etcetera, particularly in parts of Europe and the Middle East, [or] people escaping to get away from the conflict. The effects of weather – drought, flood, storm, particularly in Asia and the Island nations. Every time we have a large event, whether it be the Olympics or World Youth Day, we always get people who say, 'Well, this isn't too bad, we will stay in Australia' … I think those sorts of things are going to escalate rather than diminish over the next couple of years.
>
> *(Interview 23, NSW Police Force Local Area Commander)*

The financial and human costs of policing migration

Conducting immigration status checks, assisting DIAC compliance officers to execute warrants, and taking unlawful non-citizens into police custody all have an impact on police resources. Although DIAC training modules for police indicate that Form 1275 'Police Record of Immigration Detention' is to be completed for every person detained under Migration Act powers, police participants in the migration policing study were not aware of this process as a source of information. Similarly, researchers were told that no systematic data was available on police involvement in the execution of DIAC warrants. The apparent absence of accounting data reflects a lack of external scrutiny over police involvement in migration policing and suggests that there is no cross-agency charging for these services. Immigration enforcement was not portrayed by police interviewees as an unwarranted drain on police resources. This perception might be based on the modest amount of immigration-related work undertaken, and also the perceived trade-off in having Migration Act powers available as a policing resource. One exception to this widespread acceptance was provided by the commander of a highly diverse neighbourhood, who was concerned not only about the resource implications of immigration enforcement, but also about the 'humanity' of holding administrative detainees overnight in police cells:

> Whilst it is not a substantial risk to us because we have a cell complex and it is manned – staffed – there is obviously an issue with having someone incarcerated for a long period of time in a police holding cell…. So there is resource implications as well as humanity implications that are obviously very problematic for detaining people.
>
> *(Interview 6, NSW Police Force Local Area Commander)*

Questions of humanity also arise in a less visible way, in relation to the 86 per cent or so of immigration checks conducted on Australian citizens or lawfully present non-citizens. Police requests for documents sends a message of non-belonging that may have accumulating implications both for trust in police and feelings of security within the wider community. As Waddington (1999: 55) has explained: 'Whatever the reason for any particular stop and search, it has the latent function of asserting police authority and reminding those on the receiving end of their effective non-citizenship.'

From the data available it is impossible to discern the precise context in which the recorded ISS checks have been made, and therefore whether the individuals concerned were aware that their right to be present on Australian soil was under scrutiny. An unknown proportion of ISS checks will be made in the context of criminal investigations where the suspect will not be present, may concern movement records rather than immigration status, and may involve Australian citizens whose whereabouts on a particular date is at issue. Set against this context in which some over-counting of what might be termed 'messages of non-belonging' occurs, immigration checks conducted by police that are not referred to the ISS (for example, because a passport is provided which satisfies police of the individual's lawful status) will probably not be recorded in this, or any, system.

In response to federal proposals that immigration enforcement responsibilities in the US be delegated to local police, the American Police Foundation noted that:

> [p]olice executives have felt torn between a desire to be helpful and coopera-tive with federal immigration authorities and a concern that their participation in immigration enforcement efforts will undo gains they have achieved through community oriented policing practices, which are directed at gaining the trust and cooperation of immigrant communities.
>
> *(Khashu 2009: xi)*

Very few such concerns were expressed by senior NSW police officers interviewed for the migration policing study. The sole exception was the local area commander responsible for policing a residential area that was home to a number of long-established and emerging migrant communities, who understood that family members or other members of their community might be heavily invested in supporting unlawful non-citizens:

> You could say to yourself in all honesty immigration officials should perhaps be doing a lot of that stuff themselves. But it is left to the police to do because there is an image problem associated with chasing Johnny through five blocks of units and crash-tackling Johnny to the floor.... And if there is an image problem, then why should we get involved in it when it can actually be done by somebody else?
>
> *(Interview 6, NSW Police Force Local Area Commander)*

Although even this commander conceded that 'we don't mind having a bad name if it is in the interest of justice', his preference was that DIAC should deal with purely immigration-related apprehensions. Other commanders acknowledged damage to police–community relations as a hypothetical drawback of police involvement in immigration enforcement, although they tended to believe the problem did not exist in their command:

> I think there is probably a whole range of potential negatives. Potentially you can be seen to be picking on people from different backgrounds. You don't want to target people or alienate communities. So you know there is potential for unrest in your community if you are continually undertaking immigration checks. [Interviewer: *Do you have a sense of whether that is an issue?*] Not at all, no.
>
> *(Interview 18, NSW Police Force Local Area Commander)*

> Sometimes we get some pretty bad press from the blockies about, you know, locking up a busload of immigrants who are there to pick their grapes because they've got no one else to do it.... But in saying that as well, you get the other side of the story where people are saying that, you know, people are working for, you know, for a pittance and taking work off tax-paying Australians ... So, yeah, I don't really see it as a negative. And the other aspect is we don't have ... any pockets of the community that have hard links to unlawful citizens within our command. So there's no locals that would be – I would imagine would be upset by the fact of any unlawful citizen being detained.... If anything, I think it'd be the opposite.
>
> *(Interview 24, NSW Police Force Local Area Commander)*

Ultimately, even the officers who identified possible drawbacks associated with their involvement in migration policing believed that they had no option but to accept these responsibilities as part of their role:

> You know there certainly may well be a view that if somebody is here and they are a breadwinner, and they have got a family here, and of course from that family's perspective, it may well be – come to pass that they were detained for being illegal ... they might take it as an affront. But I'd come back to it and say that it is the role of the police to enforce the law. If those people are here against the law well then so be it. [Interviewer: *And you don't have any perception ... that it's an issue among the community here?*] Not at all, not at all.
>
> *(Interview 29, NSW Police Force Local Area Commander)*

There is a lack of data on both enforcement patterns and community responses upon which either local area commanders or researchers could base their judgements about the impacts of migration policing on community relations. One commander was confident that no problems had arisen in his area as a result of migration policing, because there had been no complaints of that nature (Interview 23, NSW Police Force Local Area Commander). This interviewee noted there were 'incident fields for immigration matters' within the police database but did not know how to search for them. The commander who expressed concern about the community implications of migration policing was the most mindful of the lack of systematic data:

> [Immigration enforcement] is considered to be a secondary thing; it is pushed aside and we all do it. It is just a force of habit. And because I don't get any of that data, I wouldn't know. So I don't even know if I have got a problem.
>
> *(Interview 6, NSW Police Force Local Area Commander)*

The police interviewees endorsed the view that high levels of community trust are needed in order for crime to be reported to the police. In fact, the current emphasis on intelligence-led policing means that the reporting of crime from all sections of the community is seen as crucial in guiding proactive deployment strategies, not only in providing an appropriate response for victims:

> It is about educating people to realise that in Australia there is a huge difference between a victim and an offender, and they need to know that in order for us – they need to know how we do things, how the police force works. And that is by – if a matter is reported it builds a picture for us. If a couple of matters occur then it affects our deployment. That is how we decide how we are going to deploy our police best. If we don't know about it, we are unable to address it.
>
> *(Interview 40, NSW Police Force Headquarters)*

However, the practice, discussed earlier, of conducting immigration checks on individuals who report their victimisation to police, seems not to reflect the 'huge difference between a victim and an offender' pointed to by this senior officer. Individuals who are 'victims' with respect to criminal law, but effectively 'offenders' with respect to immigration law, therefore occupy a tenuous position within this neat dichotomy. Ultimately, enforcing immigration law appears to be widely accepted as an inevitable part of the police role, and the view was put by this same senior officer that negative community impacts need to be dealt with through community education rather than changes in police practice:

> They need to understand that we have little choice in many issues such as immigration. However, I do think that it does have the potential to portray us somewhat negatively in communities ... we need to take a very educated and learned approach to these sorts of things by making sure that prior to enforcement there is education about what we are about to do.
>
> *(Interview 40, NSW Police Force Headquarters)*

The material presented in this chapter has demonstrated that the role of state police in policing the internal border is historically embedded and normalised within NSW. Although the enforcement of immigration is far from a central priority for senior police managers, or even among operational police who report on average making three or four immigration status checks per year, the overall police effort makes a significant contribution to the identification of unlawful non-citizens. Police also perform coercive functions that DIAC officers are unable or unwilling to perform. Police in NSW have a documented history of disproportionate targeting of their public order powers towards marginalised groups, particularly Aboriginal youths and other young people. However, there is no substantive data on the way in which immigration checks are performed, either as part of street stops or elsewhere. In the absence of observational data, community interviews or official records, the community impact of the migration policing functions performed by members of the NSW Police Force remains an important unanswered question.

5

NEGOTIATING THE CRIMINAL–ADMINISTRATIVE NEXUS

Getting rid of problem people

In the previous chapters, a picture has emerged of unlawful non-citizens being discovered largely through opportunistic encounters, rather than as a result of the organised efforts of police to detect them. However, where unlawful non-citizens are also criminal suspects, police are likely to adopt a more active role in determining their fate. The idea of 'getting rid' of problem people who are found to be unlawfully present, as opposed to pursuing criminal prosecutions against them, arose frequently in the interviews:

> The aim is that [the police] have, like, a bag full of tools that they can utilise to get the best result. You know the best result is not always ending up in a charge, it may well be the case that if the person is an illegal it may be just easy – you know this person we think is a recidivist offender, what is the point of them languishing? Just let's get rid of them.
>
> *(Interview 40, NSW Police Force Headquarters)*

Reliance on expulsion of people for the purpose of population control is not a new phenomenon, as Walters notes in his historical review of deportation practices: 'in its inception it is an administrative not a juridical measure. It is an instrument to protect and sustain public order and tranquility, akin to the removal of a nuisance' (Walters 2002: 281). Walters likens this practice to an international version of the poor laws, which were intended to return problematic people to their appropriate sovereigns. This tactic could also be viewed as a transnational form of the 'move-on' power within criminal law (see Chapter 4), which has been enthusiastically embraced by police in NSW. Throughout the research interviews, police consistently reported that they

believed that the administrative removal of criminal suspects who are unlawfully present is in the public interest in cases where the criminal matters are
not serious, and/or the chance of criminal conviction is low:

> Maybe if we didn't have enough to charge this person criminally, maybe we
> would check that everything is … is totally correct with their current status,
> and whether or not that should be reviewed. Because, you know, at the end
> of the day if … if they're doing the wrong thing and there's any sort of scope
> of getting them out of the community that's what you aim to do.
>
> *(Interview 24, NSW Police Force Local Area Commander)*

> Well, it depends on what the crime is. If it is a serious crime, something
> like a robbery, a homicide, a sexual assault, something of that nature, we
> pursue the criminal avenue, because it's in the public interest to do so. If
> it's only a two bob matter, like a minor theft or a less serious assault, some-
> thing where there is no prospect that the person is going to do any serious
> jail time, even if convicted, we would go down the immigration road and
> just remove them from the country.
>
> *(Interview 23, NSW Police Force Local Area Commander)*

In the US, immigration authorities have used similar reasoning as an incentive
to entice local police into adopting an immigration enforcement role. Appearing
at a national policing conference, a senior figure from the US Immigration
Customs and Enforcement Office, James Pendergraph, was quoted as saying, 'If you
don't have enough evidence to charge someone criminally but you think he's
illegal, we can make him disappear' (Amnesty International 2009: 4). The evidence
from this study suggests that NSW police have discovered this route to a quick
'result' for themselves. A federal police officer interviewed for the study also
described administrative removal as a 'resolution strategy', adding: 'If I've got a
target that I don't think I'm going to have a successful prosecution against, I would
consider his visa status (Interview 65, AFP).

It was clear that in the circumstances described above police preferred administrative measures because of the limited due process rights in place, compared with
negotiating the perceived obstacles of the criminal justice system:

> I suppose the police, when they are making their enquiries, generally tend
> to think – well, is there an easier way of getting rid of this matter? Say if they
> arrest somebody for a minor offence – shoplifting – this is only an example.
> What do they need to do? They need to process the offender, fill in a court
> attendance notice, then they go to court, take the fingerprints.… Or do they
> then turn around and say this person is an unlawful non-citizen, let's detain
> them, let's get Immigration to come and pick them up and take them to
> Villawood?
>
> *(Interview 35, NSW Police Force Headquarters)*

Another local area commander summed up the advantages of administrative removal in the following terms: 'It's quicker, it's cheaper, because we don't pay for it. So a lot of the time it's a highly satisfactory solution to the problem' (Interview 23, NSW Police Force Local Area Commander). DIAC liaison officers posted to the NSW Police Force also presented these cooperative processes in a positive light:

> I guess it would be a high-range traffic offence or minor drug possession or something like that where it would maybe carry a fine in court, and we have had the person available for removal and rung police and said, look this is the situation, Mr X is available for removal, and plans are being made for that person to be removed in two or three days time. Do you mind? No, and I mean we just call back to confirm when the person is being removed.
>
> *(Interview 51, Sydney DIAC)*

In the case of serious offending, senior police were more likely to consider that extracting punishment through the criminal justice process was expected of them, rather than allowing culprits to 'escape justice':

> It is a pretty sad situation for the community that they can't rely on the police to be law enforcers because there is an available option of having somebody deported. And I think that that is quite a valid argument for any democratic society to be able to identify those people who should be put before the court and not allow them to escape justice.
>
> *(Interview 6, NSW Police Force Local Area Commander)*

But relations between police and the court process were complex and could betray a well-known distrust among police of the court system to deliver justice. In some cases, removal might even be seen as a more just outcome in cases where police expect that the court system 'won't give them a full whack of the law' (Interview 6, NSW Police Force Local Area Commander). This suggests some recognition that removal entails a punitive aspect which Pratt (2005) refers to as 'immigration penality'. The victim's wishes could reportedly be another consideration supporting removal rather than criminal prosecution, and, according to the informant quoted below, might be seen as an alternative form of punishment:

> There are circumstances where you may communicate with a victim of a crime and they agree in the interests of criminal justice it is better just to let the person be deported and not keep them here. So their punishment may be that they were shipped out of the country, never to reoffend in a particular matter again. So they don't go to jail or they don't get a massive fine for their offence, but they go out of the country and they can't come back into the country.
>
> *(Interview 39, NSW Police Force Headquarters)*

While administrative removal in the absence of a criminal conviction would not necessarily preclude the possibility of return entirely, the interviewee quoted above explained that issuing an arrest warrant would ensure that the suspect's name would remain on an alert list, preventing them from entering the country under the same identity in future. This strategy therefore injects a criminal justice element into the process even in the absence of criminal prosecution, which in turn feeds into future border enforcement practices. In other cases, police suggested that it would be strategic to pursue both criminal and administrative avenues, with each option acting as a backup for the other, in order to achieve the desired result:

> Certainly it may well be that you do both, you know. You would put some-body before the court, and then at the same time you would be referring them to DIAC.... If the seriousness of the offence was such that they were to be retained in the country they would remain here on the basis that they have been given some sort of temporary visa until their matters were dealt with and then move on.
>
> *(Interview 29, NSW Police Force Local Area Commander)*

> If it's a serious offence you are just not going to deport. Like there still has to be a penalty, there still has to be a process because there is nothing to say, 'Oh, we are not going to worry about that serious assault, we will just deport them' – there is nothing saying that they won't challenge their deportation and be granted provisional residency or something. So you really need to be mindful that the charge does actually have some bearing on the process.
>
> *(Interview 40, NSW Police Force Headquarters)*

Getting rid of 'peripheral players' through administrative removal was a popular tactic even with specialist units within the NSW Police Force who dealt with serious and organised crime:

> If, for example, if they are at the bottom end of the scale we will use the fact that they are unlawful to get rid of them, and we used it quite effectively back in 2001. There was a group of predominantly Chinese students ... doing lots and lots of extortions on the Chinese restaurants. At the end of the day there were a lot of charges laid, but there was a number – they were just peripheral players. Working with [DIAC] very successfully, [DIAC] with-drew their student visas and deported them.
>
> *(Interview 36, NSW Police Force Headquarters)*

Administrative removal aligned well with this unit's modus operandi, which often involved disruption tactics that were seen as a necessary trade-off in order to protect the public. As this officer explained: 'we will use anything we can ... so if we can disrupt them instead by getting them out we will use that ... because sometimes you have to let the prosecution go and just protect' (Interview 36, NSW Police Force Headquarters).

The widespread preference among police for the administrative pathway was often predicated on seemingly exaggerated (or perhaps merely outdated) perceptions of the ease with which removal could be achieved: 'We would contact Immigration and say, we think this person's a dodge, and then they would say, yes they are, no they're not, we would detain them, they would come and get them and they would be gone' (Interview 40, NSW Police Force Headquarters). However, a specialist officer who worked closely with DIAC noted the unrealistic expectations of many police in wishing to resolve minor criminal matters expeditiously:

> Now there is – whether it is from the previous government or not – the perception is that if you commit an offence and you are on a student visa that you should be kicked out of the country. Well, it doesn't work that way.
>
> *(Interview 35, NSW Police Force Headquarters)*

As reported in the previous chapter, some police are aware of the more considered approach now taken to administrative removal in the post-Palmer era, and generally frustrated by it. One AFP officer spoke for many when he complained about a 'flow-on effect' arising from the fact that 'we just don't have that ability years ago where [DIAC] could detain somebody and remove them. That in some ways solved the problem of certain people' (Interview 66, AFP).

Prosecutorial versus removal momentum

In contrast to the scenario outlined above, it emerged from discussions with police prosecutors that pursuing a prosecution of an unlawful non-citizen could involve trying to hold back the tide of immigration enforcement. The mentality propelling police towards prosecution has been described as 'prosecutorial momentum' in relation to criminal cases (McConville *et al.* 1991). However, even in the so-called post-Palmer era for DIAC (see Chapter 3), the route to criminal prosecution looks like a long-distance steeplechase when compared with the sprint to the finish that characterises the DIAC removal machinery. The 'removal momentum' (Weber and Landman 2002) that arises from the automated character of immigration law can only be slowed down by the grant of a CJS certificate under s 148 of the Migration Act:

> I don't think they [DIAC] have any discretion in the matter. I think they must proceed with the deportation process unless and until a stay certificate is obtained.... And in fact I have heard anecdotally of a matter where a person was deported, notwithstanding they are facing serious criminal charges, and the police then had to try and extradite the person from the country that he was sent back to.
>
> *(Interview 38, NSW Police Force Headquarters)*

It was evident from this case, recounted by an experienced police prosecutor, that incursions by immigration authorities into criminal prosecutions could be a risky business for the defence side as well:

> We were prosecuting a fellow for a couple of criminal offences, and they were fairly minor offences, and he had been in custody with bail refused ... at which point his lawyer made an application for him to be released on bail, and I did not oppose that application. However, what she hadn't turned her mind to was that immigration would then grab him and throw him out of the country, and that is what happened. He was deported.
>
> *(Interview 38, NSW Police Force Headquarters)*

Applications for CJS certificates are handled by an executive unit of the NSW Police Force that reports directly to the Police Commissioner, who is one of only three senior figures in the state administration empowered by law to sign them. The interviewees reported that CJS certificates are used infrequently – perhaps 10 or 12 times a year. This was thought to be, in part, because investigating officers in LACs who are responsible for initiating such requests are often not aware of their existence, or may not be aware of the defendant's immigration status. In addition, the legislation itself contains powerful disincentives to apply for CJS certificates because of the requirement that the organisation applying for the visa must meet the financial costs of keeping the individual in the country, whether in the community or in detention. Within the NSW Police Force, this cost is borne at the LAC level, ensuring that applications are only likely to be made in relation to serious matters:

> You wouldn't recommend to the Commissioner that he sign a Criminal Justice Stay certificate preventing somebody from being deported for a minor matter. No, so it has to be in the interests of society. And as an organisation who enforces the law you have to do things that are, well, financially responsible. So you draw a line in the sand as to whether it is worthwhile spending the money to keep someone here.
>
> *(Interview 39, NSW Police Force Headquarters)*

By passing these financial burdens on to those seeking to interrupt the removal process, the immigration system is given precedence in law and policy and is affirmed as the fast and efficient method for dealing with unlawful non-citizens who transgress the criminal law. To reinforce even more clearly where the onus lies, s 153 of the Migration Act states that the removal or deportation of a criminal suspect where no CJS certificate or court warrant is in place does not constitute contempt of court, thus indemnifying immigration authorities against charges of overly zealous enforcement.

Another layer of complexity is injected into the equation since the issuing of a CJS certificate by police triggers consideration by DIAC of whether to grant the defendant a CJS visa. If no visa is issued, and the suspect is not being held in police custody, they may be retained by DIAC in immigration custody. However, if they have been granted bail by the courts and released on a CJS visa, an individual is still free to depart the country. These factors add an additional level of risk for police officers who are seeking to prevent the removal of an unlawful non-citizen:

> It is up to them and their commander to work out whether they want to run the risk, the risk involving keeping that person here … what is the likely outcome going to be if [DIAC] grant the visa? Are they just going to the airport and get on a plane and leave and never come back?
>
> *(Interview 39, NSW Police Force Headquarters)*

An interviewee from the AFP expressed the same concern that defendants granted CJS visas by DIAC 'just disappear again and continue on with what they were doing' (Interview 66, AFP).

While instances of absconding were another source of disgruntlement among some of the police interviewed, the senior officer responsible for dealing with CJS certificates was critical of the reliance on immigration detention as a means of holding criminal suspects: 'Whilst police at the coalface may like to hold people, may like immigration to hold those people until they are ready to proceed, that is not what the role of immigration is' (Interview 39, NSW Police Force Headquarters).

Making people illegal

In this section we move from the detection of unlawful non-citizens among criminal suspects to police efforts to actively reconstitute lawfully present criminal suspects as illegal. Frustration with recidivist offenders or 'troublemakers', coupled with a lack of faith in the criminal justice system to instigate effective remedies, has led police at times to dig more deeply into the resources offered by immigration law. Non-citizens who are lawfully resident on valid visas cannot be summarily removed when identified by police as criminal suspects. However, legal powers exist under s 501 of the Migration Act to cancel permanent resident visas on 'character grounds' (see Chapter 2). In contrast to the more routine cancellation of temporary visa classes, s 501 cancellations result in permanent banishment from Australia. This provision was introduced explicitly to enable the expulsion of even long-term lawful residents who are immune from criminal deportation under other cancellation powers such as ss 200 and 201. As with general removal figures, the numbers of departures from Australia following a s 501 visa cancellation peaked during the early 2000s when the Liberal Immigration Minister Philip Ruddock was at the helm. In recent years statistics on character deportations have been omitted from DIAC annual reports, but Figure 5.1 shows that visa cancellations on character grounds are once again beginning to rise. Although the numbers are

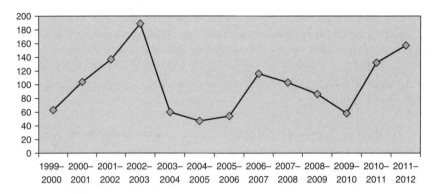

FIGURE 5.1 Cancellations of permanent visas on character grounds 1999–2000 to 2011–12.

Source: DIAC Annual Reports 2000–12.

relatively low, the law and practice of character deportation raise many significant socio-legal and human rights issues.

The powers to cancel permanent visas are exercised by the immigration minister and delegated to specialist officers within DIAC. However, police can actively contribute towards 'making people illegal' (Dauvergne 2008) by bringing them to the attention of DIAC. This provides another resource for police to solve local problems of crime and disorder through the ejection of non-citizens who are in compliance with immigration law but offend against criminal law. The test provided in the legislation (see Box 5.1) allows individuals to be judged to be of bad character for an expansive list of reasons, including past and present criminal conduct, past and present general conduct, likely future conduct and by association with disreputable others.

BOX 5.1 THE CHARACTER TEST UNDER S 501 OF THE MIGRATION ACT

(6) For the purposes of this section, a person does not pass the *character test* if:

(a) the person has a substantial criminal record (as defined by subsection (7)); or
(b) the person has or has had an association with someone else, or with a group or organisation, whom the Minister reasonably suspects has been or is involved in criminal conduct; or
(c) having regard to either or both of the following:

    (i) the person's past and present criminal conduct;
    (ii) the person's past and present general conduct;
    the person is not of good character; or

(d) in the event the person were allowed to enter or to remain in Australia, there is a significant risk that the person would:

(i) engage in criminal conduct in Australia; or

(ii) harass, molest, intimidate or stalk another person in Australia; or

(iii) vilify a segment of the Australian community; or

(iv) incite discord in the Australian community or in a segment of that community; or

(v) represent a danger to the Australian community or to a segment of that community, whether by way of being liable to become involved in activities that are disruptive to, or in violence threatening harm to, that community or segment, or in any other way.

Otherwise, the person passes the *character test*.

In effect, the provisions represent the substitution for arguably objective legal rules and universal human rights norms with subjective normative judgements based on 'community values'. As Rimmer (2008) points out:

> The criteria represent Australian values in the sense of excluding the sort of people we apparently do not want. But it is a very narrow and subjective view. Australia is better served by basing any criteria on objective human rights standards agreed throughout the world.
>
> *(Rimmer 2008: 6)*

These practices exemplify the convergence of criminal and administrative paradigms (or 'crimmigration' – see Stumpf 2006); the emergence of 'pre-crime' practices aimed at pre-empting harm (Zedner 2007); and the impetus towards the separation or banishment of those designated as social 'enemies', which has been dubbed 'enemy penology' (see Krasmann 2007). Section 501 therefore constitutes a veritable 'super-power' of neoliberal risk-based governance grounded on the attribution of perpetually conditional belonging to those without legal citizenship.

The ministerial directions that set out legally binding guidance for DIAC officers on the application of the discretion to cancel permanent visas under s 501 have been subject to frequent changes over the past decade. The appeal body, the AAT, is equally constrained by these rules, but is free to come to a different conclusion in a given set of circumstances. The first version of these guidelines, Direction 17, was found to be unlawful because it unreasonably fettered the discretion of the appellate authorities (Bostock 2011). Its replacement, Direction 21, allowed the deportation of many long-term residents without due regard to mitigating factors, and was revised by the incoming Labor minister in June 2009. Direction 41 allowed for the consideration of a range of mitigating factors, and removed the vague reference to community expectations. This has reportedly led to more cancellations being set aside, which has attracted community criticism in relation to what is seen as the lenient treatment of serious offenders (Bostock 2011). Another change of minister ushered in further changes in the form of Direction 55, which came into effect in September 2012. Notably, the conciliatory clause under 'General Guidance' in Direction 41, which states that 'In some circumstances it may be appropriate for the Australian community to accept more risk where the person concerned has, in effect, become part of the Australian community' (para 5.2[4]), has been replaced by a series of statements that specify a hierarchy of risk categories based on length of residence and seriousness of offending. This hierarchy specifies those whose presence may be tolerated, and those whose perceived likelihood of inflicting harm is so serious 'that *any risk* of similar conduct in the future is unacceptable' (para 6.3[3], emphasis added). The overall tone of Direction 55 reverts to an almost unilateral focus on community protection and the assertion of Australia's sovereignty:

> Australia has a sovereign right to determine whether non-citizens who are of character concern are allowed to enter and/or remain in Australia. Being able to come to or remain in Australia is a privilege Australia confers on non-citizens in the expectation that they are, and have been, law-abiding, will respect important institutions, such as Australia's law enforcement framework, and will not cause or threaten harm to individuals or the Australian community.
>
> *(Direction 55)*[1]

NSW police officers interviewed for the study seemed prepared to play their part in patrolling the boundaries of citizenship in line with this DIAC policy. In the words of one senior police officer: 'We will advise that they have broken the law and that we personally don't deem them as a suitable person to be here' (Interview 39, NSW Police Force Headquarters).

In practice, the most widely used provision in criminal cases not involving national security is s (6)(a) (see Box 5.1), which establishes that a 'substantial criminal record' is the criterion for failing the character test. A substantial criminal record equates to a sentence of 12 months imprisonment or more, or two or more prison sentences that add to at least two years. The more pre-emptive possibilities provided by the legislation seem to be reserved for the denial of entry visas to people outside Australia or for visa cancellations on national security grounds, of which the discredited action driven by the AFP against Dr Mohammed Haneef is the best-known example (Pickering and McCulloch 2010). In relation to s 501 deportees, the most contested aspect of this practice has been the ejection of long-term residents, many of whom have families and established social networks in Australia, which they lack in their place of origin (Commonwealth and Immigration Ombudsman 2006; Senate Legal and Constitutional Affairs Legislation Committee 2006).

None of the interviewees believed that there was an established strategy within the NSW Police Force of actively seeking the cancellation of resident visas, although there were some indications of a growing awareness of this possibility:

> It's probably a little bit more used than it would have been over the previous years because it is more known. And yes it has got a bit of publicity and it can

be a useful tool, because really prevention is better than cure in relation to crime, and if you can prevent the crime by sending the person – deporting the person provided they meet the criteria, provided the minister goes down that road, provided that there is enough there for that to occur, well it happens but it is not a very quick process.

(Interview 35, NSW Police Force Headquarters)

DIAC officials also believed that individual police officers were becoming more aware of the possibilities for character deportation, although perhaps not of the details of the legal procedures involved: 'I think that most police officers are very aware of the 501 cancellation and power, and they are very quick to call and ask for visas, ask about the possibility of a visa being cancelled' (Interview 51, Sydney DIAC). Moreover, there were some indications that DIAC was behind a push to systematically increase awareness among police of these options:

We need to be using all the mechanisms that are in place for us to be able to deal with [crime]. And if one of those mechanisms is immigration, and using our powers under the Migration Act, well so be it. But we need to prompt them to think along those lines, because it is only really a matter of doing it once or twice and then they think and they get it and they do it.... We want to see them prompted. The Department of Immigration want to see them prompted to ask them questions.

(Interview 35, NSW Police Force Headquarters)

According to one senior police officer who dealt with serious crime, she had drawn the line at seeking visa cancellation in relation to a number of African refugees who were present in Australia on permanent protection visas. Although legal avenues exist to revoke these visa types, deportation was an intensely practical strategy for her, aimed at disrupting criminal activities. In the case of refugees, practical matters often precluded their deportation:

There is nowhere to send them to.... So we knew that, so we didn't get on our soapbox and say, 'They shouldn't be here'. They are bad refugees, they are bad refugees – because they have nowhere to go. So we knew we would have to deal with them.

(Interview 36, NSW Police Force Headquarters)

As with removals of individuals who are already in breach of immigration laws, the visa cancellation process can also produce uncertain outcomes, especially given the increased observance of due process rights that characterised the period during which the interviews were held:

The minister has given police directions as well in interpreting that, so there is a whole framework around that that is looked at, that the person is given natural justice, they are advised that we are considering cancelling and given an opportunity to comment on that and to provide reasons why they think their visa shouldn't be cancelled.... So all that is taken into account and weighed against their criminal history, and you may have a number of mitigating circumstances that weigh against a very long criminal history.... I think the police would like to see that and use it in some cases, but it is not just a simple thing of saying, yes they have a long criminal history, we will cancel the visa.

(Interview 51, Sydney DIAC)

Several of the state and federal police interviewed believed that the wrongful deportation of Mohammed Haneef, mentioned above, along with other high-profile s 501 cases, had been the catalyst for the more cautious approach to visa cancellation that was now in evidence. As well as being frustrated with what they saw as unnecessary barriers to visa cancellation and removal, police also reported confusion over the thresholds (in terms of seriousness of offending) at which s 501 could be applied. This was said to be the subject of a 'file' that had been sent by the NSW Police Force to the ministerial level in order to 'get clarity on why [the policy] has changed' (Interview 36, NSW Police Force Headquarters). Police also reported that sentencing practices had changed to accommodate immigration considerations which, if true, would represent a considerable intrusion of immigration law into the criminal justice process:

There is a real issue about what is the threshold, what is the benchmark for someone to be deported. And if you fit the criminal benchmark then there is a whole range of other benchmarks that you need to meet. You know it is all over the shop at the moment.... People are being convicted for stabbing people, for malicious wounding. They are going before courts. They are getting 12 months jail when ordinarily they would get five years, but the magistrates are making comment that they would be deported when they get out so they are going to give them a lesser sentence. They spin out the other end and they are still sitting here in Australia and it is getting frustrating for the police to continually put up with these crooks.

(Interview 18, NSW Police Force Local Area Commander)

There was some awareness among the senior police interviewed that establishing a pattern of offending was an alternative option where no single sentence met the threshold for cancellation:

[Interviewer: *But with visa cancellation, correct me if I am wrong, you would need to have a conviction, wouldn't you?*] Not necessarily, because quite often it is the case that it is established that they perhaps may have offended previously elsewhere. Or if there is a pattern of behaviour.

(Interview 40, NSW Police Force Headquarters)

Focusing on patterns of behaviour that fall short of criminal convictions shifts the locus of moral judgement away from the seriousness of a particular criminal act towards the identification of people whose ongoing character flaws are considered to render them unworthy to remain in the Australian community. But the pathway to character deportation in the absence of serious convictions was not an easy one, as described by this AFP officer:

> I've got an instance in an old drug matter where effectively the crook pretty much got away with a lot of his activities. … He's a drug dealer with no real chance of rehabilitation. He's a bad man. He's not going to stop … I wasn't very hopeful. To get someone deported on character grounds is extremely difficult. If you've got a conviction, fine, they go, that's no problems. It's pretty straightforward. But to try and get someone deported by us saying, 'We suspect this is how they derive their income, we suspect this, we suspect that' – it's not really going to fly too well. It may.
>
> *(Interview 65, AFP)*

'A very effective policing strategy'

Maria Brown and her son 'Prince' were considered by NSW state police to be bad people who did not deserve the benefits of living in Australia. The cancellation of their resident visas was reported in dramatic style in the Sydney tabloid newspaper *The Daily Telegraph* (see Box 5.2).

BOX 5.2   SAMOAN MOTHER AND SON FROM HELL

The Daily Telegraph

Rhett Watson and Angela Saurine, November 15, 2008

At least two more people are likely to be deported after a Samoan mother and son had their visas cancelled yesterday for destabilising an entire Sydney suburb … Ms Brown had been in the country 11 years, her son 10, and both appeared to have quickly drawn the notice of police. And the warning coming from those within the force is that at least two others connected to the pair could face a similar fate. "We're going to pull them apart one bit at a time. It's a very effective strategy," one investigator said.

Source: http://www.dailytelegraph.com.au/news/samoan-mother-and-son-from-hell/story-e6freuy9-1111118040815

The media commentary surrounding these cases confirms that police adopted a deliberate strategy to pursue character deportation in order to resolve the local policing concerns surrounding this pair. The mother and son had entered Australia when Prince was 13 years old on New Zealand passports which entitled them to unlimited 'special category visas', and had then accrued a string of criminal convictions over a 10-year period. Prince Brown had served substantial prison terms for robbery and several assaults, including the assault of a police officer. His mother had received several 12-month prison sentences, primarily for drug-related offences, which had been suspended. Their resident visas were cancelled under s 501, after which they each applied for a review of the decisions by the AAT. In fact, police in NSW were so determined to secure the deportation of Maria Brown that, according to the AHRC, four police officers 'attempted to elicit a signature from her to consent to her immediate removal from Australia without providing her with an opportunity to seek legal advice or to apply for a review of the cancellation decision' (AHRC 2012: 25).

NSW Police Commissioner Andrew Scipione was cited in media reports suggesting that the strategy of pursuing visa cancellation might be used again, noting that '[p]eople who do not respect the laws of this country do not deserve to enjoy the privilege of living here' (Watson and Saurine 2008). When asked about this case during the research interviews, one senior officer denied that this was a systematic strategy, suggesting instead that police were occasionally forced to take these actions because of the failure of the courts to contain repeat offenders and the 'softer' approach to criminal deportation taken by DIAC under the Labor administration:

> It is very, very, very difficult, very difficult. That was only sheer frustration and, dare I say it, political pressure.… So one's actually gone, one has left the country and one is fighting, so – And again that's one of the frustrations from the cops was [having] no knowledge about being told these people are being released and going back into the community. A much softer approach now, which does have an impact on serious crime.
>
> *(Interview 18, NSW Police Force Local Area Commander)*

The case also achieved notoriety in New Zealand. While not downplaying the pair's history of serious offending, a feature article in *The New Zealand Herald* noted the growing number of New Zealanders who were the subject of 'increasingly aggressive attempts by Australian authorities to be rid of unwelcome visitors' (Fisher 2009). Prince Brown was quoted in the same newspaper article as telling the Tribunal that police 'should do something about the "murderers, rapists and paedophiles roaming the streets" before trying to remove someone who was trying to change, and take care of his family'.

Evidence put forward by the NSW Police Force played a central role in defeating the separate applications pursued by Maria and Prince Brown (*Maria Brown v Minister for Immigration and Citizenship* [2009] AATA 78 per Professor GD Walker No 2008/5492 and *Prince Brown v Minister for Immigration and Citizenship* [2009] AATA 79 per Professor GD Walker No 2008/5494). Detective Inspector Con Galea told the AAT that Commissioner Scipione had raised the possibility of deportation, not only to deal with the Brown family but also as a state-wide deterrent. Ministerial Direction 21 was still applicable at the time. The possibility of a general deterrent effect is listed as one of three factors in that Direction relevant to the protection of the Australian community (at para 2.5), although it is considered to be 'not a conclusive factor in itself' (para 2.11). This provision injects a penal mentality into the operation of immigration law that is most often associated with criminal sentencing, and does so through an entirely administrative instrument promulgated by the immigration minister. While considered an independent body which is often an irritant to government and administrators (Bostock 2011), the AAT could be described as a hybrid institution which embodies many of the features of the 'crimmigration' thesis (Stumpf 2006). In its decision in the case of Maria Brown, the AAT made the following defence of the applicability of deterrence motives in this case:[2] 'While visa cancellation is not intended as a punishment, para 2.11 of the direction plainly contemplates that the prospect of it will operate to deter similar conduct in much the same way as the threat of punishment does' (*Maria Brown v Minister for Immigration and Citizenship* [2009], para 189).

This decision in relation to the Browns was clearly premised on the perceived failure of the courts to deal with persistent offenders. The position expressed by police in the review hearing for Prince Brown was summarised by the Adjudicator in the following terms:

> Jail sentences were only periodic and the offender would return to the area after a relatively short time and might resume previous criminal activities. Deportation, however, was a major deterrent that would send a message all over the New South Wales non-citizen criminal population. It would improve the community perception of safety.
>
> (Prince Brown v Minister for Immigration and
> Citizenship *[2009], para 91)*

In relation to Maria Brown, Galea's evidence to the Tribunal was even more explicit in identifying the messages of deterrence directed to Pacific Islander communities:

> This was a high profile case and the outcome was relevant to the question of general deterrence. The applicant had escaped imprisonment and therefore appeared to operate with impunity. Visa cancellation would have an immediate impact on the Pacific Islander population and other non-citizens. People would feel safer and would be more likely to report crimes. The demand on police resources would be much reduced.
>
> (Maria Brown v Minister for Immigration and
> Citizenship *[2009], para 131)*

In fact, based on his 'personal experience', Detective Inspector Galea claimed that this deterrent effect was already occurring since 'certain categories of violent and drug crime had diminished markedly in the Campbelltown area since the applicant and her son had been detained at Villawood under threat of visa cancellation' (*Maria Brown v Minister for Immigration and Citizenship* [2009], para 191). The statements reported above identify the nature of this policing strategy as one that is directed uniquely at the lawfully present, non-citizen population.

One of the most contentious aspects of the drafting of s 501 concerns the power to cancel permanent visas on the basis, not merely of past serious offending, but also of a demonstrated *pattern* of less serious offending and other anti-social or dishonest conduct. Prince Brown's history of imprisonment met the objective test of 'serious offending', although the arguments against visa cancellation put to the AAT on his behalf noted the time elapsed since his last term of imprisonment. However, Maria Brown had eluded imprisonment, having received several suspended prison terms. In both cases the NSW Police Force sought to establish a *pattern* of criminal and general conduct based on broad references to community sentiment and on police intelligence, even where it was admitted that the intelligence was difficult to verify:

> [Prince Brown's] visa cancellation was widely publicised and people wanted him deported permanently. The extensive intelligence reports revealed an overwhelming theme of violence and intimidation by the applicant in the area, resulting in a reluctance to make formal complaints or give evidence ... It was hard to judge whether such reports were 100 percent accurate, but they had been used in the past as the basis for covert operations that had proved successful.
>
> (Prince Brown v Minister for Immigration and Citizenship *[2009], paras 90, 93*)

While the proceedings of the AAT in these cases assumed a crime-fighting character, the rules of evidence demanded in a criminal court did not apply. In fact, para 1.10(b) of Direction 21 allows that even *acquittal* for a criminal offence may be taken as evidence of bad character, undermining one of the fundamental tenets of criminal justice. CCTV footage of an assault that had not resulted in conviction was presented to the Tribunal and the failure to achieve convictions was attributed to community fear of the pair and a concomitant reluctance to bring complaints to police. The police profile of Prince Brown was said to contain '23 adverse reports for 2008 alone, including some after [his] receipt of the notice of intention to consider cancellation' (*Prince Brown v Minister for Immigration and Citizenship* [2009], para 191). Despite acknowledging the possibility that some of the reports were 'malicious falsehoods', the Tribunal reasoned that 'when there is a substantial number of reports from a wide variety of sources all detailing similar conduct, the probability that the picture created is true markedly increases' (*Maria Brown v Minister for Immigration and Citizenship* [2009], para 168). Untested allegations could be considered 'evidence' as long as there were enough of them. By the same token, community perceptions were also cited by the applicants to provide evidence of their good character. This included a petition with 81 signatures urging the Tribunal to allow the pair to remain in Australia.

Two further appeals were made to the Federal Court on behalf of Maria Brown alleging lack of procedural fairness at the AAT (*Brown v Minister for Immigration and Citizenship* [2009] FCA1098 (29 Sep 2009) per Edmonds J, NSD 187 of 2009 and *Brown v Minister for Immigration and Citizenship* [2010] FCAFC 33 (20 April 2010) per Moore, Rares and Nicholas JJ, NSD 1185 of 2009). In summarising the police evidence, Edmonds J noted that claims of a reduction in drug reports, violent offences and social tension in the neighbourhood since the applicant had been detained, and arguments about the reluctance of her victims to complain for fear of reprisals appeared to be accepted by the AAT 'notwithstanding that the relevant police witness conceded under cross-examination that he had no statistics to prove those assertions and conceded that intelligence is "not absolute fact"' (*Brown v Minister for Immigration and Citizenship* [2009], para 54). The Court concluded that the AAT was entitled to consider this information, but found that there was 'real doubt' that the police intelligence reports had been central to the Tribunal's conclusion. The Court concluded instead that the applicant had failed the character test under ss 501(6)(c)(i) and (ii) due to 'the number and nature of the offences for which she had been convicted from 1999 to 2006' (*Brown v Minister for Immigration and Citizenship* [2009], paras 67, 68). This is consistent with the findings of an exhaustive examination of s 501 cases brought before the AAT conducted by Bostock (2011), in which she concluded that the seriousness of the crime was the major determinant of the decision to either affirm or set aside the visa cancellation. This indicates a significant penetration of penal thinking (not paralleled by the importation of criminal procedure) into an otherwise administrative domain.

Visa cancellation under s 501 can also be based on perceptions of likely future offending. Much of the police evidence put before the AAT in the Brown case hearings was framed in terms of 'pre-crime' risk perceptions (Zedner 2007). In relation to Prince Brown, the Tribunal was told that, 'while there was no vendetta against the applicant, he was identified as a risk and was the subject of targeted investigations as a person of interest' (*Prince Brown v Minister for Immigration and Citizenship* [2009], para 92), who was said to associate with known lawbreakers (para 1.5 of Direction 21). In fact, a police suspect targeting management plan (STMP) had assessed him as an 'extreme risk' (para 87).

The next step in the police case against Maria and Prince Brown was to move from assessments that they were at 'high risk' of future offending, to establishing their inability or unwillingness to reform. Evidence of incorrigibility then leads inexorably to the conclusion that permanent banishment is the only solution to the threat posed to the community. As evidence of his attempts at rehabilitation, Prince Brown argued that growing up as a teenager in a low socio-economic area had to some extent dictated 'the way one views life' and 'his choice of friends' (*Prince Brown v Minister for Immigration and Citizenship* [2009], para 17). This argument located the source of his offending in the disadvantaged circumstances imposed by his life in

Australia. In relation to his prior offending he argued that he had served his time and alleged that local police had been trying for years 'to pin anything they could on him' (para 23). Perhaps most relevant of all to questions of his incorrigibility, he argued that 'Australia was supposed to help people with such problems, but instead they were seeking to remove the problem instead of accepting how he had been rehabilitated' (para 26). A number of character witnesses testified that Prince had made a 'complete turnaround' and was a 'terrific mentor to the youth'. Other witnesses described Maria Brown as a 'great mother' who might look 'intimidating and scary' but was in reality a 'kind, soft, caring person'.

Weighing the evidence for and against the likelihood of recidivism by Prince and Maria Brown, the Adjudicator in both cases noted that in *Lam and Minister for Immigration and Multicultural Affairs* [1999] AATA 56 at [51], AAT President Mathews J had said, 'Once a person has shown a disregard for the law, it can never be said that there is no risk of re-offending' (*Maria Brown v Minister for Immigration and Citizenship* [2009], para 180; *Prince Brown v Minister for Immigration and Citizenship* [2009], para 141). It was held in relation to Maria Brown that there was 'little evidence' of rehabilitation (paras 198, 204, 217). In the case of Prince Brown, the evidence of his rehabilitation was said to be 'fragmentary' (para 189) and 'subjective' (para 190). On the other hand, police intelligence reports were deemed to be 'also relevant to the risk of recidivism' and could not be dismissed even though they were of 'somewhat uneven reliability' (*Prince Brown v Minister for Immigration and Citizenship* [2009], para 148). In relation to Maria Brown, the AAT concluded that 'the community would expect that the visa of a person with such a serious and sustained criminal record, [who] is at significant risk of re-offending, and who shows little evidence of rehabilitation should be cancelled' (*Maria Brown v Minister for Immigration and Citizenship* [2009], para 198).

The guidance set out in para 2.12 of Direction 21 regarding how 'expectations of the community' are to be determined in relation to s 501 visa cancellation is extremely vague, and simply states that '[d]ecision-makers should have due regard to the Government's views in this respect', as if some level of community concern and expectation were self-evident. Criminal offending by non-citizens is portrayed in the guidelines as a breach of trust. While it is reasonable to expect that anyone present on Australian territory should obey the laws of the land, this reference to trust emphasises the contingent nature of the tolerance accorded to non-citizens and seems to expect a higher standard of compliance with the law than is achieved by citizens. The moral and legal irrelevance of the citizen/non-citizen distinction was powerfully conveyed by the Federal Court in 2011 when overturning the cancellation of a permanent resident visa in relation to Swedish citizen Stefan Nystrom.[3] The judge concluded: '[The applicant] has indeed behaved badly, but no worse than many of his age who have also lived as members of the Australian community all their lives but who happen to be citizens. The difference is the barest of technicalities' (*Nystrom v Minister for Immigration and Multicultural and Indigenous Affairs* [2005] FCAFC 121 (1 July 2005) per Moore and Gyles JJ at [29] para 2.4).

The intent of the discussion presented in this section is not so much to consider the merits or otherwise of the actions of NSW state police to secure the deportation of Prince and Maria Brown. The main aim is to illustrate the dynamics of a parallel policing and justice system that applies uniquely to non-citizens, merges criminal and immigration elements, but disregards many of the established principles of criminal justice applied in criminal settings. Both the merging of criminal and administrative paradigms and the pursuit of removal and deportation by state and federal police as forms of enemy penology are neatly reflected in the following statement by a senior NSW police officer: 'Is this the kind of person that we want in the country?... If they don't abide by the rules they get shipped out' (Interview 39, NSW Police Force Headquarters). Prince and Maria Brown have now returned to New Zealand. The AHRC subsequently ruled that Maria Brown's Migration Act *detention* prior to her return had not been 'proportionate to the Commonwealth's legitimate aim of protecting the Australian community from non-citizens who pose an unacceptable risk to the Australian community' (AHRC 2012: 3), but noted nevertheless that her departure was classified as 'voluntary' (6).

6

CREATING A UBIQUITOUS BORDER

Active and passive borders

This chapter charts the construction of a structurally embedded border within Australia which recruits a range of agencies into a migration policing role. This expanded border includes law enforcement agencies other than state police, industry regulators, service providers and private citizens. Migration policing agencies can play an *active* role in migration policing in which unlawful non-citizens are identified directly through systematic data exchange negotiated under MOUs, requests by DIAC for disclosures under s 18 of the Migration Act, or incidentally in the course of the agency making enquiries about an individual's immigration status to DIAC. At the same time, they may play a *passive* role whereby the behaviour of non-citizens with unlawful or uncertain immigration status is shaped by the fear of being detected by these agencies, so that some of them decide to present themselves 'voluntarily' to immigration authorities. These active and passive dimensions of the embedded border rely, respectively, on strategies of surveillance and attrition – or, alternatively, through surveillance and the avoidance of surveillance.

Like all surveillance projects, the functioning of the embedded border depends on control over identity, which in turn acts as a gateway to entitlement. As Deleuze has argued, 'surveillance is now detached from discipline, being primarily concerned with the distribution of entitlements based on identity' (Deleuze 1992 cited in Haggerty *et al.* 2011: 233). The active embedded border retains a disciplinary dimension, referring non-compliant individuals to immigration authorities where they face visa regularisation or exclusion. But where migration policing agencies operate as 'switch point(s) to be passed in order to access the benefits of liberty' (Rose 2000: 326), the embedded border reinforces the boundaries of belonging indirectly by patrolling the boundaries of entitlement.

Although universal detection is no doubt a 'surveillance fantasy rather than a realistic political endeavour' (Aas 2011: 342), the vision is one of a ubiquitous border that maximises detection by structurally embedding migration controls deep within the regulatory machinery of the neoliberal state and what remains of the welfare state, sorting the entitled from the unentitled, and systemically producing seemingly 'voluntary' reporting. A ubiquitous border is not necessarily an inescapable one, but one that functions by systematically shutting off points of access in order to achieve an accumulating exclusionary effect. As explained by this senior police officer:

> We are not a nation where you are stopped and your papers are checked, so as a result [immigration] is difficult to police. However, when these people go to hospitals and things like that, it is those routine things where presentation of documents is required where usually the apple cart starts to spill.
>
> *(Interview 40, NSW Police Force Headquarters)*

These developments suggest a shift away from the open deployment of coercive power against unlawful non-citizens that characterised the 'pre-Palmer era' of immigration enforcement, towards a broadly based neoliberal agenda of responsibilisation in which coercive state practices are cloaked in a mantle of legal rationalism and individual choice.

Identifying 'crimmigrants'

Australian Federal Police

Whereas state police encounter unlawful non-citizens in a wide range of contexts, and are driven primarily by a local crime control and order maintenance agenda (see Chapter 4), the AFP's involvement in immigration enforcement is concentrated in specialised areas such as the prevention and prosecution of people smuggling, human trafficking, large-scale immigration fraud and labour exploitation. The AFP has an MOU with DIAC covering information exchange and assistance on investigations relating to these offences, and a DIAC liaison officer is permanently embedded within the AFP Identity Fraud Team. Although the team's role extends beyond identity fraud, this positioning indicates the importance placed by both the federal police and DIAC on controlling identity. The fact that the AFP is constituted at the federal level means that its organisational links with DIAC on immigration matters are in some ways closer than the links reported between the NSW Police Force and DIAC. When asked about the circumstances in which AFP officers work alongside DIAC officers in the field, one AFP informant gave a description which aligned AFP officers far more closely with an immigration enforcement perspective than did any account provided by NSW state police:

> The team leader of the sex trafficking team over there will give me a call and notify me when they're going out. We work very closely with her.... If I've got someone available – it depends on operational commitments – then I'll tell my team members and we'll just go along as immigration officers, like

assisting Immigration. [Interviewer: *So you are actually considering yourself as being designated officers under the Migration Act?*] Yes, we don't really highlight the fact that we're police. If we got asked then we'd identify ourselves as police, but we're not going to the door as police.

(Interview 65, AFP)

Its focus on organised criminal activities means that the AFP is only likely to play a role in the detection of unlawful non-citizens if they are involved in serious criminality as either offenders or victims. The working unit most likely to encounter unlawful non-citizens is the Transnational Sexual Exploitation and Trafficking Team (TSETT) which has close links with the so-called Sex Team within the Sydney DIAC Compliance Office. Unlike the involvement of state police in immigration-related operations, where officers often perform a general security role and assist in the apprehension of high-risk individuals, it was reported that the assistance of the AFP was requested in these contexts to facilitate evidence gathering for intended prosecutions.

In contrast to state police who refer requests about immigration status to the ISS, the AFP liaison officer posted to DIAC reported having direct access to DIAC-run information systems (Interview 66, AFP). Other AFP officers were said to have access to the movements database, but only the liaison officer has permission to access visa information. This reportedly included not only information about immigration status, but also copies of visa applications, details about family members, photos and histories about how people came to be in Australia. This detailed information is available for individuals from countries designated as high risk who are denied access to online ETAs, and for all international students. Information of this kind was said to be of value in criminal and national security investigations, highlighting the exchange of data that occurs between these federal agencies that merges crime control, security and immigration control technologies. Overall, the role of the AFP in detecting unlawful non-citizens for the purposes of expulsion is a highly prescribed and marginal one, but the organisation features strongly as an exemplar of wider developments in 'crimmigration'.

Courts and prisons

The considerable resources that have been devoted to establishing a specialist group within the Sydney Compliance Office to monitor court proceedings involving non-citizens shows some elements of the trend towards 'pre-crime' strategies that were discussed in the previous chapter. As reported in Chapter 3, members of the specialist Remand Team regularly attend court sessions in order to monitor criminal cases which might meet the criteria for s 501 character deportation. It seems that DIAC officers take the initiative in gathering this high-value information, often via very labour-intensive means. No mention was made of MOUs or regular data exchange with court administrators, so the usual means of accessing information is through the perusal of court lists. No interviews were conducted with court officials, but a tentative conclusion can be drawn that the court system remains largely independent of the proactive efforts of DIAC to identify deportable individuals from among the population of criminal defendants.

Prisons, in contrast, although administered at the state rather than federal level, are part of the broader criminal justice machinery and might not be expected to display the seemingly independent stance adopted by the courts. In the US, places of incarceration down to the level of small-scale jails run by local sheriffs have been recruited into the '287(g)' programme to identify deportable migrants and hold them for collection by federal immigration authorities. In Britain, a 'hubs and spokes' system has been put in place which is intended to concentrate 'foreign' prisoners into particular institutions where policies exist to attempt to identify those who are potentially deportable (Anderson *et al.* 2011; Bosworth 2011; Kaufman 2012). Similar, though much more low-key, strategies are also in place in NSW, aimed at streamlining communication between prison authorities and the DIAC Remand Team.

Members of that team reported liaising with the Sentence Administration section within the NSW Department of Corrective Services (DCS) on a regular basis. This central administrative unit is responsible for ensuring the timely release of time-served prisoners across the state and managing transitions into Migration Act custody pending deportation for those with existing DIAC orders. Our DCS informant reported that the numbers of prisoners being held under Migration Act powers had dwindled since the early 2000s, when prisons had regularly dealt with the 'overflow from Villawood' (Interview 59, DCS).[1] At the time of the interview in 2009, we were told that it was most common for prison administrators to be asked to hold time-served prisoners for short periods of up to a day, pending their collection by DIAC. Migration Act powers might also be used to hold remandees who have been granted bail and would otherwise be released. Time-served prisoners who have appeals pending about the cancellation of their visas might also be released into the community on bridging visas granted by DIAC. The DCS informant believed that these arrangements were occurring more often than previously, and attributed this trend to increased knowledge within the prison system about immigration matters:

> Our information sharing is perhaps more successful, so we are a lot more aware of the immigration stuff so we chase it a bit more aggressively nowadays ... we just want to make sure that if somebody is required for deportation then we will try to facilitate it.
>
> *(Interview 59, DCS)*

This DCS informant advised that 190 prisoners had been released to DIAC custody in the two years prior to the interview (107 in 2007 and 83 in 2008), more than in previous years.

The identification of potential deportees proceeds through regular data matching carried out under a longstanding MOU, and also via more ad hoc methods initiated by prison staff:

> On a monthly basis we provide a list of everyone who has been received into Corrective Services custody and we give that to Immigration and they must do a data match.... Also ... at their reception interview, [a prisoner] might indicate willingly or sometimes we might guess by an accent or a surname that he may be not an Australian citizen and certainly not born here, and that will generate a separate individual request where we might clarify their immigration status.
>
> *(Interview 59, DCS)*

Just as Kaufman (2012) has reported in relation to the identification of deportable individuals among 'foreign' prisoners in the UK, it seems that ad hoc checks are likely to be initiated by Australian prison staff on the basis of subjective judgements about belonging and 'Australianness' which are not dissimilar from those reported in Chapter 4 in relation to NSW state police: 'So it's imprecise ... [they] might speak with an Australian accent but have a Chinese surname. It might generate a request to immigration just to double check' (Interview 59, DCS). In the absence of perceptual cues, more systematic information-based methods could be relied upon:

> And you have people who would appear that they are Australian but are in fact born – have been here so long that there is no discernable difference. And unless they tell us, volunteer that information, we would sometimes be unaware. However, in that monthly report that we send to Immigration that is sort of our backup, so we might find out a bit later, but rely on Immigration pretty much to tell us.
>
> *(Interview 59, DCS)*

A lack of resources was nominated as the main obstacle to more systematic checking at the time of admission of prisoners, putting pressure on admitting staff to make judgements about the need for ad hoc checks based on a precautionary logic: 'if you sound Chinese or look Chinese, even if you just look non-Anglo Australian, just to cover ourselves at a jail level' (Interview 59, DCS).

DIAC informants also claimed that police sometimes bring convicted individuals to their attention in a 'haphazard way', although contact with police at the post-conviction stages was said to be minimal. But information about liability to deportation was reportedly less likely to come from the courts, as information on citizenship and immigration status is not included in documentation generated at the time of sentencing. Timely identification of non-citizen prisoners who are permanent residents facing visa cancellation was considered highly desirable from a prison management point of view, since their presence is seen to 'affect the whole place because they may become an escape risk' (Interview 59, DCS). These prisoners would automatically be classified in a higher risk category, indicating a significant intrusion of immigration law into the administration of criminal justice. Individuals found to be on temporary visas were thought to be of less concern, presumably because they are seen to have less to lose through their expulsion.

Railcorp transit officers

Ticket and identity checks on both long-distance and commuter trains have been widely used in both Europe (Leapman 2005) and North America (Bernstein 2010) to identify unlawfully present individuals. This practice has not been reported publicly in Australia; however, transport systems have become highly securitised spaces where proactive checks for drugs and weapons have been sanctioned by state governments in the name of community safety (see Chapters 2 and 4). This concern for public safety, and the premium placed on cost recovery in state-operated transport systems, has spawned the establishment of various quasi police forces operating on trains in particular. In NSW, train services are provided by Railcorp and the security personnel they employ to detect fare evasion and prevent incivilities are known as transit officers. The introduction of these officers has not been without controversy. In 2006, the NSW Ombudsman reported that oversight of these officers was inadequate considering their considerable police-like powers and in the face of ongoing complaints about serious assaults committed by transit officers and their harassment of refugees and other young people (NSW Ombudsman 2006).

The Railcorp representative interviewed for this study reported that Railcorp transit officers were deployed on the basis of intelligence reports, to address issues as diverse as fare evasion, anti-social behaviour, vandalism and even terrorism (Interview 67, Railcorp). Transit officers were described by this senior manager as exercising a quasi-policing role, with a primary aim of detecting and preventing fare evasion on the rail system. The NSW Police Force is a close collaborator with Railcorp on criminal matters such as vandalism. Private security guards also operate on NSW trains, and transit officers were described as being 'positioned somewhere in between NSW police and contract security guards' (Interview 67, Railcorp). Transit officers are authorised to issue penalty notices for a number of offences under the Rail Safety Offences Regulation and the *Rail Safety Act 2008* (NSW), with authority delegated from the Independent Transport Safety Regulator. In relation to conduct contained in this legislation, transit officers have significant powers to require offenders, including individuals found to be travelling without tickets, to provide their name and address; to issue on-the-spot fines; and to give move-on directions. These powers resemble in many respects the scenarios that were found to lead to immigration checks by NSW state police. Transit officers may request documentation to prove identity, but have no powers to compel compliance with that request. The recovery of on-the-spot fines – a major objective for Railcorp – was therefore reported to be poor.[2]

The Railcorp informant advised that transit officers often worked alongside police in 'revenue protection' operations organised by NSW Police Force Commuter Crime Units. Similar operations were said to be run within the bus system with the State Transport Authority as the main partner (Interview 22, NSW Police Force Commuter Crime Unit). These operations rarely involved DIAC as an active partner and Railcorp's focus was reported to be entirely on maximising revenue. But intelligence analysis could occasionally give rise to immigration-related concerns. The informant cited one example of an organised operation among a group of international students to fraudulently produce transport concession cards, from which immigration issues had arisen.

Although passports can be proffered as proof of identity, transit officers were said to have 'no specific instructions on immigration or migration issues' (Interview 67, Railcorp). If anything, they were reportedly less likely to take action in relation to individuals perceived to be 'international visitors' who are found to be without a valid ticket. Transit officers have limited access to the NSW Police Force COPS database to check identity, which – it was suggested – might potentially flag migration issues.[3] However, it was clearly not part of the remit of transit officers to carry out these checks. If police attend a matter referred to them by transit officers, it was thought likely that additional checks for outstanding warrants, and possibly immigration status, could be made by them.

From the perspective of this informant, the detection of unlawful non-citizens was a 'hit and miss' affair 'with the exception of the dedicated enforcement and investigative programmes that DIAC have in place' (Interview 69, Railcorp). Due to the presence of state police patrolling the same spaces, it appears that transit officers have not yet been drawn into a migration policing role. In the next section I consider a range of regulatory agencies and public service providers who play a much more significant role in the detection of unlawful non-citizens than any of the law enforcement bodies discussed in this section.

Structurally embedding the border

Australian Taxation Office

The detection and prevention of fraud has attained a prominent place in neo-liberal governance across a wide range of contexts. To that end, ATO personnel possess wide legislative powers to enter premises without a court-issued warrant and seize documentation where there is reasonable cause to believe tax evasion is occurring. The compliance activities of the ATO bring them into contact with unlawful non-citizens most often in relation to their efforts to detect unpaid taxes within the so-called cash economy. A senior ATO official interviewed for the migration policing study advised that taxation officers deal with immigration matters through their participation in the Cash Economy Working Group chaired by DIAC, when conducting external data-matching exercises in accordance with the ATO's risk identification strategies, and when dealing with referrals from other agencies and public 'dob-ins'. The ATO's compliance activities are highly risk driven, and occasionally identify tax avoidance risks associated with particular visa types:

> So if, for instance, we identify a risk around 457 visas[4] – which we have – then we need to investigate that risk from two viewpoints. Basically one is the revenue risk, and the other one is the reputational risk, because there is a reputational risk to Australia and to the tax office if there is something happening that shouldn't happen and we do nothing about it. So we need to examine that visa and people from that viewpoint.
>
> *(Interview 60, ATO)*

The ATO's interests intersect with immigration compliance solely in relation to recovering unpaid taxes. This could apply to visa overstayers or individuals on tourist or other temporary visas that do not allow them to work, or to individuals working in excess of the mandated hours, such as international students. Ethnically defined businesses such as restaurants were said to be one target for ATO investigations, since labour is considered more likely to be 'imported' through transnational networks and operate outside regulatory frameworks in these workplaces. Joint operations with DIAC arising from the ATO's involvement in the Cash Economy Working Group had also included airport cleaning services and the security industry. Other high-risk industries, in terms of unreported income, include retail, accommodation, hospitality, tourism and the taxi industry:

> I would think probably at least once every year each airport in Australia has a joint raid and the cars come along and the police check the licences, and DIAC check if they are legal, and Centrelink check if they are on benefits, and the RTA checks if the vehicle is roadworthy and at the end of the line is the Tax Office who sees whether they have got an ABN [Australian Business Number].
>
> *(Interview 60, ATO)*

Unlawful non-citizens in receipt of low cash wages were said to be of much less interest to the Tax Office than employers who pay their wages from undeclared income. In contrast, DIAC's interest in joint operations was focused on the immigration status of the workers themselves. It was reported to be commonplace for tax issues to take second place to the enforcement of immigration law in relation to illegal workers, and the ATO informant was sanguine about the potential failure to recover taxes: 'You know if the people are getting paid cash, for a starter, until they have to lodge a tax return they haven't committed an offence' (Interview 60, ATO). In any case, people on temporary work visas and holiday work visas often leave the country of their own accord before their failure to pay tax is detected. Migration agents involved in overseas hiring practices that include an element of tax evasion are classified by the ATO as posing the biggest risk of all to revenue.

The ATO has a number of MOUs with DIAC, and the ATO informant confirmed that the organisation exchanges data according to documented privacy protocols. He offered the following scenario as an example:

> I think what [DIAC] are looking for is anyone who is in breach of their visa. Now there is a couple of ways they can do that. One is just seeing who, for instance, is filing tax returns. If you are filing a tax return in Australia for two years and your visa is only for one year then that is a pretty obvious giveaway. So I think that sort of data they can get.
>
> *(Interview 60, ATO)*

An ATO data specialist confirmed that addresses were the only information provided to DIAC from their client records and was exchanged via the secure Fedlink system. At the time the research interview was completed in 2009, no records of immigration status or even nationality were being kept on the ATO's systems. However, 'front-end' checking, similar to that reported by Centrelink, had just been established to automatically check applicants for tax file numbers against DIAC records for overseas visitors. This was recognised as being at odds with past practices where questions about the legality of earnings and lawful presence of the taxpayer were not considered to be Tax Office business. This data-matching initiative was said to be driven by DIAC concerns about s 457 work visa holders setting up their own businesses, which would be in violation of their visa conditions. Another proposal, apparently raised through the Cash Economy Working Group, was for checks of tax compliance history to be made before granting s 457 visas to employers seeking to hire temporary overseas labour. Data exchange between federal agencies had developed to the point where authorised DIAC officers have limited access to ATO data via the UNCLE (Unlawful Non-Citizen Location Enquiry) system without the need to issue individual s 18 notices, for example in relation to data matching against the DIAC Overstayers List.

The motivation for the ATO to engage in these information exchanges is related to the possible dividend in identifying fraudulent taxation activities:

> Well, what we find, it is non-compliance across multiple obligations. So if somebody's, like, doing migration fraud and bringing people in, quite often they will be involved in tax fraud as well. So we find there is a lot of commonality in terms of our clientele.
>
> *(Interview 60, ATO)*

Requests from the ATO for data held by DIAC were reported to be more likely to involve individual case work rather than aggregate data matching:

> I am not sure if we have ever requested anything specifically around bulk data. We do individual data sharing around individual cases, for instance. We have quite strong links with DIAC, like if people are going overseas we can issue a

Departure Prevention Order to stop them from going overseas. That is through DIAC. We can ask for record alerts if somebody comes back to Australia who owes the Tax Office money. Sometimes they can be held at the airport until they pay it or all sorts of things. Around case work, for instance, we might get a tip-off that a restaurant is employing illegal immigrants. Quite often through our Working Group we will say to DIAC, you know here is some names of people running a restaurant, here is some names of people who work there, you know. What information have you got on those people?

(Interview 60, ATO)

Requests may also be made to DIAC where it is suspected that tax file numbers relating to individuals who have left the country are being used fraudulently to obtain tax refunds. Where criminal activity such as identity fraud is identified, different sections of the ATO come into play and a more 'aggressive approach' can be adopted. Intelligence about serious criminal activity could lead to joint operations involving a wide range of agencies. The ATO informant cited an example concerning fraudulent tax activities in the rural town of Griffith, including allegations of sexual slavery, which led to an operation involving the ATO, the National Crime Authority, the AFP, the Australian Crime Commission and DIAC. However, the aspect of ATO's migration policing role that was most integral to the structurally embedded border is its capacity to exchange electronic data. This trend was so apparent, not only in relation to exchanges with DIAC but also with other government agencies, that a dedicated team has been established by the ATO to monitor the many MOUs under which these requests are made and to mediate the exchange process, including at least one individual with the title 'Data Matching Gatekeeper'.

Roads and Traffic Authority

The NSW Roads and Traffic Authority (RTA) is responsible for managing the state's traffic and road network and for promoting road safety. At first glance, its remit seems far removed from a migration policing role, and yet the information the agency collects on drivers' licences is a valuable asset in identifying unlawful non-citizens. No interview was conducted with the RTA for the migration policing study. However, the RTA was mentioned by members of DIAC, the NSW Police Force and other organisations as an agency that participates in joint operations (for example, in relation to the taxi industry) and provides data regularly in relation to unlawful non-citizens. As with other government agencies, the RTA is legally bound to respond to DIAC information requests under s 18 of the Migration Act in relation to suspected unlawful non-citizens. In addition, notifications may be made by the RTA to DIAC on a voluntary basis in the course of processing applications for drivers' licences:

For example, RTA has on their forms that you need to provide evidence and if there is a case where a client's unlawful or they think they are, they'll ring us. So it's – but there's certainly no – it's not compulsory for them to report them. 'Cause I guess one of the main things to keep in mind is [that] being an unlawful non-citizen isn't an offence.

(Interview 49, Sydney DIAC)

Beyond these ad hoc notifications, which appear to be incidental to the process of requesting information, DIAC Compliance has some online access to RTA's information systems, as reported in Chapter 3. The RTA also plays an important regulatory role in relation to the taxi industry, which has been a major employer of unauthorised labour. The inclusion by the RTA of a requirement to establish immigration status on applications for taxi licences, at the request of DIAC, was said to have played a significant role in increasing compliance within that industry:

> Another example is the Ministry of Transport in NSW for taxi drivers. They need to fill out a form that's an authority to drive form and they need to attach evidence that they have permission to work … which has reduced the number of unlawfuls in that industry…. So it's initiatives like that which obviously greatly help the department.

(Interview 49, Sydney DIAC)

The RTA therefore plays a significant role in constructing the embedded border, by cutting off avenues for employment, and directly identifying unlawful non-citizens through data exchange.

Local councils

In NSW, as well as providing services, local councils have a range of regulatory responsibilities related to building standards, health and public safety. In the interviews conducted with other agencies that have a more direct interest in immigration enforcement, local authorities were sometimes identified as useful partners in inter-agency operations because of the legal powers they hold to enter and inspect properties. Research interviews were conducted with officers from two local government areas in Sydney, whose very different roles occasionally involve them in immigration enforcement.

One of these officers with a background in corruption investigation described his primary objective as detecting and prosecuting persons operating brothels or massage parlours in breach of the development consent – for example, by having excess numbers of workers on the premises, or breaching trading hours or fire regulations. He claimed to come across unlawful non-citizens or 'persons with questionable status' engaged in sex work at least once a month. In his experience, what could appear to be merely regulatory breaches – such as having workers residing, or even hidden, on the premises – often pointed to the existence of more serious criminal activities such as debt bondage. In fact, this informant saw his role as acting to disrupt this broader criminal activity. He was active in initiating multi-agency operations, and also participated in joint operations organised by partner agencies, including the NSW Police Force, the AFP, DIAC, Centrelink, the ATO and the NSW Fire Brigade. He claimed to have a 'very good working relationship, particularly with DIAC', who he said was 'always quite keen' to participate in operations that might identify unlawful non-citizens (Interview 61, Local Council). In turn, he was pleased to attend operations where it was expected that breaches of local government legislation would be identified.

In line with the argument made by the ATO interviewee that non-compliance often manifests 'across multiple obligations', this council officer argued that violations in one domain often act as a 'marker' of non-compliance in associated areas. He expected that immigration-related work would increase in the future, particularly since sex work is likely to be a 'drawcard' for Asian workers facing difficult economic conditions in their home countries. An MOU was being negotiated with DIAC at the time the interview was conducted, which this informant expected would expedite this partnership, saying it would enable 'some very timely and accurate intelligence to flow to DIAC' to support joint operations (Interview 61, Local Council).

The other council employee interviewed for this study performed a different role, and provided a contrasting view of the desirability of collaboration on immigration matters. His background was in environmental health and he reported that he spent most of his time acting on reports of noise, overcrowding, odour and other breaches of planning regulations. He also spent time inspecting brothels, usually in response to complaints from members of the community, and mostly without the presence of other agencies. He had responded on several occasions to requests to accompany local police and DIAC officers on 'raids' of brothels, where the aim was to identify people with unlawful status and/or people being held against their will. Only one of those actions had raised matters of interest to him, in this case a serious fire safety issue:

> The brothel owner there had a system where he was able to lock the doors electronically by a remote control device, which is a breach of fire safety regulations.... The thing is that he was directed to remove that, and he suggested that it was to stop his premises being robbed. The suggestion was more so to stop the illegal sex workers escaping.
>
> *(Interview 10, Local Council)*

This council officer had also participated in a major joint operation involving a problematic residential location that had been subject to a number of complaints of illegal building works that had subdivided the apartments into what he called 'dog boxes'. The majority of the people living in the premises were Chinese nationals, many with unlawful immigration status. DIAC and the NSW Police Force were also interested in these premises in relation to the organised production of fraudulent passports. The council officer expressed surprise at the scale of the operation that had been mounted over what he described as 'just a few units', reporting that the preliminary briefing for the operation had involved a large number of DIAC officers, local police and members of the Asian Crime Squad, as well as staff from the Departments of Health and Social Security. Obviously influenced by his professional perspective, he was cautious about whether councils should play a role in these kinds of operations, and concerned about the impact of such operations on community relations:

> I suppose we have a social role to play. It's a difficult one though. [This] is Australia's most multicultural community. Yeah, I mean that could be somewhat problematic ... but the reality is that they have probably seen the fact [that] the councils do have a lot of local intelligence ... as well as having a raft of regulatory powers that they are able to use.
>
> *(Interview 10, Local Council)*

This informant was also concerned that law enforcement agencies often overestimate the powers possessed by councils to take action under the *Environmental Planning and Assessment Act 1979* (NSW), and said that he had 'actually offered to brief the police in terms of what our powers actually are – just so that they have a greater awareness of what we are able to do, and what we are not able to do' (Interview 10, Local Council).

Centrelink

Centrelink is a federal agency that exists primarily to administer welfare payments. The agency routinely checks the immigration status of claimants, since visa class is a legislated criterion for eligibility for certain benefits. Centrelink has highly developed procedures to provide welfare support for refugees who are approved for settlement, and liaises closely with DIAC via the intermediary of Migrant Resource Centres to provide these services. But it has no mandate to deal with people on temporary visas: 'The basic requirement to receive a Centrelink payment is [that] you must be an Australian resident. So if they are an unlawful resident, unfortunately we can't help them' (Interview 9, Centrelink). One of the few exceptions was said to be the 'innocent illegals' – that is, children born in Australia to unlawful non-citizen parents and who are entitled to payments: 'That is the only time we will be dealing with a non-lawful migrant ... normally the illegal immigrants, they will not even come to the Centrelink office' (Interview 9, Centrelink).

Centrelink is not required by law to advise DIAC if it believes that a social security claimant is unlawfully present, but may do so incidentally or even unintentionally in the course of conducting investigations under the MOU between the two agencies. What is known as 'front-end' checking, whereby the immigration status of claimants is checked at the time of their application for benefits, was believed to be so effective that the discovery of unlawful non-citizens among existing Centrelink claimants almost never occurs. According to this informant, dob-ins from the public were the most likely source of suspicions about Centrelink clients who might be unlawful non-citizens. In such cases this information would be passed on to DIAC after initial investigation within the organisation.

More often, DIAC requests information from Centrelink, such as an address for a specific person whom DIAC believes to be unlawfully present or in breach of their visa conditions, which enables DIAC compliance field officers to make home visits. Another reported contact point with DIAC was through its business integrity section that deals with serious fraud – for example, in relation to an unlawful non-citizen trying to use someone else's identity. Although the term 'data matching' was used, the Centrelink informant in this study confirmed that immigration status checks are carried out on an individual basis under part 5 of the *Social Security (Administration) Act 1999* (Cwlth), which enables the collection of information from third parties according to agreed privacy protocols.

Centrelink was said to have direct access to DIAC databases via an MOU. It is one of the few organisations, along with the AFP, for which this level of IT integration was reported:

> We do have a database which is provided by Immigration, which basically tells us what sub-clause visa is eligible for payment and who does have to wait for two years and all that stuff.... And there's also something else on our system where we can do their movements, basically. You know, when they arrive, when they left the country and when they come back, all that.
>
> *(Interview 9, Centrelink)*

It was reported that information on movements into and out of Australia is used mainly to assess the entitlement of pensioners who live or spend part of their time overseas. Immigration data is also used to check place of residence in situations where it is suspected that false information and documentation have been provided, since ensuring correct identity and residence is the lynchpin of Centrelink's approach to fraud control. Because eligibility for benefits can change over time, data-matching checks are also conducted at strategic times, such as when claimants travel overseas.

Along with other government agencies included in the migration policing study, Centrelink was found to have a highly developed risk-based approach to compliance, driven by organisational intelligence, and featuring strong links to the AFP and prosecution authorities. One Centrelink informant described the agency's relationship with DIAC as based on 'mutual risk and cooperation' (Interview 62, Centrelink). As with the taxation office, joint operations in which Centrelink participates with other agencies tend to be initiated by the Cash Economy Working Group. And, also in common with the ATO, the participating agencies are driven by their own organisational interests:

> We do have other things like a Memorandum of Understanding with regard to the cash economy. Now certainly that is a lot of activity we undertake with DIAC because we have mutual interest in that area, that risk ... not interested in the same people, but people in the same industry, if you like.
>
> *(Interview 62, Centrelink)*

According to our informant, more than 100 such operations might be conducted in any one year, not all of them involving DIAC, and some of them desk-based rather than in the field. One example was a joint operation targeting harvest workers in which DIAC, ATO and Centrelink investigative officers worked together to identify individuals of interest to one or more of the agencies.

While the Centrelink employee working at the local level who was interviewed for the migration policing study felt that Centrelink should not have any role in identifying unlawful non-citizens (Interview 9, Centrelink), 'mutual risks' had clearly been identified at higher levels, and it seemed that links with DIAC were being strengthened at the time the research was conducted. In fact, staff in the Sydney Compliance Office claimed that an agreement had just been made with Centrelink to post a Centrelink liaison officer permanently within DIAC.

Health services

Other service providers were occasionally mentioned during the interviews as sources for the identification of unlawful non-citizens. Hospitals, in particular, were said to be associated with the location of some 'problematic' cases (Interview 45, Canberra DIAC). The events that led to the wrongful detention and deportation of Australian citizen Vivian Solon (see Chapter 3) began with her admission to a Queensland hospital in a dazed and confused state, after being found injured in a park. According to one of the official inquiries that followed the discovery of her wrongful removal to the Philippines, she was then involuntarily admitted to the Richmond Clinic Psychiatric Unit, from where a social worker later advised the immigration authorities that she might be an illegal immigrant (Foreign Affairs Defence and Trade References Committee 2005). A senior police officer interviewed for this study also mentioned that a lot of 'illegals' had been identified in a particular LAC in which he had worked previously, because of the presence of a major hospital (Interview 40, NSW Police Force Headquarters).

No hospital administrators were interviewed for this study, but researchers were advised by the Sydney Compliance Office that hospitals hold information about people trying to access services without Medicare entitlements, which could facilitate the identification of unlawful non-citizens. In addition, compliance enquiries might lead investigators to seek hospital records, whereby it sometimes transpires that people being sought by DIAC are deceased, or are using the identity of a deceased person.

Internationally, health professionals have been implicated in a wide range of immigration enforcement activities, from certifying deportees as fit to travel in the UK (*Lancet* 2008), to reporting unlawfully present individuals to authorities under the French Pasqua laws (Fekete 1997), and have also been at the forefront of resistance to this type of distortion of their healthcare role, for example in the Netherlands (Van der Leun 2003). However, mandatory reporting legislation, even where it is opposed, undermined or repealed, is likely to leave a legacy and encourage enforcement-minded or compliant practitioners to take this action voluntarily.

The role of health providers in Australia in assisting in the detection of unlawful non-citizens, either knowingly or incidentally, remains an important area for further study. This should include the role of primary healthcare professionals as well as the involvement of major hospitals, since the necessity for doctors to extract payment under the national healthcare system has the potential to identify individuals who have no legal entitlement to stay.[5]

Universities as visa police

Managing students through PRISMS

Due to their dependence on international fee-paying students, universities around the world are heavily involved in the business of immigration compliance. At the time of writing, several prominent universities in the UK are embroiled in bitter battles over the blocking of visas for their international students due to the alleged misuse of student visas (Vasagar 2012). In Australia, it is most often vocational colleges and other tertiary education providers that fall foul of the regulatory requirements stipulated under the *Education Services for Overseas Students Act 2000* (Cwlth) (ESOS Act) (Marginson *et al.* 2010). Many of these provisions concern the standard of education provided, rather than matters to do with individual student compliance. As explained by an informant from the Department of Employment, Education and Workplace Relations (DEEWR) which has responsibility for ESOS regulation, the department's regulatory focus is primarily on the education providers themselves:

> I think the ESOS framework is broader than just students. Essentially it is designed to maintain the good reputation of the overseas education industry. It is a regulatory framework so it governs the obligations that are on providers to perform in a certain manner in order to preserve that good reputation. So I guess that is the primary function.
>
> *(Interview 64, DEEWR)*

The DEEWR has its own compliance team which, like DIAC, works under the guidance of a 'risk matrix'. While the team's emphasis is on investigating the possible non-compliance of education providers themselves, some of this activity feeds into maintaining the integrity of the visa monitoring system. Management of the complex visa system for international students is achieved via a computerised system, PRISMS (see Chapter 3). The process of granting an international student visa begins with an educational provider issuing a Confirmation of Enrolment (COE), on the basis of which DIAC issues the visa. The prevention of visa fraud was a major impetus for the development of the system, which provides a high level of monitoring and control compared with other visa types:

> Well, one of the big introductions was the electronic Confirmation of Enrolment records. So, prior to that the whole process of getting students into the country was open to fraud because they had paper-based enrolment

records ... now we have a system where the provider will issue a Confirmation of Enrolment, the student will get the piece of paper; however, the record is also on the system.... So when a COE is issued it is issued for the duration of the course and those dates are what immigration use to grant the length of the visa. So they allow a reasonable amount of time for students to settle in the country beforehand and then a certain amount of time for them to, say, graduate, receive a qualification at the end of the period of study.

(Interview 64, DEEWR)

PRISMS was described in an evaluation of the ESOS Act as 'the bridge between education and migration' (Phillips KPA and Lifelong Learning Associates 2005: 185). The evaluators considered it to be unique in the world because of its integration of education provider and migration information, although the reporting functions were said to be weighted towards migration control and to be under-used in relation to provider compliance. While this highly automated system may have improved efficiency and reduced intentional fraud, it is also capable of triggering visa cancellation automatically on the basis of information recorded or not recorded on PRISMS, in a manner that our DEEWR informant described as 'scary'. Official inquiries and independent research conducted over the past decade have identified many areas of injustice and inflexibility in the international student visa system arising from this automated system and also from the strict limits placed on paid work (Marginson *et al.* 2010; Phillips KPA and Lifelong Learning Associates 2005; Senate Education, Employment and Workplace Relations References Committee 2009; Senate Legal and Constitutional Affairs References Committee 2006).

Education providers from the primary to the tertiary level are responsible for maintaining records of students' attendance and academic progress that are key elements of the conditions for student visas, although the requirement to report on attendance is waived for universities. Universities play no role in monitoring the involvement of students in paid work. PRISMS is said to be based on 'exception reporting', meaning 'that everything is going according to plan ... unless you tell us otherwise' (Interview 64, DEEWR). The system can be 'told otherwise' by omission, in cases where academic progress information is not uploaded. Initially, this would auto-generate a 'section 20' letter which would be sent by the educational provider to the student, advising them that they were in breach of their conditions and requiring them to report to a DIAC Compliance Office within 28 days. In response to concerns about the high levels of cancellation of student visas, the Migration Regulations were amended in 2005 to allow 'exceptional circumstances beyond the student's control' to be taken into consideration in relation to prima facie breaches of the attendance and progression requirements, where formerly cancellation had been automatic. Cancellation is still automatic, however, in relation to breaches of the 20-hour work limit (visa condition 8104), the enforcement of which remains the responsibility of DIAC Compliance. Because of the inflexibility of the PRISMS machinery, a requirement was introduced in 2007 with amendments to the ESOS Act for universities to institute internal counselling and review processes before initiating this enforcement process, with these steps reinforced by on-screen prompts:

> Now there have been changes to the system in terms of recording and really tightening up the appeals processes. So a student has to have access to an internal appeals process if they are going to get reported on.... If they use that and it fails they can opt to use an external appeals process.... And on the system they can't actually complete, they can't literally create that trans-action that says you have been reported until they have gone – yes we have done this, yes we have done this, yes we have done this.
>
> *(Interview 64, DEEWR)*

Some states were said to have an Education Ombudsman who provides an addi-tional source of external review; otherwise the appeal would proceed to the Migration Review Tribunal where grounds for appeal are extremely restricted in relation to most cancellation powers.

In addition to changes in procedural safeguards, refinements have been made to PRISMS to reduce the likelihood of education providers unwittingly making changes that place a student's visa in jeopardy. These safeguards operate through a series of on-screen warnings, the need for which hints at a history of high-consequence mistakes by university administrators:

> OK, so it gives you a warning: 'Submitting a student course variation will result in automatic cancellation of this student's student visa if the student does not report to the DIAC office within 28 days.' So that is the serious part. [The warning also asks:] 'Are you sure?' Because before all those ques-tions came in it was quite a lot easier to do this, and so it is highly unlikely now [that] a provider is going to do this in error.
>
> *(Interview 64, DEEWR)*

Despite these additional safeguards, PRISMS still retains considerable power to identify and generate illegality. The DEEWR informant, who had responsibility for the integrity of data on the system, listed '12 or 15' different reasons that require education providers to report students to immigration authorities, noting that much of the inves-tigative task that had once rested with DIAC had been devolved to them:

> We do a lot of the investigation now. But pretty much it is a serious con-sequence ... unless they have got a very, very valid reason, you know 99.9 per cent of the time they will probably get their visa cancelled.
>
> *(Interview 64, DEEWR)*

While the DEEWR has ultimate responsibility for maintaining student enrolment records, the informant insisted that the department has no responsibility at all in relation to student visas.

Outside PRISMS there was said to be no broad data-sharing agreements concerning international students. About 100 specialised DIAC officers have direct access to PRISMS – presumably compliance officers responsible for responding to notifications about visa breaches. Assisting the compliance effort was seen to 'contribute to the broader goal' of maintaining the good standing of the international student industry and to support a 'whole-of-government' approach to maintaining the integrity of the visa system. In relation to individual student compliance, while the DEEWR retains a technical role in maintaining international student data for use by education providers and DIAC, the role of policing international student visas in relation to academic requirements has been largely devolved to the providers themselves.

Students or suspects?

The most relevant section of the ESOS Act for education providers is visa condition 8202 which concerns attendance and academic progress. The requirement to monitor these conditions has sparked the development of a complex bureaucratic infrastructure within universities that interacts with the DEEWR and DIAC through PRISMS. Most universities – aware of the crucial importance of international student fees – maintain an international student office which provides at least initial support to newly arriving students. Separate from this, student records offices are required to provide regular reports to the DEEWR via PRISMS about international student enrolments and visa compliance and issue 's 20' notices to students in breach of their attendance and progress conditions. Since academic records are usually maintained separately, entering academic progress data on PRISMS requires a considerable administrative effort that is usually handled by specialist university employees.

The number of visa cancellations related to visa condition 8202 increased from 3,986 in 2000–01 to 7,049 in 2001–02 following the introduction of mandatory reporting via PRISMS, and this figure reached 8,241 by 2003–04 (Contractor 2004). While arguing that the number of cancellations compared with the number of visas granted was 'minute', an evaluation report claimed that student cancellations in Australia accounted for a third of cancellations across all visa classes (Phillips KPA and Lifelong Learning Associates 2005). The additional safeguards for students introduced in 2007 might be expected to reduce these numbers, but there are still aspects of the system that are highly automated and seemingly relentless. Section 20 notices advise students to report to DIAC within 28 days to explain their failure to comply with the conditions; and failure to report (perhaps because the notice is not received?) results in automatic cancellation. Universities are also required by the ESOS Act to maintain an up-to-date record of international students' residential addresses, and to notify DIAC of any change or discontinuation of a programme or application for leave (visa condition 8533).

An employee at a major Australian university whose role was to support international students argued that cooperation with DIAC over visa compliance is essential for the welfare of international students:

So if we don't understand the rules then obviously we can't let the students know. If anything that the students then do wrong then they will be punished, then they will get into trouble. So I suppose we have to definitely cooperate with them.

(Interview 55, University Student Adviser)

At this informant's university, the employee responsible for reporting breaches through PRISMS worked within the same section that provides support to international students. This enables support staff to identify students who are not progressing with their studies and are in danger of breaching their visas.

Although the reporting requirements are mandated under the ESOS Act, the actual procedures used were said to be entirely at the discretion of individual universities. A particular area of contention raised in the interviews is the threshold at which non-achieving students should be reported:

So sometimes they [the DEEWR] will be good and say – 'It is a university, it is up to you to decide what are your progression rules'. So for us, for instance, we won't report them until they have been suspended. But if you look at that, someone could be failing for the last six sessions before we report them because they can fail badly and then they get better one session and then they fail again. So they keep going back and forth without being suspended. But honestly they are wasting a lot of time. Should we report them earlier? But maybe they can get back on track.

(Interview 55, University Student Adviser)

The processes around monitoring academic progress are a longstanding feature of major universities and apply to all students. But referrals made on this basis to academic advisers involving international students are inevitably tinged with the possibility of expulsion for the students, or at least significant and expensive disruption to their study programme:

I mean in a way you don't want to scare them, but I suppose the consequences are quite real.... The fact that they physically go there [to DIAC] shouldn't really be punished that way. So generally speaking, well in the last couple of years I think it is alright. If people do turn up they will say OK we had better leave the country and go home and reapply. And sometimes students will contact us and then we will try and get whatever documents they need to help them to get them to come back here.

(Interview 55, University Student Adviser)

One student who attended the migration policing session run by the author at an international students' conference[6] had represented students at hearings triggered by their lack of academic progress. She commented that academic staff were often unaware of the implications for international students of their studies being suspended, and seemed not to appreciate that they had a duty of care to support students in not breaching their visas. When asked in a mini-survey how important it is for universities to cooperate with DIAC, she was the only one of 23 students who identified a possible conflict of interest between the university's role as an educator, on the one hand, and as a visa policing agent, on the other: 'By law, it seems important. However, when judged against welfare implications for individual students, I think it must be very difficult for unis to choose between compliance and duty of care if detention or deportation will be the consequence' (Interview 58, Student Representative).

This informant also recounted a number of cases in which students at her university had experienced serious visa problems that were outside the remit of the university's monitoring requirements. For example, students had been known to be detained under the Migration Act if found to be working in excess of the strict weekly limit. Others had been forced to abandon their studies because their parents' visas, on which they were listed as dependents, had been rejected. This included situations in which the parents were long-term residents, but had not been accepted for permanent residence status. Quasi-parental support for unaccompanied students under the age of 18 was also identified as a serious issue, but only applied to a small proportion of university applicants. Overstaying could occur where students had completed secondary school in Australia before progressing to university, but were unaware of the need to renew their visa. It could also arise when academic failure extended the length of time needed to complete a course of study.

Student advisers reported sometimes becoming involved in serious investigations relating to missing students, including the possibility that students might 'disappear' into immigration detention:

> If we have a parent, for instance, call up and say I haven't heard from my son for the last two years or something.... So we can actually then check – not enrolled – the address – maybe you could even go to that address and obviously the person doesn't live there.... The person could be in the detention centre and no one would know.
>
> *(Interview 55, University Student Adviser)*

However, as in other areas of immigration enforcement, student advisers and representatives alike discerned a 'softer' approach by DIAC in the post-Palmer era: 'I suppose because they are interested to let international students stay on as permanent residents ... they don't actually punish people as such or scare people as much' (Interview 55, University Student Adviser). Other changes in how international students are dealt with were attributed to the improved use of IT by DIAC, so that fewer mistakes are made and students can negotiate some aspects of their visas electronically. Another informant with responsibility for student records believed that compliance processes were actually getting stricter, which he saw as a good thing because this was associated with improved efficiency of the online systems so that legal status could be established more readily and more serious problems avoided (Interview 56, University Administrator).

The National Liaison Committee (NLC) supports international students and lobbies for educational policy reform. The NLC representative interviewed for the migration policing study recognised that student visas are often used to come to Australia for purposes other than study, and believed that increasingly strict border controls and the tightening of conditions surrounding the acquisition of permanent residence are related to this misuse. Nevertheless, he was concerned about the punitive outcomes for individuals who are actively studying but still fall foul of the strict controls:

> If the cause of the breach is for lack of information, then I don't see the reason why they should be punished, and that's our argument with the government department in terms of when the student breaches their visa. What is the cause of it? Was it intentional, or was it unintentional? … So, again, unless the student comes to us and gives us the inside story or the real story, otherwise it's quite hard for anyone to know why the student had to be put into the detention centre.
>
> *(Interview 57, Student Representative)*

While supportive of immigration enforcement that is aimed at maintaining the integrity of the international student system, the NLC representative was also adamant that more discretion needed to be built into the enforcement system to prevent injustices to individual students who come to Australia to broaden their horizons and secure their futures in a globalising world.

Responsibilising private citizens

The duty to 'dob'

The techniques employed by immigration authorities to encourage members of the public to report unlawful non-citizens are hardly subtle. DIAC has created an anonymous telephone hotline – the 'Dob-in Service' – and named it in a way that links it to the informal vernacular of grassroots 'Aussie culture'.[7] A free-call telephone hotline was initially introduced in 2004. The ministerial media release announcing the launch quoted then Minister for Immigration Amanda Vanstone as saying that illegal workers 'take employment opportunities away from Australians' and urging the public to assist her department in 'tracking people down'.

Fifty thousand calls were reportedly made to the hotline by the end of 2005.[8] In the 2004–05 reporting year, 3,186 unlawful non-citizens (17 per cent of the locations for that year) were located through reports to the dob-in line (DIMIA 2005). By 2011–12, 18,900 dob-ins, or pieces of fraud-related information received from the public, were recorded by DIAC nationally (DIAC 2012). This figure is considerably down from the 47,432 notifications reported in DIAC's 2006–07 Annual Report (DIAC 2011: 119), suggesting perhaps that propensity to report may be sensitive to the general political climate, which softened somewhat after 2007. By way of comparison, following an advertising campaign entitled 'Support the System that Supports You' aimed at encouraging the reporting of suspected welfare fraud, Centrelink recorded a record high of 118,490 reports from the public in the 2005–06 financial year (Karvelas 2007). Most of these reports received no further action, but around 7 per cent resulted in a reduced payment and a further 2 per cent in complete cancellation of benefits.

At least half the notifications processed through the CIMU within the Sydney DIAC Compliance Office were said to arise from dobs. This does not include reports made in person at the Client Services counter. The CIMU reported receiving about 350 allegations per month by telephone alone at the time of the interviews, the majority from the general public. A Migration Series Instruction (MSI-292: at 3.6.1) reminds immigration officers that third party information 'might emanate from a malicious person and may not be the whole truth'. CIMU staff saw their role in the first instance as filtering and then 'value adding' to this information by interviewing complainants and obtaining additional documentary information where possible: 'Now if there's not enough information to work it up we'll archive it.… If we get enough information then we will value-add through doing our own checks and we use section 18 of the Act for that' (Interview 49, Sydney DIAC). Cases judged to require further action may be referred to Compliance Field Teams (often regarding workplace issues) or the CERT in low-risk cases (often where residential premises are concerned), and sometimes to specialist teams such as the Employer Awareness Team, the Fraud Team or the Complex Case Team. There were said to be 'less dobs' now than there used to be (Interview 48, Sydney DIAC), although they still feature as a significant source of information about potential immigration breaches.

The migration policing study focused on institutional practices so it cannot shed any light on dob-in practices from a community perspective. It might be surmised that the profile of a DIAC 'dobber' would be an Australian-born person of Anglo or European origin. On the other hand, according to DIAC officials, unlawful non-citizens are most likely to be found living among lawfully present non-citizens, which raises the possibility that other non-citizens or even co-nationals may join the ranks of the dobbers. ECLOs employed by the NSW Police Force who were interviewed for the study recounted instances in which the dob-in line had been used as a tool by local members of migrant communities to pursue personal vendettas or as a threat to maintain control over individuals with unlawful, uncertain or fragile immigration status.[9] Sydney compliance officers also suggested a range of motives for dobbing based on revenge, moral rectitude, or feelings of insecurity:

> [Officer 1] In some cases it's very personal and they've got a grudge against the person. [Officer 2] In some cases it's people who feel like they – I guess like they want to do the right thing. [Officer 1] Very strongly. Yeah, and they don't like it when they see someone else gaining an advantage unlawfully. [Officer 2] Also people who are concerned about their jobs being taken. I think we get that quite regularly.
>
> *(Interview 49, Sydney DIAC)*

Dobbing in to DIAC was apparently seen by some members of the public as analogous to calling the police, with an expectation that a swift response would follow:

> [Officer 1] I think a lot of clients ring in and also assume that we have more powers than what we actually do. And sometimes then we do try to explain that to them, because you know they assume that they can just give you an address where someone's working and then you can just go out tomorrow. [Officer 2] They think we've got police powers.
>
> *(Interview 49, Sydney DIAC)*

The NSW Police Force also receives reports from the public through its own channels about suspected unlawful non-citizens. The commander of an ethnically diverse area in Sydney expressed the view that 'illegal citizens' were often protected by the family and other members of the community 'because they are actually the ones who arranged to get them here' (Interview 6, NSW Police Force Local Area Commander). However, ECLOs who worked closely with communities believed reports were often made from within migrant communities for a range of personal and strategic reasons, and up to 50 per cent of operational police in some areas reported having checked someone's immigration status following a report from a member of the public (see Chapter 4). One senior officer summed it up as follows:

> If someone is here illegally the community will either try to protect them or oust them. And I think by and large a lot of people are of the view, or have this mistaken belief that the community want to always protect people who are here illegally. And it is not the case. They are just as worried about them being here as everybody else. So we need to provide a safe environment for those people to tell us what they know, but at the same time protecting them … we need to be able to facilitate them telling us when they want to tell us, because they do tell us.
>
> *(Interview 37, NSW Police Force Headquarters)*

The ATO and Centrelink also operate public reporting facilities that enable members of the public to report suspected tax evaders and benefit cheats, and exchange community-sourced information related to 'shared risks' (Interview 60, ATO). One informant claimed that Centrelink's Australian Government tip-off line receives 120,000 reports a year, of which 'some' are likely to be related to immigration matters (Interview 62, Centrelink).

Contributions to the dob-in line are self-motivated, and departmental instructions forbid compliance officers from offering any financial incentive for information. This is both its strength (from a public administration point of view) and its weakness (in terms of reliability of information, and possible adverse community impacts). Questions have also been asked about whether the effort required to investigate similar hotline reports has been a waste of public resources

(Dux 2005). At a Budget Estimates Hearing on 26 May 2004, soon after the dob-in line was established, Minister Vanstone reported that around 23 per cent of calls at that time were referred to further investigation. The cost of running the service was said to be a mere $10,000. Since that time, specialist information units have been established to 'value-add' to all information sources. CIMU officers interviewed for the migration policing study claimed that up to 75 per cent of allegations were followed up in some way but said that many reports are difficult to confirm. Even where the information obtained is insufficient to pursue individual cases, it was argued that the data might still assist in building intelligence about trends in non-compliance; so it seems that DIAC's reliance on community information has become integral to its intelligence-led approach.

One Canberra-based DIAC informant noted that citizen reporting was likely to be weighted towards what he considered to be less serious or systematic breaches:

> We only get tip-offs from the general public. So they're more alert to things like sham marriages. Whereas someone who's involved in some organised fraud is not likely to give you a tip-off about themselves or the fact that they're working in – in some…. So I think part of the fact that that's a bit distorted because we only see the stuff that the community sees and is willing to report about.
>
> *(Interview 44, Canberra DIAC)*

The phenomenon of dobbing in unlawful non-citizens exemplifies what Khosravi (2010: 75) has described as the border that exists 'in the minds of people'. While there may be an expressive element in the act of dobbing based on revenge, dislike or fear, the possibility of anonymity also gives the dob-in line the mechanistic quality of the 'morally cleansing circuitry' Lippert (2002: 498) has described in relation to Crime Stoppers programmes, whereby tips are received from 'persons one can never meet or know by name'. The age-old practice of informing is thereby transformed and systematised into a seemingly effective technology of population control in which migrant communities, to some extent, police themselves:

> A lot of people will try to use that to, you know to stick the knife in somebody they don't like. So there is always that. So that is where investigation is very important because you have to discern the credibility of what you are being told and all that sort of stuff … the community does to a large degree police itself because people just want to live in peace at the end of the day.
>
> *(Interview 37, NSW Police Force Headquarters)*

Disciplining 'dodgy employers'

Private citizens may also encounter non-citizens by employing them. The legal requirement on employers to check the immigration status of workers is an important element of DIAC's 'educative' compliance strategy. This transfer of responsibility onto Australian employers has been facilitated by an online database, VEVO, which provides immigration status information about prospective employees. The number of VEVO checks made by employers has increased dramatically, from 245,000 in 2007–08 to 1,146,774 in 2010–11 (DIAC 2011: 161). Through VEVO, Australia seeks to regulate its workforce on the basis of legal entitlement, through a system resembling third party policing (Mazerolle and Ransley 2006) in which employers are co-opted into a migration policing role through the threat of civil or criminal sanctions. Since 2007, ss 245AA to 254AK of the Migration Act have specified that a person commits a criminal offence by employing someone who lacks legal entitlement to work. This system might be thought of as the equivalent of carriers' liability sanctions operating at the external border.[10] Similar mentalities and technologies of governance are therefore in evidence in the internal and external borders.

Although the primary goal of the employer sanctions regime is to prevent unlawful working, enquiries to the VEVO system leave a record which can be acted upon by DIAC if necessary:

> It tells [the employer] whether the person is lawful or not, and it also gives us information whereby we can use that information if we want to prosecute under the employer sanction legislation. If they knowingly employed that person – we could locate them on the premises.
>
> *(Interview 42, Canberra DIAC)*

It is not clear whether the VEVO system might also provide intelligence that could assist in identifying and locating potentially removable individuals. With most of the migration policing work delegated to employers, compliance officers direct their efforts primarily for 'dodgy' employers (see Chapter 3). The Sydney DIAC office has a specialist team within the Business Compliance Unit that works with industry to deliver a training programme called 'Employer Awareness' that provides advice about the employer sanctions legislation and explains the VEVO system. The team also uses risk-based techniques to identify non-compliant employers who may be liable to prosecution, reportedly after one or more warning notices have been issued. DIAC managers believed that this preventative work, also involving industry regulators, has paid significant dividends within the targeted industries:

> Virtually throughout Australia now most of the taxi licensing authorities are doing immigration checks … so using those sort of methods has had a quite high … quite a good return…. To get the security guard's licence in New South Wales, you know, they must conduct an immigration check and that's been very effective…. From our point of view, that industry's been completely, virtually tidied up.
>
> *(Interview 45, DIAC Canberra)*

The Fraud Control and Investigations Branch within the business compliance function of the DEEWR also contributes to industry regulation. A departmental spokesperson declined to be interviewed but confirmed by email that their organisation works locally with DIAC through information exchange at individual, not aggregate, levels and on joint operations of mutual interest, and interacts at a national level through the Cash Economy Working Group. The branch investigates fraud across a range of DEEWR employment-related programmes, but was reportedly most likely to encounter unlawful non-citizens among the skilled worker programme who are unlawful by virtue of having obtained their visas fraudulently.

The operation of the employer sanctions system was reviewed for DIAC in 2011 (Howells 2011). The review concluded that the number of illegal workers in Australia had been growing since around 1998 and that existing sanctions and educational efforts had proven to be ineffective. A large part of the problem, according to Howells, was the precedence accorded to the administrative removal of illegal workers, at the expense of pursuing prosecutions against those who employ them:

> The principal reason for the failure of the *Employer Sanctions Act* provisions is that the 'best evidence' of breach would almost always come from the workers themselves but their evidence is affected by their complicity or independent culpability under section 235 of the *Migration Act* 1958. They would normally be removed from Australia 'as soon as reasonably practicable' as required by section 198 of the *Migration Act* 1958. The cost and the administrative inconvenience of detaining them pending a trial would be prohibitive.
>
> *(Howells 2011: 14)*

The solution proposed by Howells was the introduction of a 'strict liability' civil offence which would simplify evidentiary requirements and provide a stronger deterrent. Traditional criminal sanctions were considered to have a poor record of effectiveness in this context. Howells argued that the curtailing of illegal working through deterrence was necessary for the protection of workers and the integrity of the labour market, but was also identified as performing an important symbolic function linked to the internal performance of Australian sovereignty: 'The absence of an effective deterrent against the employment of non-citizens who do not have permission to work is an abrogation of Australian sovereignty and a contradiction of the otherwise orderly pattern of migration' (Howells 2011: 12). Responsible employers are therefore expected to align themselves with principles of good governance and even national security, and to become incorporated into the administrative state through the assiduous checking of immigration status. The Howells report noted that the financial costs and inconvenience that might be associated with the introduction of a stricter regime would be spread across employers, taxpayers and Australian workers as a whole, and concluded that these intrusions are needed to mitigate against the risks of an unregulated workforce:

The costs and inconveniences to employers of being obliged to ask whether a prospective employee has permission to work and to check whether non-citizens do have permission must be balanced against the cost being borne by the whole of our society in dealing with global population and displacement issues and international security risks. The inconvenience said to be the likely result of any change to the regime of sanctions does not outweigh the benefits to be gained from having a more secure labour market and the prevention of exploitation and other abuses. The cost will also be borne by the taxpayer through the provision of VEVO and other services.

(Howells 2011: 15)

In this report, identity management emerged as the key technology underpinning the regulatory system – an objective that Howells noted would be hampered by the historical opposition of the Australian population to carrying an identity card:

Australian citizens will need to shoulder their part of the inconvenience by being prepared to obtain adequate forms of identification for employment. In the absence of a comprehensive system of identification individuals will have to take responsibility for establishing their identity.

(Howells 2011: 15)

At present, only 'suspected non-citizens' are required under s 188 of the Migration Act to provide evidence of their identity and/or entitlement to remain in Australia if requested to do so by an authorised officer. Expanded employer sanctions would therefore potentially encroach not only on relations between employers and employees, but also on the established boundary between citizen and non-citizen.

After the release of the Howells report, the government moved quickly to introduce new legislation to toughen the employer sanction regime. The main elements of this legislation include significant strict liability civil penalties to supplement existing criminal sanctions (which are now most likely to be used for large-scale and systematic fraud), new evidence-gathering powers, and the extension of liability to a wider range of employers, agents and contractors. The ministerial press release that announced the new laws asserted the government's commitment to 'get tough on dodgy employers' in order to 'punish those who wilfully exploit foreign workers' (Bowen 2011). This political rhetoric appears to assign 'dodgy employers' a similar folk devil role in relation to the internal border that is occupied by people smugglers in relation to the external border.

From the internal to the internalised border

If published statistics are to be taken at face value, it would appear that non-citizens with unlawful or uncertain immigration status are flocking to DIAC either in the hope of regularising their visa status, or anxious to accept a plane ticket home at the expense of the Australian taxpayer. This is the picture of 'voluntary' presentations painted by DIAC compliance staff during the interviews and published in DIAC's annual reports. These presentations are reported to be the largest, and the fastest growing, source of locations of unlawful non-citizens. In 2011–12, 12,672 unlawful non-citizens were identified by DIAC following their presentation at DIAC offices, and voluntary presentations accounted for 82 per cent of unlawful non-citizens located (DIAC 2012). However, the 'voluntary' label conceals many layers of monitoring and status checking that is the genesis for many of these contacts. One example is the s 20 notices issued to international students (discussed above) which require them to report to DIAC offices within 28 days. Although compliance staff resist the idea that they actively 'monitor' temporary visa holders, notices to report are likely to be issued in many other circumstances too, so that much of this so-called voluntary reporting is effectively manufactured.[11]

In the post-Palmer era, DIAC invests significant resources in providing information and encouraging voluntary compliance with visa conditions in order that individuals can avoid become unlawful in the first place. However, with opportunities for unskilled work visas, family reunion and other means for extending lawful stays dwindling, visas are in short supply. Presentation at a DIAC counter may therefore be more like gambling on a long shot than a careful and voluntary cost/benefit calculation. Moreover, the department's own research shows that levels of trust among departmental 'clients' remain low despite what DIAC staff see as significant changes in their approach.[12] The complexity of the immigration system also leaves many individuals confused about their immigration status and fearful of making enquiries. An ECLO employed by the NSW Police Force recounted a situation where individuals who were awaiting the outcome of their applications for refugee protection had been 'moving around for years' trying to evade detection, but were found to have lawful status (Interview 41, NSW Police Force ECLOs).

The task of incentivising individuals whose whereabouts are unknown to DIAC to report voluntarily presents a particular challenge. Although public statements about the lack of entitlement of unlawful non-citizens are not a significant feature of public discourse in Australia as they have been in many other countries, one senior DIAC manager interviewed for the migration policing project revealed that strategies intended to 'make life difficult' for unlawful non-citizens were being systematically pursued:

> Already someone that's overstayed and disappeared and has no entitlements and Medicare benefits or … any form of social security benefit or anything like that, so they're very dependent on employment.… We're shifting where our resources apply and also we're … we're looking to these other ways of … making life difficult for people … so that they come in and see us.
>
> *(Interview 45, DIAC Canberra)*

The embedding of the border through an ever-expanding network of immigration checks that control access to essential services and opportunities, backed up in some cases with harsh sanctions for providing services to those without entitlement, creates a border that relies on attrition rather than active detection. It is a border drawn around unlawful non-citizens themselves, intended to separate them from all that is necessary to sustain a reasonable life. It seems that the strategy of 'intent management' that has been evident for some time at the external border has also infiltrated the internal border (Pickering and Weber 2013). While the actions of service-providing or licence-granting bodies may bring particular unlawful non-citizens to the attention of DIAC, as discussed above, none of these organisations are, as yet, obliged by law to report. Their obligation is rather to deny access to employment or services. They have become nodes in a system of entitlement that is increasingly controlled by technologically mediated switch points. This network of exclusion is intended to make it so difficult for unlawfully present individuals to sustain their existence that seemingly voluntary presentation becomes the only viable option.

Just how abject and precarious the conditions of life need to become before those living without the security of lawful status decide to self-police is likely to vary depending on an individual's access to community support, their knowledge of DIAC practices and the strength of their disincentive to return to their country of origin. Determined overstayers and other unlawfully present individuals will have many strategies for resisting pressures to report. But where the removal of all options to sustain one's existence is achieved, the border is effectively internalised and the construction of 'voluntarism' is complete.

7

A NODAL CARTOGRAPHY OF MIGRATION POLICING NETWORKS

Network morphology

Categorising migration policing networks

Having identified a range of migration policing agencies in the previous chapters, in this chapter I consider the operation of migration policing networks as a whole. Migration policing networks identified in this study are overwhelmingly constituted by state and federal agencies, deriving from what Shearing and Wood describe as the 'first sector' (Shearing and Wood 2003). The most direct role is played by law enforcement agents who are 'designated officers' under the Migration Act but the layering of federal, state and local levels of government within some migration policing networks suggests some diffusion of responsibility across the government sector. Commercial and non-governmental organisations (that is, the second and third sectors respectively) are noticeably absent except where legislation requires their participation, as in the case of employers and education providers. Finally, voluntary dob-ins from members of the public also contribute to the identification of unlawful non-citizens. However, these actions are ad hoc and not formally incorporated into migration policing networks in any enduring way.

Security networks have been categorised in many other ways. Dupont (2004) has identified four ideal types: *local* (involving information exchange between traditional and non-traditional social control agencies and local communities, mobilised to address local security concerns); *institutional* (relatively closed, inward-looking networks established to pool resources and improve the coordination of the efforts of existing government agencies); *international* (which mirror the structure of the institutional model, but extend beyond borders and increasingly incorporate non-government actors); and *virtual* (information-based networks which transcend space and time). The migration policing networks identified in this study fall most clearly into the virtual and institutional categories – categories that are clearly not mutually exclusive.

There is no sign yet in Australia of the local 'Immigration Crime Partnerships' that have been formally established in Britain and sold to the public as mechanisms that 'address community concerns on migration' (Wilson 2012), nor of the local-level migration policing arrangements negotiated with police in the US (Provine 2013). Moreover, the federal structure of governance in Australia means that such *formal* developments at local levels are highly unlikely to occur. This does not preclude local variations in forms of inter-agency collaboration, as observed between different NSW Police Force LACs, or the establishment of MOUs between DIAC and local governments, as reported in NSW. The reporting of suspected unlawful non-citizens by residents to local police is arguably an example of a local dimension to migration policing, although hardly qualifies structurally as a 'network'.

Among the migration policing practices examined in this study, the detection and investigation of human trafficking, systematic fraud and exploitation are most likely to involve an international dimension, but these aspects were not fully explored since the focus here is on the detection of 'ordinary' unlawful non-citizens. Networks involving both state and federal authorities cooperating on the detection of unlawful non-citizens could possibly give rise to some of the cross-jurisdictional complexity associated with international networks.

Migration policing networks might also be categorised as either *operational* networks (similar to Dupont's 'institutional' category), which depend on the sharing of resources, skills and legal powers; or *informated* networks (corresponding to 'virtual' networks), which operate in 'informated spaces' (Sheptycki 1998) through the exchange of electronic information. These networks are distinguished primarily by the technologies employed. But clearly neither can exist or function in isolation from the other. A joint operation involving DIAC, the NSW Police Force, the ATO and Centrelink, for example, will require an exchange of intelligence information in the planning stages, in order to define objectives, agree on tactics, identify risks and obtain the necessary legal authorisation; and will probably rely on accessing the official records held by one or more of these agencies in real time once suspect individuals have been identified. At other times – such as in relation to aggregate data-matching processes, or where an agency's records relating to a particular individual are requested by investigators from another agency – the informated networks operate across agencies in ways that are less closely associated with any particular operation.

A third category, of *strategic* networks, can also be identified from the interview data, and these involve representatives from different agencies at both the state and federal level meeting regularly to discuss policy-related matters of mutual concern. The examples of such networks provided during the interviews include the Cash Economy Working Group and the Police–DIAC Practice Management Network which will be discussed later. It might be contested that these structures are merely high-level inter-agency committees, but their direct links to inter-agency operations, particularly in relation to the Cash Economy Working Group, arguably qualifies them as functioning networks, or even as high-level nodes in wider operational networks.

If a temporal dimension is added, migration policing networks can also be categorised according to their longevity. Most of the time, operational and informated migration policing networks are ad hoc and time delimited, being negotiated and constituted as needed. Compared with these one-off or irregular operations, strategic networks exhibit continuity over time through the conduct of regular meetings involving a relatively stable contingent of member agencies. However, information exchange networks may also be more enduring, as in the case of the regular cross-agency transfer of enrolment and compliance information about international students effected through the online PRISMS, the ongoing liaison between the Sentence Administration section within the Department of Corrective Services and the Sydney DIAC Remand Team over the release of potentially deportable prisoners, or the regular data matching between ATO records and the DIAC Overstayers List.

Moreover, traces of the operational networks deployed for a particular joint operation may persist over time, in readiness for a repeat performance involving the same organisational players. This was most apparent in relation to specialised units such as the NSW Police Force Commuter Crime Unit, which participates in regular 'taxi operations' in Sydney, for which the partners, targets and tactics are all well rehearsed. Embedded liaison officers perhaps provide the best example of ongoing operational networks. Although they represent only a bilateral exchange between agencies (as with many of the information exchange practices identified), liaison officers function as sites for the mobilisation of information and resources across multiple sites within and between agencies, thus fulfilling the definition of a node provided by Burris *et al.* (2005).

Migration policing networks also display varying degrees of formality and informality. This characteristic is related to the temporal dimension outlined above, since ad hoc operations are often described as 'informal', as exemplified in the following:

> It is almost an ad hoc arrangement, but having said that it is a cohesive group. Everyone works very well with everyone else, there is no agency rivalry or jealousy, everyone is there for the common purpose and as I say it works quite well ... in a perfect world I would probably like to see a dedicated enforcement team, permanently employed and dedicated into brothel and massage parlour enforcement, and that would be a joint agency team.
>
> *(Interview 61, Local Council)*

It was argued that, within a federal agency like DIAC, the requirement to build inter-agency networks at the state level calls for the flexibility offered by informal relationships:

> We set the policy here in the national office and each state and territory office is supposed to execute the policy.... But the reality of course is [that] they become little federated offices around Australia and either by

default or by osmosis, however you want to say it, they do develop their own relationships with the local police services. And now we have formal relationships with our law enforcement agencies.... But at [the] state level you have a number of relationships that are sort of like one-on-one or group-upon-group where things take place, and that I haven't been able to quantify.

(Interview 46, Canberra DIAC)

These on-the-ground arrangements were seen to contrast with the more formal arrangements between federal agencies that were invariably underpinned by MOUs (Interview 46, Canberra DIAC). The following account illustrates how NSW police officers negotiate the formal/informal divide in relation to requests for DIAC information, depending on the purpose of the request:

If it's something informal where we're trying to just do some initial legwork it ... might be someone we already have a working relationship with. If it's something we then may want to do formally we have a ... a facility where we can make [an] application.... That'll be forwarded through to the appropriate immigration section.... Probably if it was the case [that] we wanted to use it formally for court or if we had specific information or ... you know, it would be ... on a case-by-case scenario.

(Interview 24, NSW Police Force Local Area Commander)

Building cross-agency institutions

The establishment of enduring networks at the national level dedicated to planning or implementing migration policing projects indicates the growing importance placed by federal and state level agencies on the control of non-citizens. DIAC chairs and runs a national Police–DIAC Practice Management Network that meets on a quarterly basis in different states. It reports each year to the Immigration Minister and the annual meeting of state police commissioners, from where the network is said to have arisen: 'It was actually born at that level. At one of their meetings they decided that there was a need for immigration to be put more on the radar and that is where it came out of' (Interview 35, NSW Police Force Headquarters). Members from different states were said to sometimes form sub-networks to enable the transfer of successful practices from one location to another. The example cited by our informants related to the successful negotiation of an MOU in South Australia over the policing of immigration detention centres, which was being considered in NSW and Victoria at the time the interviews were conducted.

From the perspective of DIAC, it seems that concerns about police 'referrals' of the type that had led to the wrongful detentions of Vivian Solon, Cornelia Rau and others had been the catalyst for establishing the group. DIAC officers appeared keen to mobilise the considerable migration policing resource that the state police forces represent, while also expecting police to defer to DIAC's growing expertise in identity and status determination:

> As I said to you, the basic message is don't do anything, if possible, until you contact ISS in the first instance, and we'll talk you through it. Of course identity is a big issue, so that we identify the right person and we're able to hopefully have identified whether that person has got a lawful status or not.
>
> *(Interview 46, Canberra DIAC)*

DIAC largely controls the agenda, which has included topics such as Migration Act awareness training for police, the use of the ISS, and the development of forms and inter-agency procedures (Interview 18, NSW Police Force Local Area Commander). Police members also use the forum to raise issues of importance to them. Two examples provided were the lack of 'benchmarking' for visa cancellations on character grounds (discussed in Chapter 5) and police perceptions of the increasing difficulties of deporting problematic offenders (Interview 18, NSW Police Force Local Area Commander). Although the Police–DIAC Practice Management Network could be classified as a strategic network, another police officer who attends its meetings claimed not to have 'discussed any systematic things' (Interview 36, NSW Police Force Headquarters). He said that the focus remained on practical, day-to-day matters such as information exchange. Accordingly, he could not name any new directions for migration policing that had emerged from the network so far and saw its purpose as primarily relationship building:

> All jurisdictions exchange information … and as long as it complies with the legislation and there is no third party release of it without authorisation, it is used for lawful purposes, it all fits in … this network has really been put together to facilitate the relationship and improve the relationship.
>
> *(Interview 35, NSW Police Force Headquarters)*

DIAC representatives agreed that the network had not yet reached its potential to develop policy, and thought members were still grappling with the organisational complexity represented on the committee:

> Not only do you have the complexity of New South Wales police and their set-up, but you've got the complexities of the various six or seven jurisdictions that we have around Australia…. They've also got the national AFP policing where they have regional offices and they also have representatives at airports and whatever. And the AFP also have an international angle to it…. So it would be rather pretentious to say that our little committee would be able to solve those problems…. We are still in our infancy, beginning to talk about some of the broader issues that affect all our organisations and whether we, at some point in time, [can] address them.
>
> *(Interview 46, Canberra DIAC)*

The Cash Economy Working Group is another network constituted at the national level that was widely mentioned during the interviews. Its core members are the ATO, Centrelink and DIAC. Unlike the Police–DIAC committee, DIAC is not the driving force behind this working group and the position of Chair for the quarterly meetings rotates between the three agencies. One research informant offered the following account of the origin and development of the group:

> It stems from a 2001 budget measure that provided for cash economy inter-agency activity. It was a budget measure to provide specific funding to Centrelink and the ATO to work in cooperation on issues on the risks of the cash economy. Immigration were identified in the development of that programme as being an agency that has a mutual interest in this industry and they engaged from there. So from a governance point of view the working group was established to coordinate activities. Now I suppose the governance view has taken a strategic whole-of-government approach to increasing the risks associated with cash economy activities.
>
> *(Interview 62, Centrelink)*

A multi-layered governance framework had been developed in which the role of the Working Group was to provide national guidance, which regional working groups then refined and applied according to local concerns. A three-way MOU has been agreed by these organisations specifically to cover the Working Group and joint activities that arise from it, along with general cooperation on compliance activities. DEEWR, the Department of Fair Trading, state police agencies, Customs and Border Protection, and child support services were also mentioned as non-core participants.

Although united by their organisational interest in illicit working, the motivations for each of these agencies to join the network differ markedly. The ATO officer interviewed for this study explained that his organisation's interest is solely in relation to recovering unpaid taxes, and is therefore focused on employers. In contrast, while DIAC has an interest in employers who are believed to be systematically abusing the visa system, its main concern is to uncover individuals working without authorisation:

> I mean we don't have an interest in the cash economy per se, it's actually the fact that the cash economy uses UNCs[1] [sic] often as cheap labour, so that's why we use the Cash Economy [Working Group] as a source of – and why we're engaged in the unit because it … gives us access to groups that are likely to be, or have a significant number of UNCs.
>
> *(Interview 42, Canberra DIAC)*

The regional groups were said to operate largely through the exchange of written intelligence reports with the aim of identifying mutual risks and deciding whether to mount individual or joint operations:

> A lot of this information, for instance, we would get from DIAC in terms of where [unlawful non-citizens] go, you know what industries they are going

into.... So that helps us form our view as to what the risk is and which parts of the economy we need to look at. It talks about the different risks; under-payment of minimum salary, for instance. Is that a tax issue? No, but you know we put it on the board.

(Interview 60, ATO)

Several multi-agency operations had been conducted under the auspices of the Cash Economy Working Group targeting the sex industry, with varying results in terms of the core concerns of the partner agencies:

In Parramatta what they found is that most of the people were DIAC people, so DIAC did most of the business. But they did it in Wollongong and they found it was Centrelink. It was Australians doing all the work but not declaring it when they were getting Centrelink benefits. So we do do joint operations because there is some cross-over, but for us in cash economy the people who are receiving it are not the big thing at all because it is only the undeclared income which is where our target audience is.

(Interview 60, ATO)

Embedding a liaison officer within a partner organisation is another way to build an inter-agency network. While at first sight this may seem to be merely a loose, bilateral arrangement, liaison officers operating as nodes for the transmission of organisational capacities and resources produce complex patterns of information exchange which support the development of specialist technologies to facilitate them. At the time of the research interviews, the Sydney DIAC office had several liaison officers located at the NSW Police Force Headquarters and one liaison officer within the AFP, and was planning to post liaison officers within the ATO and Centrelink. As for liaison officers from other agencies located within DIAC, these included the AFP and Centrelink, and plans were said to be underway within the ATO to post a liaison officer to DIAC. A National Police Training and Liaison Coordinator was also established at DIAC headquarters as a post-Palmer initiative, with responsibility for training police in the use of the ISS and their powers under the Migration Act (Interview 46, Canberra DIAC).

Alternatively, whole units might be established with a more specialised brief to build strong connections with other agencies working in cognate areas. An example of such in relation to migration policing is the Law Enforcement Liaison Unit, based in the Canberra headquarters of DIAC. Staff in this unit are tasked with responding to requests from state and federal law enforcement bodies for information regarding criminal investigations (Interview 46, Canberra DIAC). This process was described as a one-way flow of information, whereas the liaison officers located within the NSW Police Force were there to facilitate a two-way flow. The preparedness of DIAC to commit significant resources to a one-way flow of information without an immediate return in terms of the identification of unlawful non-citizens reflects the organisational priority attached to facilitating criminal convictions of non-citizens, who may then be eligible for visa cancellation. The Law Enforcement Liaison Unit can therefore be understood as an institution of crimmigration engaged in a process of 'upstreaming' in which significant organisational resources are invested in the manufacture of future illegality.

Network dynamics

Networks can be characterised not only by their morphology, but also in terms of their dynamics. In this regard, Gelsthorpe (1985, cited in Johnston and Shearing 2003) has suggested that models of inter-agency working can be classified according to their levels of integration (see Figure 1.1 in Chapter 1). Gelsthorpe identified communication models (which are restricted mainly to information exchange); cooperation models (whereby agencies maintain separate boundaries but agree to work on mutually defined problems); coordination models (in which agencies work systematically within defined agency boundaries but pool resources to tackle mutually agreed problems); federation models (whereby agencies operate integrated services, while maintaining some areas of distinctiveness) and, finally, highly integrated merger models (in which functional distinctions begin to dissolve). The styles of inter-agency working identified in the migration policing study align with the first three levels of integration. Migration policing networks identified were often restricted to information exchange (communication models) or might involve joint action on mutually defined problems (cooperation models). The Cash Economy Working Group and multi-agency 'taxi operations' might arguably achieve the level of integrated activity that typifies coordination models.

Migration policing as knowledge work

Information sharing is an essential element of the intelligence-led tactics of all the agencies included in the study, across a wide range of roles and responsibilities. A complex legal web of privacy and disclosure rules surrounds the exchange of personal data between agencies. Electronic systems of data exchange often operate via 'electronic certificates' authorising the selective release of information to authorised individuals. Statutory requirements were said to be built into the iAsk system operated by the NSW Police Force so that a request cannot progress unless the tick box that declares that the information is required for a criminal investigation has been checked, and then the request authorised at a higher level (Interview 35, NSW Police Force Headquarters). This area is developing to such an extent that agencies invariably have specialist staff to interpret legislation, negotiate inter-agency agreements, act as organisational 'gatekeepers' and seek out information requested by co-workers. This function was particularly highly developed in the ATO:

> The first thing that happens if anyone wants data through the Cash Economy Working Group or anything else we have a data-matching gatekeeper. You

go to them, the gatekeeper says – Under the legislation we can give them that data, or no, we can't give them that data.

(Interview 60, ATO)

The ATO operates such a complex array of data-sharing arrangements that it hosts an officer from the Privacy Commission within its data-matching unit. Officers acting as brokers for these exchanges need to be aware not only of the legislation that affects their own agency, but also of the legal entitlements to data of the requesting agencies:

We are not supposed to give any information. The police, the magistrate, whoever calls here, we are not supposed to give any information about a customer. That's how tight the privacy is. We know exactly where a customer is living and all that, but we still can't give it out. They have to contact the privacy officer. In each area they have a privacy officer, they have to contact them and get the information. But they do, they do get access though, they will get access but they have to go through the proper channels.

(Interview 9, Centrelink)

In contrast to the highly rule-governed approach described by the career civil servants quoted above, it was apparent that police retain a preference for less formal methods:

Operational Information Agency, OIA – they are the conduit for our communication – more formal communication with a whole range of other agencies, both law enforcement and government. They are that formal link or that formal conduit. But three o'clock on a Saturday morning [other agencies] are all at home in bed asleep. We get onto the DOI [Duty Operations Inspector] – not just DIAC, but you name it he can contact. His base in the communications branch is – it is like the space shuttle … I reckon he'd get George Bush on the phone if he needed to.

(Interview 23, NSW Police Force Local Area Commander)

In circumstances where strong working relationships were built up, data sharing might occur on a more open basis at local levels, as reported by this local council officer with responsibility for regulating brothels:

We have a fairly good level of cooperation, and the information exchange is fairly good and open. From this end I control all the information. I maintain a very high level of security and confidentiality in relation to information I receive from outside agencies, bearing in mind that a lot of that information is at times classified, and any potential leak of information may compromise not only our operations but [also our] external agency operations … [Interviewer: *So what sort of information would you be exchanging with DIAC?*]

Look, we talk about the names of owners, the identity of owners, identity of operators of these premises, the identity of the sex workers. That would be the main type of information that we would be exchanging.

(Interview 61, Local Council)

Another example was provided of a close working relationship between specialist sections of DIAC and the AFP through which information is exchanged openly, and with an apparent sense of common purpose:

I know with the trafficking industry [it's] basically pretty much carte blanche. I work with my counterpart in DIAC. What I know she pretty much knows – across all of our jobs at any level. I mean I've got pretty much complete trust there. Don't get me wrong, outside that specific team there have been some issues in relation to information being contained.... So I'd like to know who knows the information. In relation to my direct counterparts they're very, very good. We exchange information constantly.

(Interview 65, AFP)

Where information might be relevant to a criminal prosecution, it was suggested that more formal channels would be followed. Data-sharing practices were generally accepted as a requirement for effective whole-of-government working, although they were not always viewed as equitable in terms of the amount and direction of data flow:

So New South Wales Police would have MOUs with Customs, with DFAT [Department of Foreign Affairs and Trade], with Immigration, with all these other groups.... We try and get information back, but as I said from the outset, New South Wales Police are a great collector of data ... generally speaking they get a lot more information from us than we do from them.

(Interview 35, NSW Police Force Headquarters)

This assessment was confirmed by an informant from DIAC headquarters, who was aware that the issue had been discussed at high levels:

I know from the feedback I'm getting from the [Police–DIAC Practice Management Network] that we only give them the minimum information one way, whereas police feel they're giving us most information the other way.... We may only be in a position to say 'onshore' or 'offshore', whereas police may want to know if we have a last known address, or associates, or any sort of information we may directly get with applications or things like that. We may not always be in a position to disclose that.... And that's really important about what information they're requesting – for what reason – and we're always assessing each request on a case-by-case basis.

(Interview 46, Canberra DIAC)

Regulating information flows

Despite the strict regulations surrounding formal requests for data, or perhaps because of them, DIAC data-handling specialists in the CIMU had developed strategies for finding spaces between the legal requirements. Officers explained that information could sometimes be provided when statutes would otherwise prevent its release, where the individuals concerned had agreed to an 'IP2 clause' when the data was first collected. This was readily achieved by including a disclaimer within collection forms in which individuals could indicate their consent to have that information released under certain, possibly ill-defined conditions. This was seen as a powerful tool for avoiding many of the restrictions of privacy legislation and was believed to be widely used by Centrelink and the ATO to facilitate the sharing of their data with other agencies. At the time the interviews were conducted, DIAC informants claimed that these provisions were not built into their data collection, and suggested that 'to change all the forms to get an IP2 statement would take lots of effort':

> It's an instrument of release, it's called, and the Tax Office has a similar process I think. But working the other way we don't ... we're subject to privacy legislation, which means that it has to fulfil those different criteria for us to release information for other agencies.
>
> *(Interview 44, Canberra DIAC)*

However, benefiting themselves from these generic forms of authorisation, DIAC officers could be enterprising in pressing other agencies to include these provisions in their data collection processes, in order to make the information available to DIAC. An example of this form of persuasion was given by one senior DIAC official when describing his dealings with the licensing body for the taxi industry:

> And what I advised them at that point in time was that if you were to include questions relating to a person's right to work in Australia, which certainly you're entitled to do, if you're going to give them permission, and then ask them by signing the application [that] you acknowledge and provide your consent for [the] Ministry of Transport to check with any relevant agency or authority as to the authenticity of the information you provided ... it's a lawful exercise of the powers, no one is exceeding their authority. It's all above board, we are being quite clear and transparent with the clients in turn in speaking to them.
>
> *(Interview 47, Canberra DIAC)*

Aggregate data matching was not often reported in the interviews. One DIAC informant claimed that the organisation had neither the technical expertise nor the legal authority to engage in aggregate data matching with agencies such as the taxation office (Interview 44, Canberra DIAC). This restriction was also confirmed by the ATO representative: '[W]e can't just give [DIAC] bulk data. We have got to make certain that the use of it is within their legislation as well as ours' (Interview 60, ATO). On the face of it, this appears to contradict the information provided by the CIMU in Sydney, whose informants reported that the unit carries out data-matching procedures between ATO records and the DIAC overstayers file (Interview 49, Sydney DIAC). The crucial difference with this example may be that the DIAC information to be matched relates to individuals for whom a reasonable belief that they are unlawful non-citizens has already been formed by virtue of them appearing on the list, which would satisfy the legal criteria for inter-agency exchange. Indeed, the informants consistently said that aggregate matching in the form of a 'fishing expedition' aimed at identifying unlawful non-citizens without prior suspicion is not permitted under the current legislation.

Changes to the legislation that would open up new possibilities for intelligence exchange and data mining were seen as both highly desirable and politically achievable:

> In terms of the bigger picture of an exchange of information for intel gathering or you know … or even identifying patterns or whatever else, it is really a problem. I mean it'd be fairly simple in a sense to change the Tax Act with the right people in place in parliament and get it through and that would enable us to, for example, to match tax declaration forms with … files produced every fortnight to match to people on welfare benefits, the same thing could happen for visa holders who are not supposed to work. So you just run a match, all the visa holders that are not supposed to work against all the PDFs[2] in the tax office and you'd have the start of a compliance regime based on detection activity – as opposed to relying on tip-offs from the general public saying, oh that person's on a visa and they're working 20 hours a week.
>
> *(Interview 44, Canberra DIAC)*

The exchange of information between state and federal bodies was reported to work less smoothly than that between two federal bodies. A DIAC inform- ant described a situation in which he had been forced to argue with a state police officer, who was insisting on receiving information that he was not authorised to provide, that the Australian Constitution determines that federal legislation overrules state laws (Interview 44, Canberra DIAC). In turn, state police appear to operate with a strong sense of ownership of their own data: 'As I said, we are a state. Our information is our information. It might be dif- ferent between Commonwealth agencies, but our information is ours.… Everyone keeps their own information fairly guarded' (Interview 35, NSW Police Force Headquarters).

Even the internal structure within federal agencies, such as the devolution of operational organisation to the state level within DIAC, can create practical difficulties for the timely exchange of information between agencies:

> I have a regional Cash Economy group in Newcastle that operates fairly independently and one in New South Wales which operates fairly independently, and you talk to them about what is happening in Canberra and they don't know. And that has created a problem during the harvest trail because what will happen is they will start in Queensland and if you identify an issue and it is moved to New South Wales it is too late.
>
> *(Interview 60, ATO)*

In NSW, police and DIAC had reportedly resolved their data-sharing arrangements across the federal/state divide in a way that has not been achieved in other states:

> So it has worked very, very efficiently, especially in New South Wales where we implemented that. I understand it's not working as smoothly in each state and I suppose that's where it becomes difficult because when you're dealing with state bodies and dealing with federal bodies it's an inconsistent model from state to state.... Of course when you see Immigration's interactions with other federal agencies such as Centrelink and the AFP then there's a greater degree of consistency from state to state.
>
> *(Interview 47, Canberra DIAC)*

Through our examination of the considerable flow of data between agencies, migration policing is revealed to be about knowledge and risk communication to a large degree (Ericson and Haggerty 1997), with nodes in migration policing networks deployed to exchange information at both the individual and aggregate level. The flow of data between federal, state and local level agencies is not unimpeded, but is shaped by legal requirements, formal and informal practices, technical capacities and organisational interests, although the relative influence of each remains a matter for more detailed research.

Pooling resources, skills and powers

Recalling that nodes in security networks are conceptualised as sites of governance at which both knowledge and resources are mobilised (Burris *et al.* 2005), another way to analyse network dynamics is to identify the human, legal and financial resources that partner organisations are able to contribute. Almost without exception, the agency representatives interviewed for the migration policing study felt that joint operations could be of benefit in terms of advancing their own organisational goals, or supporting a whole-of-government effort. Police in rural areas appeared to be keenly aware of the additional resources that could be mobilised by involving DIAC compliance officers in police-led operations:

If we are running an operation that's based on detecting drugs … and then we get tied up with half a dozen non-lawful citizens, it takes our police off the road…. Whereas if Immigration are there [t]hey take over the unlawful citizen aspect straight away, and our police can be back focused on … on the policing issues of removing the drugs.

(Interview 24, NSW Police Force Local Area Commander)

A federal police officer interviewed for this study claimed that DIAC might be invited to participate in AFP operations in cases where unlawful non-citizens might be encountered, not because of any particular powers they exercise, but because of their training in making administrative decisions based on migration law:

It's not the detaining power, it's the visa power, the visa issue. Are these people going to be detained and sent to Villawood, or are they going to be given a bridging visa, or what's going to happen with them, essentially?

(Interview 66, AFP)

The informant from the taxation office also claimed their officers have suffi-cient powers to conduct their own operations, including the use of coercion where necessary – for example, in order to seize documents. However, as in DIAC, their investigative officers are not trained to a high level in these func-tions, so police might be relied upon in atypical cases where the use of force is anticipated:

Well, we can say, here is our powers. We are exercising those powers, we are going into that back room, we are going to look for a second set of books…. And we have done a few raids like that around tax agents doing the wrong thing. Usually it is planned, like, weeks ahead, and usually we will take federal police along because they can break in the doors and stuff. We can't … [Interviewer: *But it sounds like you have got the powers to do that?*] That's right. We have got a very wide range of powers.

(Interview 60, ATO)

Overall, in relation to joint operations, police were said to bring particular occupational skills, such as securing a location, pursuing targets, keeping the peace, use of force, forced entry and evidence gathering:

These Commonwealth officers, they would have the relevant authority to execute the order, but we just go along to assist more or less as a tool … if they wouldn't open the door, or things turned into a siege, or we got through the door and they were hanging off the balcony, or they were going to jump over the balcony to their death. All those sorts of things, and it hap-pens. So there are about a hundred good reasons to take the cops along.

(Interview 23, NSW Police Force Local Area Commander)

Pooling skills and resources is not the only benefit to be gained from inter-agency working. It was clear from the interviews that joint operations can provide an opportunity to pool legal powers in ways that enable the participating agencies to considerably extend their reach. The informants from migration policing agencies generally reported that they have sufficient powers to achieve their goals, and that they rely on partners for the skills they can contribute. However, in all cases, the application of powers is limited to specific purposes set out in legislation. As previously discussed, DIAC can request information from other agencies in respect of people who are reasonably suspected of being unlawful non-citizens, and police may do the same in relation to criminal investigations. Police or DIAC officers may enter premises to search for specified types of evidence under similar limitations, while other agencies, such as local councils, may be authorised to enter on different grounds – for example, to monitor compliance with planning regulations. It is not suggested that the practices of government officers on the ground are completely rule governed. Everyday experience and a considerable body of scholarship on discretion reveal otherwise. Nevertheless, senior officials, at least, are mindful of the legal limits placed on their organisations and the implications this has for the legitimacy of their actions. Joint operations provide an opportunity to pool legal powers in creative ways that can be legally justified, in order to open up new fronts in regulatory and enforcement practice.

The AFP's unique powers in relation to telephone intercepts and surveil-lance devices, for example, could be a valuable asset: 'If it becomes evident that those are needed then we'll take the job on. If not, Immigration usually deal with it' (Interview 66, AFP). Taxi operations are another example in which the NSW Police Force or the Department of Transport will take the lead 'because they are the agencies that specifically have the power and the authority to request those vehicles to pull over' (Interview 47, Canberra DIAC). Stopping vehicles is not an option for DIAC, this officer explained, because 'whilst we could obtain a search warrant to pull over a vehicle and search it, we'd have to have a reasonable cause to believe that the person or document that we can identify may be located in the vehicle'. In turn, rural police reported that they depend on the powers of the RTA to stop vehicles for compliance inspections at roadblocks (a context in which their own powers are apparently less appro-priate), which can then trigger their own investigations for drugs, and possibly identify unlawful non-citizens as a consequence (Interview 24, NSW Police Force Local Area Commander).

Since state and federal police are designated officers under the Migration Act they are theoretically entitled to apply any of the powers contained in that Act. This raises questions about which powers police are relying upon when they accompany DIAC on immigration-related tasks, such as the execution of internal DIAC war-rants in 'high-risk' compliance cases. In the interviews, all parties were clear that it is DIAC officers who execute the warrant in these contexts, with police providing security and sometimes a custody service. Tensions could arise, however, where operating under the auspices of a DIAC warrant placed greater constraints on police than they would normally exercise under police warrants:

> If you think there are drugs or weapons on the premises and you would ordinarily need a warrant, you will still need to seek a warrant through your own processes because you won't be covered by ours for those specific actions.
>
> *(Interview 47, Canberra DIAC)*

However, he added, this did not restrict police from exercising their own powers where the need arises 'if they can access them'.

In the reverse situation, where DIAC officers accompany police on a police-led operation, immigration officers (who are not authorised officers under any policing legislation) attend on the basis of 'consent', highlighting another grey area in relation to legal powers in an inter-agency setting:

> It would be a different matter if we were accompanying the police under a 3E warrant[3] and it was their warrant. In that instance we would be the second party to the warrant. It's their job, it's their warrant, they are in control and they are exercising their powers and we would probably be coming along as a matter of consent perhaps of the occupier.
>
> *(Interview 47, Canberra DIAC)*

Likewise, representatives of other partner agencies who are not designated officers under the Migration Act have to resort to obtaining entry by 'consent' when accompanying DIAC on operations covered by DIAC warrants:

> [Officer 1] Yeah, like if we enter a premises using a search warrant under our powers, it doesn't allow Centrelink to come in right behind us holding on to our coat tails. [Officer 2] But we can ask the owners or managers ... [Officer 1] But we would inform the owner or manager that Centrelink are with us and that – and could they speak to the Centrelink officer. And Centrelink would then request their approval to enter. [Interviewer: *And if it's denied, do they just have to wait outside?*] [Officer 1] Well, they just stand outside.
>
> *(Interview 48, Sydney DIAC)*

The AFP also reported using their warrants under the federal Crimes Act in order to assist DIAC. Crimes Act warrants authorise the seizure of evidence and do not depend on demonstrating a likelihood of encountering unlawful non-citizens:

> Well, occasionally Immigration will have investigations where they require search warrants to be executed, so we'll go out to execute them on their behalf because they don't have that power. [Interviewer: *They don't have a search warrant power?*] They can apply for a search warrant [under the Crimes Act] but the

search warrant is issued to a member of the AFP.... [Interviewer: *They obviously have a warrant that they're quite able to execute on their own*] ... They have a compliance warrant, which is essentially a warrant to enable them to go in and search for unlawfuls if they know they're there. It's been quite strict these days.

(Interview 66, AFP)

Gaps in legal authority were sometimes seen to threaten the legitimacy of joint operations. In one operation that was led by state police, local council powers were being relied upon to gain entry in a situation where the council officer doubted that there were valid grounds:

The reason that Council was there was because [the police] believed that we had the ability to gain access to the properties without obtaining a warrant. The police were also in that situation, that they had no evidence of anything criminal going on.... In reality we shouldn't have been going back to these premises unless there was new evidence to suggest that something had occurred.... The thing is that we do actually have more powers of entry than a police officer. So you have the situation where the Department of Immigration were actually standing at the door, and were quite mindful of their legal obligations, and just wouldn't enter the property.

(Interview 10, Local Council)

This description bears some similarities to the characterisation of third party policing by Mazerolle and Ransley (2006: 63): 'These police are simply "flying by the seat of their pants," there is no script for them to follow, no police department policy that they are working within, and generally very little accountability for their actions.' Inter-agency collaboration creates an entrepreneurial environment in which individual agencies can tap into the skills, resources and legal powers of partner agencies to pursue their own organisational goals. But the mobilisation of these resources across migration policing networks also raises problems related to coordination, accountability and the accommodation of different agency norms and objectives.

Network relations

As David Garland has observed, techniques of 'government-at-a-distance' raise significant new problems for states, since '[p]ower is not a matter of imposing a sovereign will, but instead a process of enlisting the cooperation of chains of actors who "translate" power from one locale to another' (Garland 1997: 182). The different actors in the chain have independent agency and may inject their own personal or institutional preferences into the process. Networked governance therefore entails an ongoing problematic of enlisting and retaining cooperation towards achieving a goal that may or may not be universally shared. Individual nodes within migration policing networks maintain their own organisational or sub-organisational objectives, and tend to cooperate in the identification of unlawful non-citizens out of a general commitment to a whole-of-government approach or whenever more specific 'shared risks' are identified. Outlining the techniques used to foster active cooperation within migration policing networks, overcome barriers and accommodate conflicts of interest is the task of this section.

Merging mentalities

The cooperation of other government departments is achieved by DIAC largely through techniques of persuasion that mobilise shared objectives. These techniques may be supplemented or regulated by recourse to law, such as the requirement under s 18 of the Migration Act for other agencies to provide information about suspected unlawful non-citizens to DIAC. Rather than acting from a shared commitment to border control, the government and non-government actors who participate in migration policing networks maintain distinct organisational objectives that sometimes converge in the identification of unlawful non-citizens, as depicted in Figure 7.1 below.

FIGURE 7.1 Overlapping targets for migration policing.

The following statement given by DIAC compliance officers illustrates how officers navigate the organisational objectives of other agencies to identify suitable partners:

> [Interviewer: *Under what circumstances do you decide to involve other agencies?*] [Officer 1] Based on risk.... [Officer 2] And also ... [Officer 1] and information ... [Officer 3] Information sharing. [Officer 1] We may consider [that] Centrelink would be useful to take with us, or the Tax Office. [Officer 3] Workcover sometimes. [Officer 1] Yeah, depending on the information, and that [the unlawful non-citizen] may be of interest to them as well. So instead of us going in one day and them going in another, all go together.... Because, clearly, a lot of the places we go to are ... [Officer 2] Cash. [Officer 3] Cash, yeah. [Officer 1] ... you know, a lot of unlawful non-citizens are actually paid cash in hand and that. And the Tax Office will clearly have [an] interest in those businesses. [Officer 2] And if we get allegations about trafficking then we obviously contact the AFP too – and they may want to come with us.
>
> *(Interview 48, Sydney DIAC)*

Once joint operations are underway, individual organisations continue to pursue their own interests:

> Usually we go along because if people like Centrelink and DIAC go along they will be looking for their own things, whereas for tax purposes we are looking for a second set of books, invoices, whatever, anything like that which will help establish what income is being undeclared.
>
> *(Interview 60, ATO)*

Despite these persisting differences in objective, one senior DIAC official argued that a new cross-agency perspective on compliance is emerging, in which government agencies recognise that multiple forms of non-compliance might be co-located: '[T]here's starting to be a different way of thinking which is ... you know fulfilling their visa requirements and making sure that people comply in the broader sense with the tax model or the welfare model or whatever else' (Interview 44, Canberra DIAC). This way of thinking was framed in terms of a whole-of-government approach, whereby organisational goals are not subverted to some overarching world view, but rather a diversity of objectives co-exist within the same operation:

> Well, the benefit of the joint operation is, as I mentioned earlier, the whole-of-government approach. So you have got every agency looking at their own specialist area. So Council will look at the licensing law approval provisions of the operating consents of brothels. The police are looking at criminal matters ... weapons and drugs found on premises. DIAC officers are obviously concerned with unlawful non-citizens or serious visa

breaches, both by the sex workers and the operators utilising the services. Fire brigade – serious fire safety issues. Centrelink … many brothels have sex workers who tend to earn significant amounts of cash on a weekly basis, however, still want to receive various social security benefits, including sole parent's pension … and obviously the Tax Office. Our understanding is that there are cases of serious non-compliance of tax laws by some of these brothels and massage parlours.

(Interview 61, Local Council)

In many cases, the incentives that shape organisational priorities are explicitly articulated, and may either be aligned or at odds with activities that contribute to the identification of unlawful non-citizens. These incentives might take the form of targets set by management or government, financial costs or rewards, or the pressure of public opinion. While it might be expected that performance measures for DIAC compliance officers would encourage the identification of unlawful non-citizens, the DIAC employees interviewed for this study insisted that the explicit quantitative incentives set by the previous administration were no longer in place and that political expectations in the post-Palmer era had shifted the agenda away from encouraging detention and summary removal and towards resolution of immigration status where possible. However, the strong focus on visa compliance still creates a powerful incentive to identify non-compliant individuals, guided by the hierarchy of enforcement targets set out in the Priorities Matrix (discussed in Chapter 3). The approval with which increases in locations and departures of non-compliant individuals are reported in departmental annual reports also suggests that the core business of the DIAC Compliance Office remains the identification of unlawful non-citizens.

Very different political priorities were identified by state-level police. For example, an officer from Commuter Crime commented:

Our main focus is the reduction of crime, and we have under our State Plan specific goals in relation to assaults and robberies, alcohol-related crime, anti-social behaviour. They are the things that we are actually looking at to reduce on the transport infrastructure, and if we can show marked improvements there, that is our biggest kick.

(Interview 22, NSW Police Force Commuter Crime Unit)

This means that the detection of unlawful non-citizens is likely to remain a largely opportunistic matter for police, although individual officers may well differ in the enthusiasm with which they pursue this task. From a police perspective, the results of taxi operations are the identification of defects, licensing issues or general traffic infringements. However, the value of joint operations might be less apparent for generalist sections of the organisation that have a range of other more pressing priorities:

I am looking at some priorities for criminal activities that could impact on people's safety. So immigration to me is way down the list. However, if an immigration officer walks through the door and says, 'Listen, we have got a major problem, we have identified a pool of illegal immigrants at location X, and that has been going on for some time', that would probably change the priority status of it. I am waiting, but I could be here for another five years.

(Interview 6, NSW Police Force Local Area Commander)

On the other hand, a senior NSW police officer with responsibility for serious crime had nothing but praise for the cooperation she had received from DIAC:

It works beautifully. I have to say in all the years we have been working together it has been a fantastic partnership. Customs are the same.... It seems to be that we are all working for the common cause, and it is certainly done on collaboration, as in 'Look we are going to do all of the karaoke bars.' And we know that we are going to load them up with a whole lot of work, and they are more than happy to come. They are fantastic.

(Interview 36, NSW Police Force Headquarters)

The federal police also reported good working relations, but clearly retained a focus on their own priorities – and the limits of their statutory powers – while working on joint operations with DIAC:

Effectively, when Immigration go in they're looking for unlawfuls. For example, if there's a brothel where I think human trafficking is going on, Immigration really want me to show that there could be potentially someone unlawfully there before they'll go in under their powers.... We'll do it from a human trafficking perspective but not from an unlawful perspective. I'll ask Immigration on any of my warrants – I'll have Immigration there because of the unlawful factor. I'm looking at human trafficking and they're tagging along for unlawfuls.

(Interview 65, AFP)

Aside from joint operations, agencies may participate in migration policing networks by sending information about unlawful non-citizens to DIAC, either on request or via voluntary 'referrals'. As discussed earlier, voluntary exchanges are usually motivated by organisational objectives, often related to fraud control and checking an individual's entitlement to services: 'For example, [the] RTA has on their forms that you need to provide evidence and if there is a case where a client's unlawful or they think they are, they'll ring us' (Interview 49, Sydney DIAC). In other cases, the willingness to report suspected unlawful non-citizens to DIAC might be driven by a commitment to a whole-of-government approach: '[W]e take a whole-of-government approach.... Our role isn't to enforce immigration offences, but we will provide assistance and intelligence ... to assist them to fulfil their obligations' (Interview 62, Centrelink).

Sometimes the main advantages of cooperating with DIAC are very specific to an agency's core business:

Mainly it allows us to classify somebody to a jail that would be appropriate for their escape risk. But also it would allow us to, if they are required for removal from Australia, or Immigration sometimes interview them prior to release and then we can have them close to where Immigration will want to see them or pick them up … it just allows us to plan a bit better.

(Interview 59, DCS)

A strong financial incentive exists for DIAC to maintain close communication with the prisons system. As the DCS informant stated, DIAC is charged $200 for every day that a time-served prisoner remains in custody pending their removal under Migration Act powers only. However, financial incentives are not often apparent as a factor influencing the dynamics of migration policing networks, owing to the apparent lack of cross-charging in operational contexts, as noted earlier. But some informants identified a different type of 'cost' that could arise from a failure to cooperate with immigration authorities:

It is not really our role to inform Immigration. We sort of feel that it is, we are just assisting, mainly for our own benefit rather than because we care about the Department of Immigration. I think we are perhaps sensitive of being, getting adverse media publicity by releasing … we are the ones who will be criticised if somebody gets out who should have been deported, when it's really not our job. That's where our response is, so we don't cop the criticism.

(Interview 59, DCS)

The discussion so far has examined the motivations for government departments other than DIAC to direct some of their resources towards the identification of unlawful non-citizens. The main non-government actors identifiable in migration policing networks, besides members of the general public, are commercial or quasi-commercial enterprises such as education providers and employers, who take on a migration policing role in response to negative, rather than positive, incentives imposed by law, as discussed in Chapter 6. However, the incentive structures in these cases are not clear-cut. While it could be argued that reporting non-compliant students might be in conflict with both the pedagogical and commercial aims of universities and colleges, a major national body representing students has actively lobbied for education providers to take greater responsibility for visa monitoring, in the belief that it is possible for the educational and welfare interests of students to be merged through the mentality of visa compliance:

From a student's point of view, why should the institution want to do that because it's really my own business. But again, from our point of view … our aim of having that in place is so that the institution would really care for the student's progress. And if you know that the student isn't doing well for the first semester, you should actually have some procedure in place.

(Interview 57, Student Representative)

Finally, members of the public play a significant role in reporting suspected non-citizens to the DIAC dob-in line on a completely voluntary basis. While there is no authority for cash rewards to be offered to informants, the promise of anonymity increases the likelihood of suspicions being reported in so far as it removes the risk of ongoing entanglement with authorities or other personal costs. Although there have been no high-profile campaigns exhorting members of the public to report suspected unlawful non-citizens, the ministerial statements that accompanied the launch of the dob-in line played on a sense of civic mindedness by portraying those who work without legal entitlement as threatening the livelihoods of legitimate others. The fact that other government agencies have noted a similar readiness among members of the public to report suspected fraudsters and cheats suggests that the preoccupation of neoliberal governments with pursuing fraud, while containing spending on welfare and public services, may be exerting a general responsibilising pressure.

Fragmentation and resistance

The inter-agency relationships identified from the research interviews were generally said to be positive. But network dynamics do not always present a picture of seamless cooperation, especially when viewed from an operational level. As noted by Garland (1997: 182), '[t]he process always entails activity on the part of the "subjects of power" and it therefore has built into it the probability that outcomes will be shaped by the resistance or private objectives of those acting down the line'. Points of resistance within migration policing networks were most clearly discernible in relation to differences in organisational culture, sometimes coupled with personal values. This sort of tension was immediately apparent between the goals and methods of NSW state police, and the occupational values of one of the local council officers interviewed for the migration policing study:

> Realistically it's not our role to do that, to get involved in accusing people of – or even making that assumption that they are illegals or not.... There is an expectation from the police in particular that they receive our information in inverted commas 'for free'. I'm very mindful of the privacy issues working for a council and not giving that information out unless it has been requested from appropriate channels.
>
> *(Interview 10, Local Council)*

As reported in the previous chapter, this officer had been involved in large-scale operations led by local police, and was clearly uneasy with the arrangements. He described some of the tactics suggested by police, such as closing off the targeted location and questioning everyone present, as 'exposing some of these people who have come from fairly harsh kinds of backgrounds' to unnecessarily hostile treatment. He also claimed that there were 'some major reservations there in terms of – number one – the lack of evidence, and the lack of procedural process, from the police point of view' (Interview 10, Local Council). This officer's accounts of his experience with DIAC were no more positive: 'I'd be honest in saying that they are probably more of an interference, more of a hindrance than a help. Because they appear not to have their act together, for something as serious as what they have been promoting' (Interview 10, Local Council). In contrast to the perspective of this council employee, who deplored what he saw as 'fishing expeditions' and a 'scattergun approach', an officer from a different local council, whose role was focused on the regulation of brothels, perceived a closer alignment with the goals and methods of his major migration policing partners:

> My view is that Council perhaps has an onus and a duty of care, not only to the employees, the sex workers of these premises, but also perhaps to the patrons of these premises. Given that it is a recognised and lawful business activity in the state of New South Wales, activities conducted within the premises are conducted in a safe manner where persons are safe from disease or the threat of harm or other crime. And equally I think there is an obligation to detect persons who aren't entitled to be working in the premises, or persons who are working in the premises who are there under duress. So I have that view, and the work we have conducted essentially reflects that view. And that view is synchronising and certainly in tune with DIAC and the police and the other agencies.
>
> *(Interview 61, Local Council)*

In turn, DIAC's procedures were viewed at times with considerable scepticism by police, not least because DIAC is able to 'type out' its own warrants with no scrutiny from the courts (Interview 11, NSW Police Force Commuter Crime Unit). The pressures of engaging in inter-agency operations also throw up tensions between police and DIAC in relation to their respective organisational norms and procedures:

> There's quite significant differences in the way that the police will exercise their powers when exercising a warrant … [We] have to educate them I suppose as to the department's restrictions within our legislation, but more important our policy outlook. Our interactions with clients are fundamentally different to police interactions with their clients. Where the police may be dealing with an offender or offenders who are suspected or are known to have committed a criminal offence, we are dealing with clients who we're seeking to arrive at an administrative outcome.… Whilst there is no doubt that the legislation provides us with some very specific and powerful authority in certain matters, the exercising of those powers is always considered as a last resort and we will always seek the client's cooperation in the first instance.
>
> *(Interview 47, Canberra DIAC)*

This complexity necessitated cross-agency briefings which were said to occur prior to all joint operations:

> In the event that it is a large operation, we'll have the operational orders drawn up. [In] any warrant applications [it] would be identified which parties will be participating within the operation. In the operational orders it will be outlined not only which parties are assisting in the operation but what their individual roles and responsibilities for the operation will be. It will make it clear to every single person operating on that particular visit or job what their role is, what functions they're required to undertake and what the limitations for their powers are.
>
> *(Interview 47, Canberra DIAC)*

One local area commander suggested that police presence during the execution of Migration Act warrants adds an element of accountability to the process, because of their greater experience in being scrutinised in relation to the execution of their own warrants (Interview 23, NSW Police Force Local Area Commander). Other observers did not always agree:

> On one of the inspections that we did, I was walking with one of the detectives, and the uniformed police had got to the door of this premises that we had identified before us, and I recall a conversation between the detective, who was the senior officer there, calling over one of the other constables, and saying, before entering the premises, 'Did you actually caution the people?' And the reply was that 'No, the door was just open and we just walked in.' And the detective had the same perplexed look as myself, because it's just a basic requirement for even a council officer, that you present yourself, you present your ID card, you announce what you are there for, because realistically all of that evidence is inadmissible.
>
> *(Interview 10, Local Council)*

Even where there is initial enthusiasm for participation in migration policing networks, there were some indications from the interviews that agencies could experience a sense of diminishing returns over time:

> So we get the intel but we tend not to attend because it wasn't as much benefit as we thought … after you have done [it] a few times you tend to clean out the people doing the wrong thing. So [there are] diminishing returns after a while.
>
> *(Interview 60, ATO)*

Although the research revealed no signs that NSW police are contemplating withdrawing their support for joint operations, individual police sometimes questioned the benefits of their involvement in migration policing. In many cases, exemplified by the statement below, this disgruntlement was a direct result of the post-Palmer reforms, which were viewed by police as placing frustrating hurdles in the way of achieving policing outcomes through immigration enforcement (see also Chapter 5):

> It used to be clear-cut – if they were illegal they would take them away. Now it takes a long time and they may be given a bridging visa, so there's no outcome. They're moving away from a draconian approach to trying to resolve the situation – not sure if they're being nice or just can't cope with the numbers. It's frustrating for police. The policies sound nice – the practical realities are different. We spent a lot of time, around six hours, for a 55-year-old woman found with no train ticket, who was identified as an unlawful non-citizen, then no result.
>
> *(Interview 11, NSW Police Force Commuter Crime Unit)*

Although the idea of a friendlier, less enforcement-orientated DIAC may not always ring true in the experience of legal representatives, refugee supporters and human rights campaigners, the view expressed above was also endorsed by the federal police:

> 'People are our business' is what they say, so people come first for them and it's more of a client services – not to upset people. They like to serve people and get things done. Which is where it's different from us. We're trying to prosecute, eliminate security threats and things like that, whereas they're trying to bring people in or assist people coming in and admitting people ... I suppose policing's very black and white, you know. This person's doing this, can we get them removed. And Immigration come in and say, 'Well, no, because of this, this, this and this. They've got legal rights which is this, this and this, and they can appeal'. And the process can drag out.
>
> *(Interview 66, AFP)*

Conflicts in organisational aims and methods have also been noted by independent commentators – for example, in relation to the expectation that education providers will monitor compliance with the international student visa system:

> A gulf exists between the education system which views student participation and progress as primarily matters of educational judgement, and DIMIA which views them as facets of visa control. Given their different goals and cultures, a tension is inevitable, but it has been unnecessarily exacerbated by the lack of specificity in the Code.
>
> *(Phillips KPA and Lifelong Learning Associates 2005: 152)*

This assessment was made before changes to the ESOS Act and associated code were introduced in 2007. The visa monitoring requirements set out in the ESOS Act were not accepted without question by the university sector. According to a 2006 media report, the Australian Vice-Chancellor's Committee rejected the initial code of practice which would have required information on international students to be sent by education providers to DIAC every six weeks, saying that the measures would 'damage their international reputation' (ABC News 2006). The 2005 review of the ESOS Act noted with respect to reporting of attendance or performance breaches that:

> Providers would strongly resist a requirement for immediate reporting on the grounds that decisions about completion of course requirements are educational matters, not immigration matters, and it can be genuinely impossible to determine whether a student is progressing satisfactorily or not till the end of the semester. They would also resist such a requirement on equity grounds (vis-à-vis domestic students), and because of the new, additional bureaucratic complexities this requirement would create.
>
> *(Phillips KPA and Lifelong Learning Associates 2005: 173)*

Commercial considerations can also lead organisations tasked with monitoring visa compliance to undermine DIAC procedures. Some education providers who were 'of concern' to DIAC at the time of the 2005 evaluation of the ESOS Act were believed to manipulate student records to conceal non-attendance. It was also argued that sympathy for the plight of struggling students motivated hesitance to report their failure to progress, with delays in reporting deliberately intended to give these students the opportunity to transfer courses or access support (Phillips KPA and Lifelong Learning Associates 2005). Different organisational priorities and perspectives have also affected the dynamic between the education regulator DEEWR, and DIAC:

> If you look at it from a whole-of-government approach we are, I guess, working towards the same objective. However, it is difficult because obviously DIAC has their DIAC hat on and see it from a certain mechanism. And the other thing that is complicating is [that] DIAC are student visa based, we are enrolment based. So we come at it, we have different hats and we come at it from different perspectives.
>
> *(Interview 64, DEEWR)*

One university-based student adviser complained that DIAC and the DEEWR 'didn't really talk to each other that much', and had attended training sessions at which representatives of the two departments argued openly with each other.'

Tensions and differences of perspective arise not only between different agencies, but also between different sections of unwieldy federal bureaucracies. A council officer complained that he was 'not overly excited' about getting calls from DIAC about joint operations, noting 'some kind of friction between investigators from Canberra and their contemporaries from the Sydney office' (Interview 10, Local Council). A research participant from the DCS highlighted poor internal communication within DIAC as one of the main difficulties with inter-departmental working (Interview 59, DCS). Senior DIAC officers also complained about a lack of national coordination within the agency:

> There's no national perspective [so] we could have something happening in one part of the country ... well, happening all over the country, but we would have different pieces of the jigsaw, which are never put together and it's clearly a weakness.
>
> *(Interview 44, Canberra DIAC)*

Indeed, the DIAC informants sometimes viewed their own federal structure as a network. For example, one Canberra-based official argued that a major aim of the Integrated Business Model (see Chapter 3) is to provide consistency in practice across the states, concluding that '[t]hen it'll be consistent across the network' (Interview 43, Canberra DIAC).

Although DIAC has invested heavily in improved IT in the post-Palmer era, shortfalls in IT capacity nevertheless create points of practical resistance in managing the flow of information across migration policing networks:

> For us, our entire system is [that] we deal with international students. But for [DIAC] you know they have got a vast number of systems that support them, and also quite archaic systems. So implementing change through their systems is quite difficult, while we can respond more immediately to the system changes ... I think there is probably a lot of capacity to look at streamlining.
>
> *(Interview 64, DEEWR)*

A similar lack of connectivity was observed by informants from several agencies that exchange information on a regular basis with DIAC:

> So we don't really have a centralised government database.... As soon as somebody came on, if they were on a visa, if they would generate an alert to Immigration, but it doesn't work that way.... We have been involved in some basic stages of sharing information with the courts and the police, sharing justice information, but it would involve either us having a new computer system, the police having a new computer system, or the courts, and none of us want to give up what we are used to, and the government's not going to fork out for a whole new one.
>
> *(Interview 59, DCS)*

With identity the lynch pin in any electronic tracking system, it is often minor differences in the recording of individual identity, or the deliberate provision of false identity, that disrupts the connections between agencies:

> You know, the system works if the customer has given everything exactly the same, then the systems can talk to each other. So a lot of the customers are 'El'

something or 'Al' something, you know, whatever. So on Centrelink records they have an 'Al hyphen' and something, and on DIAC they have 'Al' without a hyphen – it won't match.... That's exactly the same for [the] RTA as well. We have a link to the RTA as well because you know all our pensioners, they are entitled to a pensioner concession for rego [car registration] and things like that. So if they have one simple space, not even a hyphen, a space there, then that won't match.

(Interview 9, Centrelink)

Information that is potentially of interest to DIAC might not even be recorded for reasons specific to the agency holding the data, such as this example given by the ATO:

Yeah, I guess the scary thing is sometimes we will go, 'Oh they have gone overseas so we won't even bother putting the debt on'. Because if you put the debt on the system all it does is it would raise the level of debt owed to the Australian Government which is not something that we want to do. It doesn't look good, and secondly it doesn't achieve anything if they are never going to come back to Australia. But unless you put a debt on the system, DIAC probably don't know that they left without paying their tax.

(Interview 60, ATO)

As they stood at the time the fieldwork for this study was completed, migration policing networks in NSW, although aspiring to greater connectivity, were characterised by personal and inter-agency resistances, technical barriers and legal constraints. As Van der Leun noted in her study of migration policing in the Netherlands:

[I]mplementation of internal migration control measures hinges on a pluralistic and multi-layered system of actors who have their own deliberations and professional considerations. Therefore it is not realistic to suggest that these actors can simply be controlled from a distance.

(Van der Leun 2003: 173)

However, in Australia considerable efforts are in train to smooth out the process of translating power across locations motivated by a 'whole-of-government' mindset.

8

PATROLLING THE BOUNDARIES OF ENTITLEMENT AND BELONGING

Key migration policing themes

The normalisation of the police role in immigration enforcement

The checking of immigration status by police in NSW operates as an everyday adjunct to the policing of public order. Street policing in the state is increasingly driven by the proactive targeting of risky people and places, on-the-spot identity checks aimed at gathering intelligence and classifying individuals into risk categories, and the development of new information technologies to facilitate an expanding range of checks. Immigration checks are also widely seen as a normal part of criminal investigations or background checking in relation to crime victims or suspects who may be non-citizens. On the basis of the survey and interview data captured in the migration policing study, it seems that actively detecting unlawful non-citizens is not a major imperative for police, at either the managerial or operational level. However, conducting immigration checks may provide a means to achieve other policing objectives, such as verifying identity in order to serve warrants or issue on-the-spot fines, obtaining information about the whereabouts of criminal suspects at particular times (for example, whether they are inside or outside Australia), or verifying the accounts provided by individuals who present as victims of immigration-related crimes (see Chapter 4). The low 'success rate' reported in Chapter 3 of around 13 per cent of police checks which identify unlawful non-citizens (see Figure 3.2) may therefore not reflect all the operational benefits to police of using the status checking system.

On the face of it, the Migration Act gives police a licence to stop and question non-citizens in the absence of any suspicion in a manner that has no parallel for Australian citizens. The legal boundary of 'secure belonging', to use Loader's evocative term (Loader 2006), is therefore drawn firmly around citizens rather than lawful residents, although no bright line separates citizens from non-citizens in terms of perceptual cues available to police. The police informants all argued that immigration checks would *always* be secondary to other matters that might catch their attention. They claimed that checks would be triggered most often by a sense that individuals are 'out of place' once questioning had begun, and would not be initiated purely on the basis of ethnicity or appearance. The history of the policing of Indigenous people in NSW (see, for example, Cunneen 2001), and some of the responses to the operational police survey in this research, suggests that racialised bases for street stops cannot be so readily discounted. It was apparent from the police survey that many officers are not aware that they are using Migration Act powers when conducting immigration checks. It is therefore likely that, as senior police attest, immigration checking is deeply embedded within ordinary street policing and investigative practices, for which police already have ample powers (actual or imputed) to approach and question individuals in public places or to obtain information from other agencies.

The NSW Police Force sometimes initiates multi-agency operations involving DIAC, in which it is expected that unlawful non-citizens will be identified. But the police interest is said to be *always* in detecting crime or gathering criminal intelligence. The exception is when police accompany immigration authorities on DIAC-led joint operations or help to execute 'high-risk' Migration Act warrants – scenarios in which their role is primarily to maintain security and promote compliance. In these situations there is no obvious return for police other than maintaining good working relations across the federal/state divide. The historical role for Australian state police in maintaining order across a wide range of contexts, their current legal designation as officers under the Migration Act, and the non-uniformed, unarmed status of the DIAC compliance function all combine to bring this explicit migration policing work into the accepted remit of state police. While the attempted recruitment of police into immigration enforcement roles has been highly controversial in the US (Provine 2013) and UK (Weber and Bowling 2004), the casting of NSW state police as front-line definers of belonging and entitlement seems to fit quite comfortably with their historical role. Overall, it seems that immigration status may be becoming just another risk category for police in NSW – one that is not actively monitored as known offenders might be, but is available as a resource in the everyday pursuit of crime control and public order objectives.

Migration policing as a transnational move-on strategy

The use of immigration law as a resource to achieve general policing objectives is most apparent where police actively seek the removal of a criminal suspect – having identified that they are unlawfully present – by referring them to DIAC. This option was said to be preferred to pursuing a prosecution in situations where the alleged offence is relatively minor and/or the chance of criminal conviction is thought to be low. In these cases, police use immigration law as a 'legal lever' (Mazerolle and Ransley 2006). However, this is not a classic 'third party policing' scenario, since the lever is used directly against the target, rather than as a means to convince an otherwise reluctant third party to take action. In this case DIAC is the third party possessing the resources and authority to effect the removal, and is generally willing to do so. Additional safeguards introduced into DIAC practices after the wrongful detention and deportation of Australian citizens (discussed in Chapter 3) were perceived to have disrupted the previously smooth operation of this police 'referral' system. Nevertheless, the research interviews confirmed that 'getting rid' of problem people through administrative removal is likely to continue, and can be thought of as a transnational equivalent of the use of police 'move-on' powers to exclude troublesome individuals from public places, without pursuing criminal charges.

These practices have other similarities to third party policing in that civil remedies are recruited into the criminal justice arena. In this regard, the civil – or at least administrative – remedy is drawn from immigration law. This merging of immigration and criminal law also bears the hallmarks of the 'crimmigration thesis' (Stumpf 2006). One strand of the crimmigration thesis concerns the widening of the circumstances in which lawfully present non-citizens can be deported on the basis of criminal convictions. There is considerable evidence that this expansion has occurred in Australia, both in law and in practice (see Chapter 5), although the numbers deported are very small when compared with US figures or with other removal categories in Australia. Of particular interest to this study is the observation that police in NSW have actively participated in the construction of 'crimmigrants', for example, through their testimony to the AAT that Maria and Prince Brown were a danger to the community and should have their resident visas revoked (discussed in Chapter 5). In this case, the actions of the police reflect not only a crimmigration agenda, but arguably an 'enemy penology' mentality as well (Krasmann 2007), in which the physical exclusion of dangerous others is seen as a lasting and appropriate solution to local community safety problems. One senior officer lamented that the government's 'much softer approach' to visa cancellation 'does have a [negative] impact on serious crime' (Interview 18, NSW Police Force Local Area Commander), reflecting a belief that deporting crimmigrants is an effective approach to crime control.

However, in contrast to the administrative removal of unlawful non-citizens, there were no indications from the research that actively 'making people illegal' (Dauvergne 2008) would become an everyday strategy for police, if only because it had proven to be highly resource intensive. Seeking the cancellation of resident visas in relation to Prince and Maria Brown was said to be an exceptional case, driven by 'sheer frustration' with the court process and involving an element of 'political pressure' (Interview 18, NSW Police Force Local Area Commander). The 'talking up' of the visa cancellation in relation to this pair in the local media seems to have been designed to send a message to non-citizens of the possible consequences of engaging in criminal and anti-social behaviour, rather than reflecting a genuine intention to pursue criminal deportations as a regular policing strategy. On the other hand, the case of a Tongan national accused of the very serious offence of murdering a police officer (*Taufahema v Minister for Immigration and Citizenship*

[2009] AATA 898) did ignite another police campaign for visa cancellation. Bostock (2011: 164) reports that, in a rare example of public unity between the NSW Police Commissioner and the Police Association that represents rank-and-file members, both parties wrote to the Immigration Minister exhorting the federal government to 'do everything within their power to make sure that this guy does not become or remain an Australian citizen', adding that he was 'not a good character. He doesn't deserve to stay here'. While these practices appear to be isolated events at present, they reflect a desire by police to influence not only how the community is policed, but also how it is constituted.

Although police are not usually the main instigators of criminal deportations, the Priorities Matrix that guides DIAC compliance work classifies the expulsion of convicted non-citizens and all 'police referrals' as 'mandatory work' (see Appendix 3). This reflects a political will to ensure the continuing expulsion of this high-risk group, as does the establishment of a dedicated national unit to consider visa cancellations on character grounds. While the government has not announced publicly any explicit removal targets, Figure 5.1 shows that levels of visa cancellation on character grounds are rising and beginning to approach 2001 levels. Cross-agency systems for routinely identifying non-citizens who meet the legislated criteria for visa cancellation were also being pursued by DIAC at the time the migration policing study was completed (discussed in Chapter 6). On the other hand, the issuing of new s 501 operating instructions that require greater consideration to be given to mitigating circumstances has resulted in more cancellations being set aside on appeal. But Bostock (2011) reports that the Immigration Minister responded to these circumstances by increasing his exercise of executive powers to cancel permanent visas without possibility of review. Further evidence of the political enthusiasm for character deportation was provided in the aftermath of clashes in Sydney in 2012 between police and 'Muslim protestors' incensed about the circulation of the offensive video mocking the Prophet. Immigration Minister Chris Bowen appeared on national television that evening declaring the events to be 'just criminal behaviour, nothing short of that', and threatening to cancel the visas of any non-citizens against whom criminal charges were brought (Cullen 2012). He was forced to publicly retreat after the Police Commissioner pointed out that criminal behaviour is a matter for the independent prosecuting authorities, signalling that the crimmigration domain remains a zone of contested jurisdiction.

Creating a ubiquitous border

While street policing and immigration raids represent the overt face of immigration enforcement, the internal border has also gone underground. The growing interconnectivity of official databases has enabled immigration checks to be embedded at the points of public access to essential services (see Chapter 6). As Rose (2000: 326) has argued in relation to asocial forms of regulation more generally, the embedded border operates through a variety of 'switch point(s)' that must be 'passed in order to access the benefits of liberty'. The intention has been two-fold: to directly detect individuals marked for exclusion through inter-agency data exchange, and also to exclude individuals from the essentials of a liveable life, so that 'voluntary' reporting to authorities is achieved indirectly through a process of attrition.

In this study, immigration status checking was found to occur across a wide range of service providers, including social security, higher education and health services. The recruitment of government agencies into overt migration policing practices has exploited overlapping organisational objectives between the agencies (see Figure 7.1) or relied on a general commitment to 'whole-of-government' approaches to obtain cooperation. The general public has also been recruited into migration policing roles – voluntarily, in the case of reports to the DIAC dob-in line; or under threat of criminal sanctions, in the case of employers. Employers have effectively been turned into 'place managers', to use Mazerolle and Ransley's terminology (2006: 62), performing both a labour regulation and a migration policing role. In similar fashion, universities and other educational institutions have been captured by a highly developed legislative and IT framework, in which they must operate as guardians over the legitimate use of international student visas. DIAC's own description of these arrangements resonates with the idea of third party policing: 'A continuing strategy has been the focus on intermediaries such as employers, migration agents, education providers and labour hire companies who can play a major role in helping people to adhere to migration law' (DIAC 2009: 122).

The purpose of these migration policing alliances has been two-fold. First, in line with the neoliberal preoccupation with preventing public fraud (Pratt 2005), the embedded border protects public resources and delineates the boundaries of entitlement to them. Second, although there is no legal requirement for any regulatory or service agency or individual to report suspected unlawful non-citizens to the authorities, the embedded border effectively defines the boundaries of belonging. This is so because attempts to access employment or services without authorisation can bring unlawful non-citizens to the notice of DIAC (through processes outlined in Chapters 3 and 6), and ultimately lead to their expulsion. The embedded border thus contributes to both the securitisation of the welfare and regulatory systems and the securitisation of territory. Moreover, the two functions are dynamically linked, since an inability to access essential goods and services, including employment, promotes 'voluntary' reporting to DIAC, either in an attempt to obtain a more secure immigration status, or as a gesture of capitulation in cases where life under the mantle of illegality has become unsustainable. For several years, DIAC's annual reports have noted with some satisfaction an increase in voluntary reporting, which is attributed to deliberate strategies to promote this form of self-policing.

Rose (2000) has noted that constituting the subjects of governance as freely choosing agents is a key technology of contemporary governance. He states:

> Although the problems addressed by these new strategies of control are varied, at their heart lies the problem of control in a 'free' society and hence the kinds of subjects that are imagined to inhabit and deserve such a society.
>
> *(Rose 2000: 337)*

Even so, the effort to promote apparent voluntarism among those who are destined for exclusion, and are not considered to 'deserve' such a society, is curious. It appears to fly in the face of Shearing and Wood's (2003: 414) assertion that the governance of communal spaces is characterised by 'a capacity for coercion and banishment' that is openly wielded against those who lack 'denizenship status', while 'strategies and technologies of governance that are subtle, embedded, risk-orientated, and non-coercive' are reserved for accepted members.

In the case of the embedded border, it seems that subtle and risk-oriented strategies, as well as openly coercive methods, are being applied to individuals who have no claim to denizenship status. Indeed, a senior police officer interviewed for the migration policing study argued that checks conducted by service providers was a less coercive option than reliance on police checks, claiming that Australia is 'not a nation where you are stopped and your papers are checked' (Interview 40, NSW Police Force Headquarters). Yet the creation of an effectively ubiquitous border, based on information-based surveillance and geared towards 'social sorting' in terms of access to the means to sustain a reasonable life, may have an even more profoundly excluding effect because of its deeper penetration into social life.

Networks and the decentring of the state

The migration policing study identified 'operational networks' in which resources, skills and legal powers are mobilised across nodes; 'informated networks' which operate through the exchange of electronic information; and 'strategic networks' which function at a national level with a view to coordinating cross-agency collaboration (see Chapter 7). In terms of their degree of integration, migration policing networks were either restricted to information exchange or involved joint action towards mutually defined objectives. These correspond to the 'communication' and 'cooperation' models described in Figure 1.1. Operational and informated networks are often ad hoc and time delimited; examples of such are one-off aggregate data-matching exercises, and location-based joint operations run by DIAC or the police. Strategic networks such as the Cash Economy Working Group and the Police–DIAC Practice Management Network show greater continuity over time. Operational networks may also be more enduring, such as the highly structured computerised system PRISMS, which allows for the exchange of information about international students between DIAC, educational institutions, and the regulatory body DEEWR; or regular 'taxi ops' conducted by state police, DIAC and other regulatory agencies according to a well-rehearsed script. Liaison officers embedded permanently in agencies other than their own can also act as migration policing nodes, where 'knowledge and capacity are mobilized for transmission' (Burris 2004, cited in Crawford 2006: 458).

DIAC remains the driving force behind most of these developments in migration policing. In fact, much of the networking identified in the study was limited to bilateral exchanges between DIAC and other agencies in the migration policing periphery. As has often been observed in relation to public scandals and the official inquiries that follow them, it could be argued that the Palmer Inquiry has provided an expanded space of governance for DIAC to occupy, and has delivered considerable public resources for new technologies to support the further development of the department's risk-based approach. Moreover, this reinvigorated migration policing landscape has promoted entrepreneurialism within the organisation (Pickering and Weber 2013). DIAC employees interviewed for the migration policing study reported working with other agencies to promote the collection of personal data in strategic ways that will enable its lawful disclosure in future, and pressing for changes to the legislation that would create new possibilities for intelligence exchange and data matching. Police have carved out a small entrepreneurial space for themselves in pressing for the removal and deportation of 'crimmigrants', but this agenda has been somewhat curtailed by the post-Palmer reforms and the limited due process procedures introduced under the Labor government (described in Chapter 3), which are widely perceived by police as impediments.

Responsibilising techniques used to recruit other government organisations include inter-agency awareness programmes and information technologies intended to shape the behaviour of organisational actors. The threat of sanctions – both civil and criminal – is reserved for more independent agents such as universities and employers. State agencies participate on the basis of 'overlapping organisational objectives' (see Figure 7.1), and the identification of unlawful non-citizens is only ever a secondary consideration for agencies other than DIAC. As argued by Garland (1997: 182), the governmental process 'has built into it the probability that outcomes will be shaped by the resistance or private objectives of those acting down the line'. While most inter-agency relationships were said to be good, the informants identified some points of resistance. Numerous police informants complained about what they saw as the 'softer' approach to enforcement taken by DIAC in removing individuals referred to them by police. On the other hand, one local area commander, who had concerns about the impact on community perceptions, wondered why police needed to do the 'dirty work' on DIAC-led operations that did not deliver a crime control benefit for police. One local council officer who regularly combines his regulatory powers with the powers and skills of police and DIAC was enthusiastic about the mutual benefits; yet an officer from a different council with a different role and background was disturbed about what he saw as the misapplication of his regulatory powers and was critical of the lack of professionalism of police that he had witnessed in the operations he had been involved in.

Information sharing is such a rapidly developing area that all government agencies were found to have specialist staff to interpret legislation, negotiate inter-agency agreements, act as organisational 'gatekeepers' and seek out externally held information requested by their co-workers. The flow of information about potential unlawful non-citizens, both within DIAC and across agencies, is now coordinated by Compliance Information Management Units located at the state level in major DIAC Compliance Offices. These units are becoming hubs for the detection of unlawful non-citizens through IT-based information networks, which are likely to expand. However, the picture that emerged from this study is not yet one of super-connectivity or 'total surveillance' (Lyon 2001). A web of privacy and disclosure rules still surrounds the exchange of personal data between agencies, although these rules will no doubt continue to be the target of entrepreneurial activity by DIAC and other agencies aimed at maximising the potential for data flows.

In line with the views of those who are sceptical about the 'decentring' of state power in real-world examples of nodal governance (see, for example, Crawford 2006), this research found migration policing networks to be largely driven by government border control imperatives and DIAC entrepreneurialism. Although some non-governmental nodes are being recruited into migration policing roles – whether willingly, unwittingly, or under duress – none of these actors could be identified as playing an 'auspice' role, to use the terminology of Wood and Shearing (2007). This is not surprising given that border control is primarily a national, rather than a local, concern (although local variations in implementing this national agenda clearly occur). While large corporations have an interest in influencing immigration policies such as visa quotas and conditions, it was not apparent that any organisation other than DIAC is directly investing in internal border control. At present, there are not even clear signs in Australia of a market-based approach in the business of *detecting* unlawful non-citizens, as opposed to detaining or deporting them. While the 'services company' Capita has recently been awarded a government contract reportedly worth up to £40 billion to find and remove visa overstayers in the UK on a 'payment by results basis' (BBC News 2012), and the Minutemen and other vigilante groups continue to hunt down irregular migrants crossing the US–Mexico border without the need for financial inducements (Michalowski 2007), migration policing in Australia remains non-commercial and under the *auspices* of the federal government, although heavily reliant on the recruitment of an expanding network of third parties and responsibilised actors to be the *providers* of detection services. These developments are broadly consistent with O'Malley's arguments about a '*politically driven* decentring of the state' (O'Malley 1997: 368) in which the state retains the primary role in auspicing governance programmes, public agencies are managed along 'enterprise lines' and non-government partners are incentivised into governmental agendas.

Community and institutional impacts

Generating 'status insecurity'

DIAC has reportedly reoriented its compliance function to devote more effort towards resolving the immigration status of unlawful non-citizens rather than immediately seeking their removal. This research was not able to fully test this claim and was not designed to do so, but numerous statements by state and federal police confirmed that some circuit breakers had been introduced into the system of police referrals. At the same time, increased training and specialist technologies are being provided to police and the embedded border is expanding and promoting more 'voluntary' reporting to DIAC. The overall effect of these developments is to increase the efficiency of detection, while ensuring that expulsions are at least seen to be lawfully executed. Despite this emphasis on status resolution, the restrictive character of Australia's immigration laws means that regularisation will not be available to all who seek it. The latest annual report from DIAC notes that the number of individuals achieving a resolution of their status in 2011–12 increased to 10,366 from 9,352 in the previous year (DIAC 2012). Incredibly, these figures combine all types of immigration outcomes, as if the difference between being granted a visa and being required to depart were secondary to the bureaucratic goal of achieving an outcome.

The relationship between boundaries of entitlement and belonging is a disputed one within citizenship theory. Bosniak (2006) observes that, at one end of the spectrum, commentators may reject the legitimacy of admission rules altogether (related to belonging); and at the other extreme, may consider 'alienage' to be a morally relevant category that justifies exclusion from services (related to entitlement). In between these poles is a position that accepts admission rules (in other words, migration controls) but argues that they 'must be exercised within their own sphere'. In other words, '[a]dmission laws can be enforced by fences at the borders, deportation proceedings, or criminal sanctions, not, I maintain, by imposing social disabilities' (Bosniak 2006: 128, citing Fiss 1999). Aspects of the embedded border which are intended to achieve border control objectives through denial of basic services would be incompatible with this position. Bosniak also notes that individuals' concerns about membership can inhibit their access to rights to which they *are* in fact entitled – a process she describes as 'collateral damage':

> This illegality under the immigration laws, in turn, very often makes them unwilling to avail themselves of the various non-immigration-related civil and economic rights that they *have* been accorded out of fear that, by doing so, they may precipitate an inquiry into immigration status.
>
> *(Bosniak 2006: 69)*

While the specific entitlements of unlawful non-citizens in Australia were not explored in detail in the study, both the research interviews and the published statements in DIAC's annual reports about the success of strategies to induce 'voluntary' reporting confirm that the manipulation of social entitlements has penetrated deeply into the enforcement of admission rules. This combination of circumstances could be expected to create a sense of pervasive insecurity for some excluded groups, which I refer to as 'status insecurity'. In fact, the stated organisational goal to maximise voluntary reporting (Weber and Pickering forthcoming) establishes that it is expressly intended to do so.

Empirical research into the effect of policies that impose social disabilities on undocumented migrants has confirmed some of the theoretically driven concerns described above. Van der Leun (2003: 172) reported in her study of the Dutch Linking Act that '[r]espondents have mentioned several cases in which illegal immigrants do not make use of the few rights they have'. As she explains, '[e]ven under the Linking Act it is not considered decent and humane, and it could not be aligned with international treaties, to block these opportunities' (Van der Leun 2003: 172). Fear of sending children to school, using public services such as libraries and even being in public places has also been reported among undocumented migrants in Arizona (McDowell and Wonders 2009–10). The migration policing study did not include ethnographic work with communities, but some insights into the impact of status insecurity were provided through the interviews with ECLOs employed by the NSW Police Force, including this example of 'collateral damage' based on confusion over immigration status:

> People tend not to come to the police station for help. Some people keep moving houses because they know people who have been picked up by Immigration. I know of people who had been moving around for years. They were in a dubious state re. their visa … but we found out that they are actually not illegal.
>
> *(Interview 41, NSW Police Force ECLOs)*

Moreover, as Bosworth and Guild have argued (2008: 715), '[t]he marks of migration management do not stay fixed to the bodies of those to whom they were originally applied … but invariably spill over into the routine governance of the community'. In other words, 'collateral damage' may occur in terms of which individuals are impacted, as well as in terms of the rights affected. The migration policing study revealed many ways in which this 'spillover' into the lawfully present non-citizen population may occur. Immigration checks conducted by police on the streets or in investigations are poorly targeted, with around 87 per cent of ISS checks relating to lawfully present individuals or citizens. DIAC-led workplace 'raids' invariably result in the status checking of many individuals who are entitled to work and remain in Australia. The requirement on employers and service providers to check the immigration status of individuals seeking work and access to services, respectively, directs extra surveillance onto entitled as well as unentitled groups.

Whether such checks are universally applied or discretionary, it has been noted in relation to general street stops by police that the 'subjective experience of *feeling* profiled' may be just as damaging as 'the objective one of *being* profiled' (Tyler and Wakslak 2004: 254). Another well-established finding from the policing literature that might be expected to have wider currency in the context of immigration checks is that the effects of unjustified stops (or immigration checks) in terms of perceived unfairness spread beyond the impacted individuals to their families and wider communities (Bradford *et al.* 2008; Brunson and Miller 2006; Sharp and Atherton 2007; Skogan 2005, 2006).

It is reasonable to conclude that the complexity of the Australian immigration system, the unclear boundary between legality and illegality, and the overreach of immigration enforcement all combine to generate feelings of status insecurity not only among unlawful non-citizens but also in relation to anyone whose right to remain is subject to dispute. Even if the deliberate creation of status insecurity as a migration policing strategy were considered to be legitimate in relation to individuals who are in breach of immigration laws, questions remain over the effectiveness of this approach. Van der Leun (2003) determined from her detailed study in the Netherlands that irregular migrants, their community support networks, and even service providers are able to find 'loopholes' in the legislation restricting access to essential services. She concluded that the policy was not likely to succeed in curtailing illegal residence and employment, but instead risked creating a 'layer of long-term socially excluded illegal residents'. In turn, she argues, the long-term presence of legally marginalised groups may lead to other negative consequences that impact on the security of settled populations. As Zedner (2010: 385) observes, 'those with conditional immigration status are known to be particularly vulnerable to abuse, open to exploitation, subject to poor working conditions, at risk of homelessness, and it follows, more prone to offending'.

Dividing communities

While migration policing could be implicated in promoting certain types of offending among illegalised groups, it can also be a *response* to criminal offending by lawfully resident non-citizens. Deporting convicted non-citizens in the name of community safety can be seen as part of the pervasive spread of character testing across a wide range of public policy areas (Betts 1998). These practices elevate community values and politics over individual human rights and the rule of law, and it is important to ask how settled communities are positioned in relation to these practices, and how the associated risk communications impact on them. In the cases of Maria and Prince Brown, police communications were intended to warn other non-citizens of the risks they faced if they engaged in criminal or anti-social behaviour, in the belief that this would create a deterrent effect. Inevitably, these ethnically based risk communications also convey messages to the wider community about the incorrigible criminality of certain 'crimmigrant' groups. Police claimed to have the support of the community when presenting their case for deportation in the Maria and Prince Brown appeals, but it is not clear how this was ascertained.

This exclusionary mindset, if it is an accurate reflection of community feeling, raises important questions about the responsibility of communities and society at large in responding to and preventing social harm. This point is made by Grewcock (2011: 61) in relation to the cancellation of the resident visas held by two Tongan brothers who were convicted of the extremely serious offence of manslaughter of a police officer, when he notes that, 'but for the legal construction of their non-citizenship, both brothers are effectively Australian and important questions of principle remain. Can their forced removal be justified when their criminal activity and perceived risk is associated with their lives in Australia?' In the longer term, marginalising unlawful non-citizens who nevertheless remain in the community, and relying on enemy penology approaches to rid communities of undesirable individuals, has questionable value in producing security for settled populations and carries a high potential for disrupting social cohesion. The inherent duality of this 'us' versus 'them' thinking is expressed well in the following critical commentary on visa cancellation practices in Australia:

> We appear to be asking new citizens to be better than us, better than our Federal Parliamentarians, better than our lawyers and board members. We celebrate our rogues gallery of larrikins and naughty sportspeople, and yet send the message that foreigners will be rigorously scrutinised according to a magic formula we will keep hidden from them.
>
> *(Rimmer 2008: 12)*

The recruitment of members of the public into an active migration policing role by encouraging them to report suspected unlawful non-citizens to the DIAC Dob-in Service also has far-reaching implications for community cohesion. NSW Police Force ECLOs interviewed for this study believed that the threat of dobbing in unlawful non-citizens, or individuals whose immigration status is dependent on a third party, has been widely used to control and exploit immigrants in domestic and workplace settings, and to exact revenge against relatives or co-nationals. As with other branches of the migration policing network, the motives of those performing a migration policing role do not always accord with purely immigration enforcement–based objectives. While front-line DIAC staff dealing with these reports indicated in the research interviews that they are cognisant of the risks of malicious reporting, the manner in which the dob-in line impacts on the community depends on how the reports are handled by the organisation. The quality of the vetting and internal dissemination of this 'community intelligence' has been questioned, for example, in a submission by a member of 'Rural Australians for Refugees' to a Senate Inquiry in 2005:

> I also find the Immigration Dob-in Line a dangerous affront to the Australian value of the 'fair go'. Anonymous statements, often of a general nature e.g. 'So-and-so is not from Afghanistan, he is Pakistani', are accepted, apparently entered on DIMIA records and can be presented for rebuttal by the asylum seeker at RRT [Refugee Review Tribunal] interviews. If any anonymous information is accepted, it should be the job of DIMIA to check that out thoroughly.
>
> *(Berry 2005: 2)*

At hearings of that committee held on 11 November 2005 Greens Senator Kerry Nettle produced a list of cases where incorrect information had remained on people's files and later become part of important legal hearings. The account of the internal checking processes given by the senior officer attending that hearing was similar to that provided several years later by CIMU staff interviewed for the migration policing study. However, Senator Nettle remained concerned about the department's routine failure to reveal the content of allegations to the individuals concerned, or to conduct investigative interviews.

While the ultimate decisions about who will be expelled and who will be allowed to stay are made by administrators and politicians, the existence of the dob-in line and the appeal to community sentiments in justifying the criminal deportation of long-term residents combine to effectively disperse responsibility to communities for defining the boundaries of belonging. As Anderson *et al.* (2011: 547) have argued, while citizens may demonstrate broad support for immigration policies, the threatened exclusion of some individuals is still 'liable to generate conflicts amongst citizens and between citizens and the state over the question of who is part of the normative community of members'. In other words, sections of communities might seek to play an active role in defining membership according to social rather than legal considerations, in ways that may differ from the government's intentions.

Apart from groups defending the rights of asylum seekers, public campaigns against deportation are not prominent in Australia as they are in some other countries such as the UK.[1] However, consultant research commissioned by DIAC, which was intended to assist the department in dealing with 'entrenched clients' who had been resisting removal, provides a fascinating insight into how these individuals seek to include themselves within the boundaries of belonging (Hall and Partners 2012). The authors identified as a problem the fact that these intransigent individuals, irrespective of the amount of time they had spent in the country, all considered themselves to be Australian, and expressed the belief that they *deserved* permanent residence because of their community ties and contribution. While these beliefs were rejected in the report as delusional, and the immigration system was presented as objective and rule-governed, the view that citizenship rights and social inclusion should be earned is central to neoliberal governance, and is powerfully conveyed in some of the migration policing practices described above.

Setting the police in a bad light

Criminologists interested in border control are beginning to investigate the implications for established criminal justice institutions of their involvement in migration policing (Aas and Bosworth 2012). In relation to the role of police in democratic societies, Loader (2006) has noted that policing:

> communicates authoritative meanings to individuals and groups about who they are, about whether their voices are heard and claims recognized, and about where and in what ways they belong. These routine – identity denying and affirming – policing practices consequently play a significant part in reinforcing or else undermining the sense of security that flows from a feeling of effortless, confident membership of a political community.
> *(Loader 2006: 204)*

While it may be argued that the full benefits of 'secure belonging' are only due to those with legal entitlement to be present on sovereign territory, it is widely accepted that a basic level of personal security is owed to all. The long-established dual role for the NSW Police Force in protecting life and property, while also patrolling the boundaries of belonging, therefore generates a fundamental tension. When pressed on this issue, several senior police expressed concerns about the possible impacts of immigration control on police–community relations:

> It has got to have a negative impact … all of a sudden the cops have come in the door and now they are going to run through our house at a million miles an hour and try and get Johnny. And it has cost us $80,000 to get him here, and now they are going to take away all of that…. And it flows through the community that the police are taking away our loved ones.
>
> *(Interview 6, NSW Police Force Local Area Commander)*

Similar sentiments were expressed by some of the ECLOs who were aware of significant tensions in the highly diverse communities in which they work:

> It sets the police in a bad light to deal with this, particularly in cases of prostitution, seniors overstaying their visas or student/migrants working in the black market. From the police point of view, we are doing our job for the betterment of this state. However, from the community point of view, they feel strongly [that] the police is [sic] there to destroy them.
>
> *(Group interview 41, NSW Police Force ECLOs)*

However, these considerations seem to be submerged beneath a widespread acceptance of Migration Act enforcement as a peripheral but essential duty arising from the broad remit of the state police. One tragic example of a negative outcome arising from community knowledge of the police role in immigration enforcement is the death of Wah Aun Chan, an unlawfully present Malaysian national who drowned after running from police following a vehicle stop. A more widespread consequence of this dual policing role is the reluctance among non-citizens with unlawful or insecure immigration status to report victimisation to the police. In fact, the act of mobilising police services has been equated with claiming citizenship status (Waddington 1999). Similarly, Pratt has argued that '[v]ictimhood has become a new basis for claims to citizenship' (Pratt 2005: 221). In contrast, those with diminished citizenship entitlements may be less willing or able to make such a claim. During the research interviews, ECLOs often cited the example of domestic violence (DV) – particularly in situations where newly arrived women are dependent on their spouses for their immigration status – to illustrate how the police role in immigration enforcement can inhibit reporting:

> The police try to police … they are trying to encourage people to report DV. … They are too scared because their spouse is – they are new to the

country and they don't know what the law is. Their spouses use those things on them with – The police won't believe you; the police won't do anything for you because you are not an Australian citizen.

(Group interview 41, NSW Police Force ECLOs)

A senior NSW police officer interviewed for the migration policing study sought to resolve the tension between enforcing immigration law and encouraging reporting of victimisation by asserting the need to send a clear message to communities about 'the price to be paid' for violating immigration law, while stressing that 'if you do the right things you will have nothing to worry about' (Interview 40, NSW Police Force Headquarters). He illustrated this approach with reference to the policing of international students. Following a series of highly publicised attacks against Indians living in Australia, the safety of Indian students in particular became a major political priority in several Australian states, for which police were held to have the primary responsibility:

In particular within the Indian community there is a very big reluctance to report, and that is because of fear of visa violation. What we are trying to tell them is that if you are a victim of crime, you are not violating your visa.... However, if it is true that that person did instigate the event and did instigate the assault, there may well be visa implications; however, it is best to report it ... we want to try to foster reporting, because we are being told by these communities that these are a big issue.

(Interview 40, NSW Police Force Headquarters)

This rather tenuous argument depends, in part, on victims of crime having confident knowledge of their own immigration status, and on police being able to distinguish between the categories of victim and crimmigrant. Confronted with the observation that the practice of checking the immigration status of individuals who report crimes at police stations somewhat undermines this purported victim/offender distinction, this senior officer explained that the police role is to 'support the victim; however, that doesn't mean that we would ensure that that person became a resident' (Interview 40, NSW Police Force Headquarters). Not surprisingly, given this unresolved tension within the role of state police in Australia, unwillingness to report criminal incidents to police for fear of visa cancellation was raised at the Senate Inquiry into the Welfare of International Students (Education Employment and Workplace Relations References Committee 2009: para 3.12).

Historically, police in both the UK and US have had a more ambivalent relationship to border control (as described in Chapter 4). More recently, British police have joined the UK Border Agency in operations aimed at identifying deportable foreign nationals taken into police custody on criminal matters (Hamilton-Smith and Patel 2005; Muir 2012). Their apparent acceptance of this role, compared with an earlier reluctance to be involved in the enforcement of immigration law per se (Weber and Bowling 2004), may be due to the crimmigrant status of the targeted groups. In the

US, where immigration control is considered a federal function, schemes to authorise local police to carry out checks on immigration status have been controversial,
and many local police organisations have declined to take up this new mandate
(Provine 2013). A study by the American Police Foundation noted that:

> [p]olice executives have felt torn between a desire to be helpful and coopera-
> tive with federal immigration authorities and a concern that their participation
> in immigration enforcement efforts will undo gains they have achieved
> through community oriented policing practices, which are directed at gaining
> the trust and cooperation of immigrant communities.
>
> *(Khashu 2009: xi)*

The study concluded that '[l]ocal police must serve and protect *all* residents regardless of their immigration status' (Khashu 2009: xiii, emphasis in original).

The ready acceptance by the NSW Police Force of an immigration enforcement
role may be traced to their historical function as all-purpose administrators and the
primary definers of the boundaries of inclusion within a settler society (Weber 2011).
The lack of commitment by the NSW Police Force to the tenets of community policing which conflict with migration policing objectives could be another contributing
factor. The organisation has recently reverted to its habitual title of the NSW Police
Force, after briefly identifying as the NSW Police *Service*, indicating a commitment to
proactive law enforcement and a preparedness to present an aggressive image to the
public. In the research interviews it was apparent that community policing is not
foremost in the minds of local area commanders, all of whom described their local
strategies as proactive and intelligence led. When asked whether there was a conscious
awareness of adopting a community policing approach, even the commander who
expressed concern about the effect of immigration enforcement on community relations in his area sought to distance himself from this policing style, describing the
heyday of community policing in the state as the time when they stopped 'doing any
police work'. The internally contradictory response reported below illustrates the
unresolved contradictions surrounding community engagement that are apparent in
the thinking of senior NSW police:

> There is definitely a requirement that cops can actually talk to their com-
> munity and be actively involved. That, I think, definitely happens at my
> level, there is no doubt about that whatsoever. It won't happen at the con-
> stable level, but they are dealing on a practitioner level every single day
> with different ethnic groups. So they have got a community spirit anyway.
> I think it is there, I think it needs to be inculcated.
>
> *(Interview 6, NSW Police Force Local Area Commander)*

Even when senior officers were advocating strategies to increase community
reporting of victimisation, it was clear that the objective of 'intelligence gathering'
rather than service to community was foremost in their minds:

It is about educating people to realise that in Australia there is a huge difference between a victim and an offender.... They need to know how we
do things, how the police force works ... if a couple of matters occur then
it affects our deployment. That is how we decide *how we are going to deploy
our police best*. If we don't know about it, we are unable to address it.

(*Interview 40, NSW Police Force Headquarters, emphasis added*)

In the opinion of many of the police informants interviewed, immigration
checking is likely to become more deeply embedded in everyday police practice as
information technologies enhance the accessibility and accuracy of information
about immigration status. However, given its current commitment to aggressive,
intelligence-led policing, the NSW Police Force appears to have little appetite for
serious reflection about the wider impact of immigration enforcement on community trust and cooperation, and little data on which to base such judgements. At
the time the migration policing study was conducted, the greatest concern expressed
by police informants over their migration policing role was over the perceived barriers to summary removal that had arisen from politically driven reform in DIAC.

A 'softer' image for DIAC

It may seem odd to ask how immigration enforcement has impacted on an organisation that has a primary remit for border control, but recent changes in DIAC's
modus operandi, and some enduring contradictions in the agency's remit, make
this question relevant. It has been observed that immigration enforcement is
becoming more police-like in the US (Stumpf 2006) and the UK (Weber and
Bowling 2004). In Canada, Pratt (2005: 209) has noted the 'increasingly indistin-
guishable customs, immigration and law enforcement officers'. However, in
Australia, directions in immigration enforcement are not entirely congruent with
this trend. Neither the federal police nor DIAC field officers wear uniforms, allowing AFP officers to more readily 'pass' as immigration officers when accompanying
DIAC on operations, if they so choose. At the same time, DIAC appears to be
distancing itself from an openly 'police-like' role by relying on uniformed state
police to exercise force on its behalf, while it operationalises a risk-based, regulatory model based primarily on deterrence and compliance, with enforcement
reportedly the last resort. This model has some similarities with new intelligence-
led paradigms that are evident in state policing (Pickering and Weber 2013), but in
this case traces its provenance directly to other regulatory agencies such as taxation
and social security that have a long-running interest in preventing and detecting
fraud. While the most marked changes in the department's modus operandi appear
to stem from the post-Palmer reforms and the further changes instigated following
the election of a Labor government in 2007, the transition to an intelligence-led,
compliance-based model has been underway for much longer.

Since its inception as a specialist agency responsible for the development and
application of immigration policy, there has always been a tension between DIAC's

enabling and excluding functions. The shifting political emphasis of the day has been reflected in ongoing organisational name changes signalling new operational linkages with diverse policy areas such as employment, indigenous affairs, multiculturalism and even local government. The contemporary preoccupation with reinforcing the boundaries of belonging and entitlement is readily apparent in its latest iteration as the Department of Immigration and Citizenship. Whatever its name, the department has always operated on the presumption that cross-border flows can be strictly controlled – an aim that Bruer and Power (1993) assert was largely achieved until the early 1990s. According to these authors, a highly rule-based administration had been forged in the 1980s and 90s to cope with the more politicised environment of an increasingly diverse population. The 1990s then saw the department take on an 'increasingly police-like role' (Bruer and Power 1993: 120) in an attempt to regain central control in a climate of increased demand for temporary visas. These changes were underpinned by the development of 'scoring and risk-measuring systems' and more active intervention by the minister of the day (see also Nicholls 2007). Bruer and Power concluded in 1993 that conflict within the department was 'perhaps illustrated by the public image it presents. It suffers from continuing image problems' (Bruer and Power 1993: 121).

These image problems came to a head most recently in the events that culminated in the 2005 Palmer Inquiry. According to DIAC sources, unpublished research commissioned by the department since then reveals a continuing lack of trust among the department's 'clients'.[2] This suggests that, despite post-Palmer attempts to portray a 'softer' image by emphasising active status resolution and public education to promote compliance, the dual role of enforcing strict immigration law and providing an immigration 'service' is a strained one. In some ways this parallels the tension described in the previous section concerning the police, except that for DIAC this difficulty relates to its core function. One might think that the structural embedding of the border in ways that place other agencies in a front-line migration policing role would conceal the coercive functions of DIAC to some degree; but it nevertheless remains the agency responsible for following through on enforcement. The predictions made by Bruer and Power in 1993 about the relentless demand for cross-border mobility have come to pass, and Australia plays host to a larger number of temporary visitors than any other country within the Organisation for Economic Cooperation and Development (OECD).[3] However, there are no clear signals as yet of the fundamental rethinking of the distinction between citizens and others that these authors foretold:

> In the not-too-distant future, as Australia becomes more integrated into the international economy, it is likely that the department will have to modify the long-standing dichotomous distinction upon which its control function has been based – a distinction between settlers/prospective citizens on the one hand, and visitors on the other. The middle ground between these two categories has in recent years been becoming more heavily populated.
>
> *(Bruer and Power 1993: 123)*

The evidence presented here seems to suggest that the emphasis remains on tightening the boundaries of 'secure belonging' around citizenship, and strengthening the switch points that govern access to entitlements reserved solely for permanent residents and other lawfully present denizens.

Service providers as visa police

The recruitment of essential service providers into migration policing roles is bound to influence the relationship between these agencies, the public and the state. Some of the implications are associated with the risks of attempting to 'govern at a distance'. On this point, Van der Leun (2003) argued in her study of the Dutch Linking Act that the policy risked widening the gap between the construction of central border control policies and local implementation, due to active resistance and other local factors. She found that responses from service agencies could vary, with more 'professional' occupational groups tending to look for ways to circumvent restrictions. Where state funding could not be provided without proof of legal status, the restrictions were harder to circumvent, but the option remained to refer undocumented migrants to alternative community-based service providers. Van der Leun reasoned that opportunities for the 'incorporation' of illegal migrants were more restricted in strong social democracies such as the Netherlands, which are characterised by high levels of social and labour market regulation, compared with the US where opportunities for illegal working and regularisation at the time were greater. However, writing in 2013, Provine notes the closing of these 'loopholes' in the US as well, with the result that communities are losing the capacity to interact with immigrants, both documented and undocumented, as they once did. She concludes: 'unauthorized immigrants have been reframed from their earlier quiet presence as workers, parents, and community members, to subjects whose most salient quality is their (lack of) legal status' (Provine 2013: 124).

In Australia, proof of immigration status has become widely embedded in the provision of government services in ways that require further exploration in order to determine their institutional impact. The best documented example in Australia is the role of universities, who have delegated responsibility for monitoring compliance with the academic conditions of student visas (see Chapter 6). The demands of this complex visa policing role have given rise to a specialist infrastructure of administrators, student advisers and visa compliance officers within every major university. Workshop discussions with students attending the annual conference of international students in Brisbane in October 2008 revealed widespread acceptance of the role of universities as 'visa police', with only one student, who had experience advocating for international students over visa cancellations, recognising the tension between this function and the core role of universities as providers of education and pastoral care. She claimed that academics were often unaware of the implications for international students of their studies being suspended, and seemed not to appreciate that they had a duty of care to support students to meet the strict conditions of their visas (Group Interview 58, Student Representative).

A spokesperson from the NLC, which represents international students at the national level, also considered that education providers wielded enormous power over students, and were frequently at fault for suspending studies precipitately, often with very serious consequences (Interview 57, Student Representative). More procedural safeguards were said to be in place now under the ESOS Act to prevent institutions from triggering enforcement action unnecessarily, but the entrenched links between academic progress and immigration compliance mean that standard academic policies on student progress carry profoundly different meanings and consequences for local and international students.

Concluding comments

What is to be done about migration policing?

Existing approaches to achieving democratic accountability of police institutions are proving inadequate in the face of rapid change. This is largely because policing has become pluralised and fragmented (Loader 2000), and is increasingly information based and directed towards the control of suspect populations (Sheptycki 2002). The informated nature of policing networks raises new accountability questions, such as who is responsible when erroneous data is spread through a 'multi-agency intelligence sharing nexus' (Sheptycki 2002: 328). Where several agencies collaborate on joint migration policing operations, they sometimes stretch, rather than merely pool, their legal powers, so that they operate in the 'shadow of the law' (Mazerolle and Ransley 2006). In response to the challenges of pluralisation, Wood and Shearing (2007: 98) outline a range of 'nodal solutions' to 'nodal problems' such as inequality of access to market-based forms of security. Since the findings of this study are that migration policing networks do not decentre state power to any significant extent, these measures are not directly applicable to the migration policing context.

A broader accountability issue with respect to migration policing networks arises not so much from the form this policing takes, but the fact that its targets are non-citizens who have no obvious claim to the basic entitlement of 'secure belonging' (Loader 2006). It is not clear under these circumstances where the political constituency for existing forms of democratic accountability are to be found. Dauvergne has noted, '[f]or extralegal migrants seeking legal protection or redress from harms, the status of "illegal" has been almost insurmountable. This will eventually prove to be one of the most important tests of the global spread of human rights' (Dauvergne 2008: 19). It is no coincidence that the Palmer Inquiry in Australia was precipitated by the wrongful detention and mistreatment of a naturalised Australian citizen who was readily recognised as a bearer of rights, while the impact of the migration policing regime on unlawfully present and criminal non-citizens remains unquestioned. The framing of the wrongful detentions as 'mistakes' resulted in the development of more efficient forms of identification and detection, and considerable resources have been spent introducing internal quality assurance systems. However, no significant measures have been put in place to open up the migration policing machinery to the systematic, external scrutiny which would be expected in other contexts within a democratic system.

The Commonwealth Ombudsman has had a longstanding mandate to inquire into matters concerning the operation of immigration laws, but on an advisory rather than determinative basis (Bruer and Power 1993). The role of the Australian Human Rights Commission (formerly the Human Rights and Equal Opportunity Commission) was described in 1993 by Bruer and Power as 'marginal', although it may play a more prominent role now, in public debate at least, especially in relation to administrative detention and the treatment of juveniles. It became clear during the conduct of the migration policing study that there is no requirement on agencies to collect monitoring data in relation to migration policing activities, let alone to make it available on a regular basis for public scrutiny, as is required, for example, in relation to police stop-and-search practices in the UK (Shiner 2010). No readily accessible data is kept by police in relation to Migration Act warrants executed in the company of DIAC officers, Migration Act detentions by police or any aspect of street policing. The ISS operated by DIAC, which is used by police to check immigration status in the context of criminal investigations and street policing, could become a starting point for monitoring of some of these enforcement practices but there is no indication that this application of the data has been considered. As Ericson and Haggerty (1997: 18) have observed, the knowledge that is most valued within a risk-based policing system is the 'knowledge necessary to set acceptable standards of risk'. The emphasis in terms of migration policing data has therefore been on the systems for the determination of identity and inter-agency data exchange, where there are signs of pressure to erode some of the privacy restrictions that currently constrain data exchange in more speculative contexts.

One small step towards increased accountability could be to recognise immigration enforcement as a form of policing, despite its ostensibly administrative character. DIAC officers strongly resist the characterisation of their compliance functions as 'policing'. However, the enforcement of immigration law *is* a form of policing – understood broadly as population control – and should be perceived and studied as such. The capacity to evoke powers of expulsion from Australian territory will continue to give migration policing a character that is distinctive from the policing of citizens for as long as this distinction remains salient in domestic law. Meanwhile, improved accountability could be built on a foundation of increased knowledge about migration policing practices and their impacts at particular locations, drawing on conceptual tools where applicable from policing research. To this end, some ideas for further research that have arisen specifically from the migration policing study are presented in the form of an annotated list in the final section below.

Expanding the migration policing research agenda

- *Ethnographic research on community impacts*

    The migration policing study did not ascertain the experiences of non-citizens and immigrant communities directly, or tap into the wealth of knowledge held by community organisations and legal advocacy groups. Van der Leun's (2003) sociological study of the impact of the Linkage Act on undocumented migrants in the Netherlands is exemplary for its inclusion of community, service provider and institutional perspectives. Other studies that explore the strategies used by migrants to manage the consequences of their 'illegality' include ethnographic work by Coutin (2005) and studies by Calavita (2003), McDowell and Wonders (2009–10) and Schuster (2005).

- *Excavating the embedded border*

The migration policing study began life as an attempt to discover how key agencies work together actively to identify unlawful non-citizens. The extent of the embedded border, and particularly the strategy of producing voluntary reporting through the denial of services, was an unexpected discovery that could not be fully explored with the time and resources available. The role played by medical authorities and educational institutions, whether willingly or unwillingly, directly or inadvertently, would be a fruitful area for further research in the Australian context, possibly emulating some of the methods used by Van der Leun (2003).

- *Migration policing as surveillance*

The internal border increasingly operates through the exchange of information mediated by technologies of identification. This mode of migration policing can be conceptualised as a form of surveillance and contextualised within the rich literature on contemporary surveillance. The work of Katja Aas (2011) on technologies for the surveillance of 'crimmigrants' in the EU exemplifies this research genre. A committee appointed by the French Government identified the most problematic aspects of contemporary surveillance technologies as the shift from checking identity to checking behaviour, the increasing interconnection of data sources, and the collection of personal data without the individual's knowledge (reported in Mattelart 2010). This provides a useful list of normative considerations that could guide further research on internal border surveillance.

- *Identifying immigration crimes*

The migration policing study examined one dimension of the crimmigration thesis – namely, the mobilisation of immigration law in response to criminal offending by non-citizens. The role of criminal law in dealing with immigration breaches was explicitly excluded from the study due to its focus on the detection of 'ordinary' unlawful non-citizens, since criminal sanctions for immigration breaches in Australia seem to be reserved for relatively large-scale, systematic activities. This avenue is worthy of further exploration through the lens of the crimmigration thesis. The work of Ana Aliverti (2012a, 2012b) in charting the importation of criminal justice procedures and sanctions into the migration domain in the UK is a good example of research in this field.

- *Evaluating specific enforcement regimes or reforms*

Following a detailed study of detention and deportation policies in Canada, Anna Pratt observed:

> While the discussion clearly indicates the prominence of the logic of risk and risk management strategies in the development and promotion of government programs, the degree to which they have been implemented, the extent and ways in which they are used, whether they 'work' and how they differ from former practices all remain questions for further empirical investigation.
>
> *(Pratt 2005: 210)*

While the migration policing study included original empirical research, the objective was to achieve a broad mapping of inter-agency practices, and the design did not include any significant observational elements. Therefore, many of these specific questions about migration policing practice remain unanswered in the Australian context as well.

- *Discretion, occupational culture and organisational change*

The long tradition of studying the exercise of discretion by police provides many examples of research that could be adapted to the migration policing context. Chan's study of police reform in NSW (Chan 1997), and her explication of the role of police cultural knowledge in supporting or resisting those reforms, offers one model for investigating institutional change. In relation to migration policing, a key question would be: Has the much vaunted 'cultural' change in DIAC following the Palmer Inquiry really materialised, and if so, how has this impacted on migration policing practices? Socio-legal studies on the dynamics of individual decision-making, such as my own earlier work on decisions by UK immigration officers to detain asylum seekers (Weber 2002b, 2003), are another avenue for micro-level research in this field.

- *Attention to the local*

The importance of paying attention to local variations in migration policing is very clear from the work of Van der Leun (2003) in the Netherlands and Provine (2013) in the US. Due to space restrictions, detailed material collected through local police case studies for migration policing research has not been fully reported here, and there is scope for further analysis of this data. Furthermore, NSW stands out as the most active of the Australian states in migration policing, and comparisons with other less involved state police forces may be instructive. In order to gain a full understanding of local compromises, negotiations, adaptations and contexts, data gathering should be less institutionally focused than the approach adopted in the present study, and could include discussions with local non-government organisations, service providers and community groups.

- *Institutionalising discrimination through risk-based policing*

  Intelligence-led and risk-based approaches to compliance and enforcement were found to be prevalent across all the government migration policing agencies included in the study. While enthusiastically embraced as a way to prioritise the use of resources, policing by targeting risky individuals (for example, based on conviction status), risky places (in which everyone is suspect) or high-risk groups (defined, for example, by nationality) increases the risk of harassment and systemic discrimination or profiling. While intelligence-led targeting is manifest across a wide range of institutional practices, the established body of empirical research on police stop and search (see, for example, Weber and Bowling 2012) could provide a template for research that would be applicable in at least some of these migration policing settings.

- *Integrating immigration status into intersectionality frameworks*

Immigration and citizenship status are becoming pervasive forms of social categorisation that significantly affect the life chances of individuals living in developed countries. The realities of contemporary mobility mean that these categories have significance beyond a mere dichotomy of included/excluded, but also define enduring categories that range from outlaw status to hierarchies of partial, pseudo or conditional citizenship or denizenship. It follows that these legally defined categories could usefully be included alongside the more established markers of race, class, ethnicity and gender in any empirical research that is aimed at identifying social inequalities in access to services or treatment by authorities. This framing would help to elucidate expanded forms of othering within globally interconnected societies that were discussed by Weber and Bowling (2008) under the banner of 'xeno-racism'.

In societies that are no longer merely multicultural, but are increasingly globally interconnected, immigration authorities, police and expanding migration policing networks play a key role in defining the boundaries of belonging and operating the switch-points that control access to entitlements. Recalling Loader's conclusion that new strategies are needed if 'policing is to be capable of recognizing, rather than denigrating or silencing, the security claims of *all citizens*' (Loader 2006: 213, emphasis added), the challenge posed, although not answered, by this book is how this vision might be expanded to promote 'secure belonging' for all.

APPENDIX 1

OPERATIONAL POLICE QUESTIONNAIRE

Thank you for agreeing to participate in this survey about the enforcement of immigration law. We are interested in your experiences and opinions even if you have not been directly involved in immigration enforcement. Your responses are anonymous and will only be seen by the researchers.

1. What would you be <u>most likely</u> to do if someone told you they were unlawfully in Australia? (Tick one)
    □ Probably nothing
    □ Nothing unless there is also a criminal matter
    □ Contact Immigration
    □ Conduct further enquiries
    □ Report within your LAC. To whom? (please specify): _____
    □ Arrest them
    □ Other (please specify): _____

2. In your view how important is the enforcement of immigration law to the police role? (Tick one)
    □ Not important at all   □ Somewhat important   □ Very important

3. Have you ever been involved in any of the following? (Tick all that apply)
    □ Escorting someone to immigration detention
    □ Called to attend an Immigration Detention Centre
    □ Accompanying immigration departures overseas (off duty)
    □ Detaining someone in police custody for migration matters
    □ None of the above

4a. Have you ever accompanied Immigration Officers to execute a warrant?   □ Yes   □ No
b. If yes, what was your role? _____
c. Did you receive a briefing? □ Yes   □ No
d. If so, from which agency/agencies?   □ Police   □ Immigration
                                     □ Other (please specify): _____

5a. Have you ever taken part in an organized operation aimed at identifying people with unlawful immigration status? □ Yes   □ No
b. If yes, what was your role? _____
c. Did you receive a briefing? □ Yes   □ No
d. If so, from which agency/agencies?   □ Police   □ Immigration
                                     □ Other (please specify): _____
e. What other agencies were involved in the operation? (Tick as many as apply)
    □ Immigration □ Australian Tax Office   □ Australian Federal Police   □ Centrelink
    □ Local Council   □ Industry Regulatory Groups   □ Other (please specify): _____

6. Which of the following methods, if any, have you used to check someone's immigration status? (Tick all that apply)
    □ Contacted VKG
    □ Contacted ISS (Immigration Status Service)
    □ Contacted Immigration Liaison Officers (located in Parramatta Police HQ)
    □ Contacted Sydney Immigration Office
    □ Contacted Canberra Immigration Office. Which section? _____
    □ Other (please specify): _____
    □ Not applicable

7a. Have you ever done an immigration check in any of the following circumstances? (Tick all that apply)

☐ Routine traffic matters ☐ Proactive street stops

☐ Routine patrols ☐ Presenting to station as complainant/victim

☐ Not applicable ☐ Attending call to house

☐ Other (please specify): _____

b. Thinking about these situations, what factors prompted you to conduct the check? (Tick all that apply)

☐ Doubt over identity ☐ Unable to speak English

☐ Non-Australia accent ☐ Possession of foreign documents

☐ Ethnic appearance ☐ Foreign name

☐ Other (please specify): _____

8a. Have you ever done an immigration check in any of the following circumstances? (Tick all that apply)

☐ Reported by the public as suspect of crime ☐ Reported by public as illegal immigrant

☐ A report from another agency ☐ During the course of a police investigation

☐ Other (please specify): _____

☐ Not applicable

b. Thinking about these situations, what factors prompted you to conduct the check? (Tick all that apply)

☐ No evidence of suspects' identity ☐ Unable to speak English

☐ Only in possession of foreign documents ☐ Non Australian/foreign/ethnic appearance

☐ To confirm information supplied ☐ Other (please specify): _____

9. Over the last 12 months, how many times have you checked someone's immigration status:

☐ Once or twice ☐ 3-10 times ☐ 11-20 times ☐ More than 20 times ☐ None

10. Have you ever exercised power(s) under the Migration Act? (Tick one)

☐ Yes. If so, which power(s)? _____

☐ No

☐ Don't Know

11. Since you became a police officer, has time spent on immigration enforcement increased or decreased? (Tick one)

☐ Increased ☐ Decreased ☐ Stayed about the same

12. Which of the following forms of training have you completed in relation to migration matters? (Tick all that apply)

☐ Checking immigration status/ Using the Immigration Status Service (ISS)

☐ Exercising powers under the Migration Act

☐ Dealing with ethnic minority communities

☐ None of the above

13. Prior to completing this survey had you ever heard of the ISS? ☐ Yes ☐ No

14. Do you think you need further training in any of the following areas? (Tick all that apply)

☐ Using the ISS/Checking immigration status ☐ Exercising powers under the Migration Act

☐ Dealing with minority communities ☐ Other (please specify):_____

15. Use this space to list any other migration-related activities which you have been involved in and to comment on any other aspect(s) of immigration enforcement.

Thank you very much for answering these questions. Could you please tell us a bit about yourself:

Your Rank: ☐Probationary Constable ☐Constable ☐Senior Constable

☐Sergeant ☐Senior Sergeant ☐Inspector

APPENDIX 2

SUMMARY OF KEY ENFORCEMENT POWERS UNDER THE MIGRATION ACT

Section	Power
s 18	Power to obtain information and documents where reason to believe person is an unlawful non citizen
s 73	Power to grant a bridging visa
s 109	Power to cancel visas obtained on basis of incorrect information
s 116	General power to cancel temporary visas
s 137L, M	Power to revoke automatic student visa cancellation
s 137T	Power to cancel the visas of dependent family members where the primary visa holder has had their visa cancelled under s 137Q
s 140	Power to cancel related visas held by members of the family unit (or other association if discretionary power is exercised) where the primary visa holder has had their visa cancelled
s 147, 148, 158	Power to grant criminal justice stay certificates, visas
s 164	Power to cancel criminal justice visa where the holder is no longer required to be in Australia
s 178	Mandatory detention of unauthorized arrivals by sea
s 188	Power to require evidence from non citizen about legal status
s 189	Power to detain unlawful non citizens
s 196	Power to continue detention
s 198, 200	Power to remove/deport unlawful non citizens
s 251, 257	Powers of entry, search and questioning
s 258E-G	Rules for carrying out identification tests
s 261AE	Use of force
s 268BA	Requirement for education establishments to provide information
s 268CA-CZ	Power to apply for and use monitoring warrant
s 336D	Authority to access identifying information (for data matching)
s 501	Power to cancel visas on character grounds

APPENDIX 3

ABRIDGED DIAC COMPLIANCE PRIORITIES MATRIX 2007–8

Mandatory work

Non-citizens subject to adverse security assessments, convicted of serious crimes, suspected war criminals, controversial visitors

Non-citizens identified by health authorities as threats to public health

Unauthorised arrivals and people smuggling

Perpetrators of people trafficking or organized fraud against migration and citizenship law

Employers and business sponsors in breach of obligations

Referrals from police and other law enforcement agencies

Emerging issues determined by minister or senior management

Immigration detention of unlawful non-citizens

High-priority work

Identity fraud

Prevention and deterrence work to limit illegal work

Support clients in breach who are seeking to comply

Locate and remove overstayed and failed protection visa applicants who are seeking to remain in the community illegally

Resolve cases of repeat BVE holders

Overseas students in breach and suspected fraudulent institutions

Unregistered immigration assistance

Selected compliance and integrity 'hot spots' for 2007–8

Identity management – implement Biometrics at the Border initiative, capture facial images of all citizenship clients

Fraud control – identify and highlight risks within program areas with assistance of Risk Governance Group

Combating student non-compliance – conduct spot checks of educational institutions and participate in audits of educational institutions by regulatory bodies; cancel visas of students who fail to comply with attendance and performance requirements

Tackling employers abusing visa system – raise awareness of obligations, provide training in Visa Entitlement Verification Online system, refer cases to law enforcement

Remove non-citizens posing risk to community – engage with law enforcement and correctional authorities to identify people of character concern

Pursuing immigration outcomes – have single view of client's dealings with department

Source: Compliance and Integrity in Australia's Immigration and Citizenship Programs, DIAC, 2007-8.

NOTES

2 Researching migration policing networks

1 'Policing Migration in Australia: An Analysis of Onshore Migration Policing Networks', Australian Research Council Discovery Grant DP0774554, Leanne Weber sole Chief Investigator. The fieldwork for this study was completed while I was employed at the University of New South Wales.
2 The study did not examine detention practices, but it was expected that the proximity of this station would ensure a reasonable level of awareness about immigration among police officers there.
3 'Location' is the term used in conversation by DIAC officers and within official DIAC reports for the detection of an unlawful non-citizen.
4 There is a lack of published statistics about pathways through the compliance system by which to judge these claims about outcomes. This aspect of immigration enforcement is being examined in another study funded by an Australian Research Council Discovery Grant 'Exporting Risk: The Australian Deportation Project' (DP110102453), Chief Investigators Sharon Pickering, Leanne Weber, Mike Grewcock, Marie Segrave.

3 Immigration officers as migration police

1 In an address delivered in November 2005, the incoming head of DIAC Andrew Metcalfe announced that the government had committed a substantial $230 million over a five-year period 'to achieve the change process' (Metcalfe 2005).
2 By 2008, reports were appearing of a '$44 million budget gap' caused by cost blow-outs for the massive Systems for People programme (Sharma2008) and the axing of 300 immigration department jobs (ABC News 2008).
3 DIAC Budget Statements 2010–11 (provided by DIAC) include strategic outcomes such as the 'promotion of client service delivery excellence' (19); 'application assistance to people in immigration detention and eligible clients in the community' (33); 'to maximise voluntary compliance by raising awareness of Australia's immigration and citizenship laws through a variety of media, education and training programs and communication with clients, stakeholders, unions, employer and industry groups and other interested parties such as migration agents, travel agents and foreign missions, and through collaboration with other government service providers' (43).
4 DIAC's compliance priorities were last published in its overall Compliance and Integrity Plan for 2007–08. DIAC has advised that a new Compliance Priorities Plan is being developed.

5   This is the term used within DIAC and its reporting systems to indicate the detection of an unlawfully present person.
6   Australian vernacular for reports from the public, akin to the idea of 'snitching'.
7   Departmental shorthand for unlawful non-citizens.

4   Police as immigration officers

1   The term 'alien' has now been replaced by the legal category of 'unlawful non-citizen'.
2   Place names have been removed from the interview extracts in order to retain the anonymity of police commanders.
3   These 11,672 calls included 2,686 calls about matters other than immigration status (for example, checks on whether a named individual was in or out of Australia on a particular date); but the disaggregation by agency was not provided separately for these two categories of inquiry.
4   Averages could only be approximated using interval mid-points since data on the number of checks conducted was collected in the broad categories shown in Figure 4.2, rather than as exact figures.
5   For example, the higher frequency of reports from the community in urban locations and the relatively lower incidence of street stops in rural locations.
6   Victims of trafficking who might otherwise be liable for removal may be eligible for special temporary visas if they assist in prosecutions.
7   It is reliance on these internal police data sources that attracted so much criticism in relation to the wrongful detention and deportation cases discussed in Chapter 3, and prompted the development of the ISS.
8   Humphrey Bear is a popular children's television character.
9   From the training materials 'Immigration Compliance: DIAC and Police Working Together' provided to the researchers by DIAC.
10 AUSTRAC is an Australian government agency tasked with protecting Australia's financial system and contributing to the administration of justice by countering money laundering and the financing of terrorism.

5   Negotiating the criminal–administrative nexus

1   Direction No. 55 – Visa refusal and cancellation under s 501 Migration Act 1958 Direction under Section 499, para 6.3(1).
2   In a dissenting view in *Shaw v Minister for Immigration and Multicultural and Indigenous Affairs* [2005] FCAFC 106: BC200503812, considered under the original Direction 17, Spender J noted that

> the exercise of the cancellation power and removal in this case was not an exercise of executive power. It was penal and punitive in character and as such it was an invalid exercise of the judicial power of the Commonwealth by the Executive.

3   Stefan Nystrom was born in Sweden but had spent all his adult life in Australia and mistakenly believed himself to be a citizen. He was deported following cancellation of his permanent residence visa due to a history of serious offending. Following a successful appeal in the Federal Court, which was subsequently overturned in the High Court, an individual complaint was brought under the International Covenant on Civil and Political Rights on his behalf, alleging breaches of his right to family life, his right to enter his own country, and his right to equality before the law and freedom from discrimination on the basis of nationality. The UN Human Rights Committee held that he should be allowed to return to Australia (Human Rights Committee [2011] UN Human Rights Committee decision in *Nystrom v Australia,* Communication No. 1557/2007 adopted 18 July 2011), an undertaking that had not been implemented at the time of writing.

6 Creating a ubiquitous border

1 Villawood Detention Centre in Sydney is an Immigration Detention Centre operated by a private security firm under the administration of DIAC.
2 This result may also follow from the fact that transit officers – at least according to allegations by youth advocates – target young people disproportionately for on-the-spot fines which they are largely unable to pay.
3 Note that the use of the COPS database, rather than DIAC information sources, to make inferences about entitlement to remain in Australia was one of the practices that attracted virulent criticism from the Palmer Inquiry.
4 Short-term work visas associated with particular employers.
5 A report in *The Australian* newspaper on 9 November 2012 claimed that temporary visitors were 'racking up tens of millions of dollars of unpaid health bills', with taxpayers left to cover the costs of treating patients not eligible for treatment under the national scheme Medicare (Parnell 2012).
6 National Liaison Committee 23rd National Conference for International Students held in Brisbane on 6–8 October 2008. Students attending the workshop were asked to complete a questionnaire and engage in discussions about their perceptions of the role of universities in monitoring compliance with student visas.
7 In a newspaper article mocking the choice of name for the service, Monica Dux (Dux 2005) noted: 'It has none of the brave altruism associated with the more adult concept of whistleblowing. It's part of a keystone cop vocabulary and is used most effectively by children to regulate the injustices they detect in their siblings and friends', adding that the traditional Australian dislike of dobbing was being challenged by a raft of bureaucrats from a range of agencies exhorting Australians to inform about all manner of wrongdoing.
8 http://www.workpermit.com/news/2005_12_28/australia/illegal_immigration_hotline_successful.htm, dated 28 December 2005.
9 This could include individuals on visa types that create dependence on others, such as spouses or employers.
10 Under threat of substantial fines, international airlines are required to refuse boarding to 'inadequately documented passengers' attempting to travel to Australia. They are able to do this through access to the Advanced Passenger Processing system (Weber 2007) – the offshore equivalent of the VEVO system.
11 The case of recognised refugees holding temporary protection visas is perhaps the most controversial example.
12 Based on verbal information provided at an invitational seminar organised by Monash Criminology and held in Canberra on 24 October 2011.

7 A nodal cartography of migration policing networks

1 'UNC' is DIAC shorthand for unlawful non-citizen.
2 Portable Document Format – an electronic format in which documents can be saved and viewed.
3 These warrants for search and seizure are issued by magistrates.

8 Patrolling the boundaries of entitlement and belonging

1 See, for example, http://www.ncadc.org.uk/.
2 Information provided at an invitational workshop entitled Migration, Legality and Borders convened by Monash University on 24 October 2011.
3 For example, with respect to the percentage of the labour force who are foreign born, and the hosting of international students as published in the OECD publication *International Migration Outlook: SOPEMI 2011*.

REFERENCES

AAP (Australian Associated Press) (2005) 'ALP questions the validity of the Palmer report', *Sydney Morning Herald*, 18 July.

Aas, K. (2005) '"Getting ahead of the game": border technologies and the changing space of governance', in E. Zureik and M. Salter (eds) *Global Surveillance and Policing: Borders, Security, Identity*, Uffculme, Devon: Willan Publishing.

—— (2007) *Globalization and Crime*, London: Sage.

—— (2011) '"Crimmigrant" bodies and bona fide travelers: surveillance, citizenship and global governance', *Theoretical Criminology*, 15: 331–46.

Aas, K. and Bosworth, M. (2012) *Borders of Punishment*, Oxford: Oxford University Press.

ABC News (2006) 'Unis reach deal on international student checks', *ABC News Online*, 8 September, retrieved from: www.abc.net.au/news/2006-09-08/unis-reach-deal-on-international-student-checks/1258436.

—— (2008) '300 Dept of Immigration jobs to go', *ABC News Online*, 21 May, retrieved from: http://www.abc.net.au/news/2008-05-21/300-dept-of-immigration-jobs-to-go/2442818.

Aliverti, A. (2012a) 'Exploring the function of criminal law in the policing of foreigners: the decision to prosecute immigration-related offences', *Social and Legal Studies*, 21: 511–27.

—— (2012b) 'Making people criminal: the role of the criminal law in immigration enforcement', *Theoretical Criminology*, 16: 417–34.

Amnesty International (2009) *Jailed without Justice: Immigration Detention in the USA*, New York: Amnesty International USA.

Anderson, B., Gibney, M. and Paoletti, E. (2011) 'Citizenship, deportation and the boundaries of belonging', *Citizenship Studies*, 15: 547–63.

Australian Human Rights Commission (2010) 'Background paper: Immigration detention and visa cancellation under section 501 of the Migration Act', Sydney: Australian Human Rights Commission.

—— (2012) 'Brown v Commonwealth of Australia [2012] AusHRC 51', Sydney: Australian Human Rights Commission.

Banton, M. (1983) 'Categorical and statistical discrimination', *Ethnic and Racial Studies*, 6/3 (July).

BBC News (2012) 'Capita gets contract to find 174,000 illegal immigrants', *BBC News online*, 18 September, retrieved from: http://www.bbc.co.uk/news/uk-politics-19637409.

Bernstein, N. (2010) 'Border sweeps in north reach miles into US', *The New York Times*, 29 August, retrieved from: http://www.nytimes.com/2010/08/30/nyregion/30border.html?pagewanted=all.

Berry, R. (2005) 'Submission by Rosalind Berry to the Inquiry into the Administration and Operation of the Migration Act 1958', *Senate Legal and Constitutional Affairs Committee.*

Betts, K. (1998) 'The character bill and migration rights', *People and Place*, 6: 39–53.

Bigo, D. (2000) 'Liaison officers in Europe: new officers in the European security field', in J. Sheptycki (ed.) *Issues in Transnational Policing*, London: Routledge.

Bosniak, L. (2006) *The Citizen and the Alien: Dilemmas of Contemporary Membership*, Princeton, NJ: Princeton University Press.

Bostock, C. (2011) 'The effect of ministerial directions on tribunal independence', *Australian Journal of Administrative Law*, 18: 161–71.

Bosworth, M. (2011) 'Deportation, detention and foreign-national prisoners in England and Wales', *Citizenship Studies*, 15: 583–95.

Bosworth, M. and Guild, M. (2008) 'Governing through migration control: security and citizenship in Britain', *British Journal of Criminology*, 48: 703–19.

Bowen, C. (2011) 'New laws to get tough on hiring illegal workers', Press Release by Minister for Immigration and Citizenship, Canberra.

Bowling, B. and Phillips, C. (2002) *Racism, Crime and Justice*, Harlow: Longman.

—— (2007) 'Disproportionate and discriminatory: reviewing the evidence on police stop and search', *The Modern Law Review*, 70: 936–61.

Bradford, B., Jackson, J. and Stanko, E. (2008) 'Contact and confidence: revisiting the impact of public encounters with the police', *Policing and Society*, 19: 20–46.

Braithwaite, J. (2000) 'The new regulatory state and the transformation of criminology', *British Journal of Criminology: Special Issue on Criminology and Social Theory*, 40: 222–38.

Brown, D., Farrier, D., Neal, D. and Weisbrot, D. (2006) *Criminal Laws: Materials and Commentary on Criminal Law and Process in New South Wales*, Sydney: Federation Press.

Bruer, J. and Power, J. (1993) 'The changing role of the Department of Immigration', in J. Jupp and M. Kabala (eds) *The Politics of Australian Immigration*, Canberra: Australian Government Publishing Service.

Brunson, R. and Miller, J. (2006) 'Young black men and urban policing in the United States', *British Journal of Criminology*, 46: 613–40.

Burris, S. (2004) 'Governance, microgovernance and health', *Temple Law Review*, 77: 335–62.

Burris, S., Drahos, P. and Shearing, C. (2005) 'Nodal governance', *Australian Journal of Legal Philosophy*, 30: 30–58.

Calavita, K. (2003) 'A "reserve army of delinquents": the criminalization and economic punishment of immigrants in Spain', *Punishment and Society*, 5: 399–413.

Castel, R. (1991) 'From dangerousness to risk', in G. Burchill, C. Gordon and P. Miller (eds) *The Foucault Effect: Studies in Governmentality*, London: Harvester Wheatsheaf.

Castells, M. (2000) 'The network society', in D. Held and A. McGrew (eds) *The Global Transformations Reader: An Introduction to the Globalization Debate*, Cambridge: Polity Press.

Chan, J. (1997) *Changing Police Culture: Policing in a Multi-Cultural Society*, Cambridge: Cambridge University Press.

Coleman, R. and McCahill, M. (2011) *Surveillance and Crime*, London: Sage.

Commonwealth and Immigration Ombudsman (2006) *Administration of S 501 of the Migration Act 1958 as it Applies to Long-Term Residents*, Canberra: Department of Immigration and Multicultural Affairs.

Commonwealth Ombudsman (2001) *Report of an Own Motion Investigation into the Department of Immigration and Multicultural Affairs' Immigration Detention Centres*, Canberra: Commonwealth of Australia.

—— (2005) *Inquiry into the Circumstances of the Vivian Alvarez Matter*, Canberra: Commonwealth of Australia.

—— (2007a) *Annual Report 2006–2007*, Canberra: Commonwealth of Australia.

—— (2007b) *Department of Immigration and Citzenship – Reports into Referred Immigration Cases: Detention Process Issues*, Canberra: Commonwealth of Australia.

Contractor, A. (2004) 'Students expelled for working in sex industry', *Sydney Morning Herald*, 27 December, retrieved from: http://www.smh.com.au/news/National/Students-expelled-for-working-in-sex-industry/2004/12/26/1103996439790.html.

Coutin, S. B. (2005) 'Contesting criminality: illegal immigration and the spatialization of legality', *Theoretical Criminology*, 9: 5–33.

Crawford, A. (2006) 'Networked governance and the post regulatory state? Steering, rowing and anchoring the provision of policing and security', *Theoretical Criminology*, 10: 449–70.

Crock, M. and Berg, L. (2011) *Immigration Refugees and Forced Migration: Law, Policy and Practice in Australia*, Sydney: Federation Press.

Crock, M., Saul, B. and Dastyari, A. (2006) *Future Seekers II: Refugees and Irregular Migration in Australia*, Sydney: Federation Press.

Cullen, S. (2012) 'Non-Australian protestors face deportation if charged', *ABC News Online*, 17 September, retrieved from: http://www.abc.net.au/news/2012-09-17/non-citizens-face-deportation-over-protest/4265634.

Cunneen, C. (2001) *Conflict, Politics and Crime: Aboriginal Communities and the Police*, Sydney: Allen and Unwin.

—— (2007) 'Reflections on criminal justice police since the Royal Commission into Aboriginal Deaths in Custody', in N. Gillespie (ed.) *Reflections: 40 Years on from the 1967 Referendum*, Adelaide: Aboriginal Legal Rights Movement.

Dauvergne, C. (2007) 'Security and migration law in a less brave world', *Social and Legal Studies*, 16: 533–49.

—— (2008) *Making People Illegal: What Globalization Means for Migration and Law*, New York: Cambridge University Press.

Deegan, B. (2008) *Visa Subclass Integrity Review*, Canberra: Department of Immigration and Citizenship.

Deleuze, G. (1992) 'Postscript on the societies of control', *October*, 59(Winter): 3–7.

Department of Immigration and Citizenship (2007) *Identity Matters: Strategic Plan for Identity Management in DIAC 2007–10*, Canberra: Australian Government.

—— (2009) *Department of Immigration and Citizenship Annual Report 2008–09*, Canberra: Commonwealth of Australia.

—— (2011) *Department of Immigration and Citizenship Annual Report 2010–11*, Canberra: Commonwealth of Australia.

—— (2012) *Department of Immigration and Citizenship Annual Report 2011–12*, Canberra: Commonwealth of Australia.

Department of Immigration and Multicultural and Indigenous Affairs (2004) *The Department of Immigration, Multicultural and Indigenous Affairs Submission to the Senate Standing Committee for the Scrutiny of Bills Inquiry into the Government's Response to the Previous Report by the Senate Standing Committee for the Scrutiny of Bills on Entry and Search Provisions Tabled in 2000*, Canberra: DIMIA.

—— (2005) *Managing the Border: Immigration Compliance 2004–05 Edition*, Canberra: Commonwealth of Australia.

Deukmedjian, J. (2002) *The Evolution and Alignment of RCMP Conflict Management and Organizational Surveillance*, Toronto: Centre of Criminology, University of Toronto.

Dickins, L. (1995) 'Immigration issues for police: Migration Reform Act', *Policing Issues and Practice Journal*, 3: 1–15.

Dixon, D. (1997) *Law in Policing: Legal Regulation and Police Practices*, Oxford: Oxford University Press.

—— (1999) *A Culture of Corruption: Changing an Australian Police Culture*, Sydney: Federation/Hawkins Press.

—— (2005) 'Why don't the police stop crime?' *The Australian and New Zealand Journal of Criminology*, 38: 4–24.

Dixon, D. and Schimmel, J. (2002) 'What's wrong with the Law Enforcement Bill?' *Law Society Journal*, 40: 58–61.

Dunham, R., Alpert, G., Stroshine, M. and Bennett, K. (2005) 'Transforming citizens into suspects: factors that influence the formation of police suspicion', *Police Quarterly*, 8: 366–93.

Dupont, B. (2004) 'Security in the age of networks', *Policing and Society*, 14: 76–91.

Dux, M. (2005) 'The lowbrow approach to whistleblowing', *The Age* online, 18 September, Melbourne: Fairfax, retrieved from: http://www.theage.com.au/news/opinion/the-lowbrow-approach-to-whistleblowing/2005/09/17/1126750162628.html

Education Employment and Workplace Relations References Committee (2009) *Welfare of International Students*, Canberra: Commonwealth of Australia.

Ericson, R. V. and Haggerty, K. D. (1997) *Policing the Risk Society*, Oxford: Clarendon Press.

Evans, C. (2008) 'New directions in detention: restoring integrity to Australia's immigration system', speech delivered at the Australian National University, Canberra.

Ewart, H. (2005) 'Immigration Department under the spotlight', *The 7.30 Report*, ABC television programme, 19 May.

Fekete, L. (1997) 'Blackening the economy: the path to convergence', *Race and Class: Special Issue on Europe – The Wages of Racism*, 39: 1–18.

Finnane, M. (1994) *Police and Government: Histories of Policing in Australia*, Melbourne: Oxford University Press.

—— (2009) 'Controlling the "alien" in mid twentieth-century Australia: the origins and fate of a policing role', *Policing and Society*, 19: 442–67.

Fisher, D. (2009) 'Crime family banished from Aust to NZ', *The New Zealand Herald* online, 22 February, retrieved from: http://www.nzherald.co.nz/nz/news/article.cfm?c_id=1&objectid=10558021.

Fiss, O. (1999) *A Community of Equals: The Constitutional Protection of New Americans*, Boston, MA: Beacon Press.

Fitzgerald, J. (2000) 'Knife offences and policing', Sydney: NSW Bureau of Crime Statistics and Research.

Foreign Affairs, Defence and Trade References Committee (2005) *The Removal, Search for and Discovery of Ms Vivian Solon: Final Report*, Canberra: Commonwealth of Australia.

Garland, D. (1996) 'The limits of the sovereign state: strategies of crime control in contemporary society', *British Journal of Criminology*, 36: 445–71.

—— (1997) '"Governmentality" and the problem of crime: Foucault, criminology, sociology', *Theoretical Criminology*, 1: 173–214.

—— (2001) *The Culture of Control: Crime and Social Order in Contemporary Society*, Oxford: Oxford University Press.

Gaynor, T. (2011) 'US illegal immigrant population steady', *Reuters*, 1 February.

Gelsthorpe, L. (1985) *The Community Service Volunteers/Kent Initiative: Report IV*, London: Community Service Volunteers.

Gilboy, J. A. (1998) 'Compelled third party participation in the regulatory process: legal duties, culture, and noncompliance', *Law and Policy*, 20(2): 135–55.

Grewcock, M. (2005) 'Slipping through the net? Some thoughts on the Cornelia Rau and Vivian Alvarez Inquiry', *Current Issues in Criminal Justice*, 17: 284–90.

—— (2011) 'Punishment, deportation and parole: the detention and removal of former prisoners under section 501 Migration Act 1958', *Australian and New Zealand Journal of Criminology*, 44: 56–73.

Haggerty, K. D., Wilson, D. and Smith, G. (2011) 'Theorizing surveillance in crime control', *Theoretical Criminology*, 15: 231–7.

Hall and Partners (2012) *The Management of Enforced Removals from Australia: A Client Perspective*, Carlton, Victoria: Hall & Partners Open Mind.

Hamilton-Smith, N. and Patel, S. (2005) 'Determining identity and nationality in local policing', London: Home Office.

Howells, S. (2011) *Report of the 2010 Review of the Migration Amendment (Employer Sanctions) Act 2007*, Canberra: Commonwealth of Australia.

Human Rights Committee (2011) *Nystrom v Australia*, Geneva: United Nations.

Immigration Policy Centre (2012) *The 287(G) Program: A Flawed and Obsolete Method of Immigration Enforcement*, Washington DC: Immigration Policy Centre.

Inda, J. X. (2006) *Targeting Immigrants: Government, Technology, Ethics*, Oxford: Blackwell.

Institute of Race Relations (1987) *Policing against Black People*, London: Institute of Race Relations.

Johnston, L. and Shearing, C. (2003) *Governing Security: Explorations in Policing and Justice*, London: Routledge.

Joint Standing Committee on Migration (2007) *Temporary Visas … Permanent Benefits: Ensuring the Effectiveness, Fairness and Integrity of the Temporary Business Visa Program*, Canberra: Commonwealth of Australia.

Karvelas, P. (2007) 'Jump in calls to dob centre', *The Australian*, 2 March, retrieved from: http://www.theaustralian.com.au/news/nation/jump-in-calls-to-dob-centre/story-e6frg6nf-1111113084712.

Kaufman, E. (2012) 'Finding foreigners: race and the politics of memory in British prisons', *Population, Space and Place*, 18: 701–14.

Khashu, A. (2009) *The Role of Local Police: Striking a Balance Between Immigration Enforcement and Civil Liberties*, Washington: Police Foundation.

Khosravi, S. (2010) *'Illegal' Traveller: An Auto-ethnography of Borders*, Basingstoke: Palgrave Macmillan.

Krasmann, S. (2007) 'The enemy on the border: critique of a programme in favour of a preventive state', *Punishment and Society*, 9: 301–18.

Lancet (2008) 'Migrant health: what are doctors' leaders doing?' Editorial, *The Lancet*, 19–25 January, 371(9608): 178.

Layder, D. (1993) *New Strategies in Social Research*, Cambridge: Polity Press

Leapman, B. (2005) 'Immigration checks on tube passengers banned', *London Evening Standard*, 15 February.

Lippert, R. (2002) 'Policing property and moral risk through promotions, anonymization and rewards: crime stoppers revisited', *Social and Legal Studies*, 11: 475–502.

Loader, I. (2000) 'Plural policing and democratic governance', *Social and Legal Studies*, 9: 323–45.

—— (2006) 'Policing, recognition and belonging', *Annals of the American Academy of Political and Social Science*, 605: 201–21.

Loader, I. and Walker, N. (2007) *Civilizing Security*, Cambridge: Cambridge University Press.

Lyon, D. (2001) *Surveillance Society: Monitoring Everyday Life*, Buckingham: Open University Press.

—— (2003) *Surveillance as Social Sorting*, London: Routledge.

—— (2005) 'The border is everywhere: ID cards, surveillance and the other', in E. Zureik and M. Salter (eds) *Global Surveillance and Policing: Borders, Security, Identity*, Uffculme, Devon: Willan Publishing.

McConville, M., Sanders, A. and Leng, R. (1991) *The Case for the Prosecution: Police Suspects and the Construction of Criminality*, London: Routledge.

McDowell, M. and Wonders, N. (2009–10) 'Keeping migrants in their place: technologies of control and racialized public space in Arizona', *Social Justice*, 36: 54–72.

Macklin, A. (2006) 'Exile on main street: popular discourse and legal manoeuvres around citizenship', in Law Commission of Canada (ed.) *Law and Citizenship*, Vancouver: UBC Press.

Maley, P. and Taylor, P. (2010) 'Boat crisis forces visa-raid halt', *The Australian*, 16 April.

Marginson, S., Nyland, C., Sawir, E. and Forbes-Mewett, H. (2010) *International Student Security*, Melbourne: Cambridge University Press.

Mattelart, A. (2010) *The Globalization of Surveillance*, Cambridge: Polity Press.

Mazerolle, L. and Ransley, J. (2006) *Third Party Policing*, Cambridge: Cambridge University Press.

Metcalfe, A. (2005) 'Implications of the Palmer Report: future changes', *IPPA Seminar*, 25 November.

—— (2007) 'Managing risk in times of change', *Comcover's 2007 Senior Executive Risk Management Forum*, Canberra: Department of Immigration and Citizenship.

Michalowski, R. (2007) 'Border militarization and migrant suffering: a case of transnational social injury', *Social Justice*, 34: 62–76.

Migration Review Tribunal (2010) *Migration Review Tribunal and the Refugee Review Tribunal Annual Report 2009–2010*, Sydney: MRT and the Refugee Review Tribunal.

Ministry of Justice (2010) *Statistics on Race and the Criminal Justice System 2008–09: A Ministry of Justice publication under Section 95 of the Criminal Justice Act 1991*, London: Ministry of Justice.

Moore, M. and Knox, M. (2007) '"Out-of-pocket" workers lose visas', *The Sydney Morning Herald*, 19 September, retrieved from: http://www.smh.com.au/news/national/outofpocket-workers-lose-visas/2007/09/18/1189881513652.html.

Muir, H. (2012) 'Border Agency teams up with police in drive to target foreign criminals', *The Guardian*, 5 October, retrieved from: http://www.guardian.co.uk/uk/2012/oct/05/border-agency-police-foreign-criminals.

Muller, B. (2005) 'Borders, bodies and biometrics: towards identity management', in E. Zureik and M. Salter (eds) *Global Surveillance and Policing: Borders, Security, Identity*, Uffculme, Devon: Willan Publishing.

Neighbour, S. (2011) 'Comment: Hazara asylum seekers', *The Monthly*, June.

Neocleous, M. (2000) *The Fabrication of Social Order: A Critical Theory of Police Power*, London: Pluto Press.

Nicholls, G. (2007) *Deported: A History of Forced Departures from Australia*, Sydney: UNSW Press.

—— (2008) 'Immigration's culture war', *Inside Story*, 2 November, retrieved from http://inside.org.au/immigration-culture-war/.

NSW Ombudsman (2000) *Policing Public Safety: Report under s.6 of the Crimes Legislation Amendment (Police and Public Safety) Act 1998*, Sydney: New South Wales Ombusdman.

—— (2006) *Annual Report 2005–06*, Sydney: New South Wales Ombudsman.

—— (2008) *Review of the Police Powers (Drug Detection Trial) Act 2003*, Sydney: New South Wales Ombudsman.

NSW Police Force (2012) *Annual Report 2011–12: Serving the State of New South Wales*, Sydney: New South Wales Police Force.

O'Malley, P. (1997) 'Policing, politics and postmodernity', *Social & Legal Studies*, 6(3): 363–81.

Palmer, M. (2005) *Inquiry into the Circumstances of the Immigration Detention of Cornelia Rau*, Canberra: Department of Immigration and Multicultural and Indigenous Affairs.

Parnell, S. (2012) 'Visitors sending our health bills sky-rocketing', *The Australian*, 9 November, retrieved from: http://www.theaustralian.com.au/national-affairs/health/visitors-sending-our-health-bills-sky-rocketing/story-fn59nokw-1226513360318.

Phillips KPA and Lifelong Learning Associates (2005) *Evaluation of the Education Services for Overseas Students Act 2000*, Canberra: Department of Education, Science and Training.

Pickering, S. (2005) *Refugees and State Crime*, Sydney: Federation Press.

Pickering, S. and McCulloch, J. (2010) 'Counter-terrorism policing and the Haneef case', *Policing and Society*, 20: 21–38.

Pickering, S. and Weber, L. (2013) 'Policing transversal borders', in K. Aas and M. Bosworth (eds) *The Borders of Punishment: Criminal Justice, Citizenship and Social Exclusion*, Oxford: Oxford University Press.

Pinkerton, C., McLaughlin, G. and Salt, J. (2004) *Sizing the Illegally Resident Population in the UK: Home Office Online Report 58/04*, London: Home Office Online Report 58/04.

Pratt, A. (2005) *Securing Borders: Detention and Deportation in Canada*, Vancouver: UBC Press.

Preston, J. (2010) 'Number of illegal immigrants in US fell, study says', *The New York Times*, 1 September, retrieved from: http://www.nytimes.com/2010/09/02/us/02immig.html.

Proust, E. (2008) *Evaluation of the Palmer and Comrie Reform Agenda, Including Related Ombudsman Reports*, Canberra: DIAC.

Provine, D. M. (2013) 'Disappearing rights: how states are eroding membership in American society', in M. J. Guia, M. van der Woude, and J. van der Leun (eds) *Social Control and Justice: Crimmigration in the Age of Fear*, The Hague: Eleven International Publishing.

Quinton, P. (2011) 'The formation of suspicions: police stop and search practices in England and Wales', *Policing and Society*, 21: 357–68.

Reiner, R. (1997) 'Policing and the police', in M. Maguire, R. Morgan and R. Reiner (eds) *The Oxford Handbook of Criminology*, Oxford: Clarendon Press.

—— (2000) *The Politics of the Police (3rd edition)*, Oxford: Oxford University Press.

Rimmer, S. (2008) 'Character as destiny: the dangers of character tests in Commonwealth law', *Weekend of Ideas*, Manning Clark House, Canberra: Australia Institute.

Roach, K. and Choudry, S. (2003) 'Racial and ethnic profiling: statutory discretion, constitutional remedies, and democratic accountability', *Osgoode Hall Law Journal*, 41(1): 1–36.

Robson, C. (1993) *Real World Research: A Resource for Social Scientists and Practitioner-Researchers*, Oxford: Blackwell Publishers.

Rose, N. (1999) *Powers of Freedom: Reframing Political Thought*, Cambridge: Cambridge University Press.

Rose, N. (2000) 'Government and control', *British Journal of Criminology: Special Issue on Criminology and Social Theory*, 40: 321–39.

Sassen, S. (1996) *Losing Control? Sovereignty in an Age of Globalization*, New York: Columbia University Press.

Schuster, L. (2005) 'The continuing mobility of migrants in Italy: shifting between places and statuses', *Journal of Ethnic and Migration Studies*, 31: 757–74.

Senate Education, Employment and Workplace Relations References Committee (2009) *Welfare of International Students*, Canberra: Commonwealth of Australia.

Senate Legal and Constitutional Affairs Legislation Committee (2006) *Inquiry into the Provisions of the Migration Amendment (Designated Unauthorised Arrivals) Bill 2006*, Canberra: Commonwealth of Australia.

Senate Legal and Constitutional Affairs References Committee (2006) *Administration and Operation of the Migration Act 1958*, Canberra: Commonwealth of Australia.

Sharma, M. (2008) 'Immigration plugs $44m budget gap', *Australian IT*, 7 February, Canberra, retrieved from: http://www.theaustralian.com.au/australian-it-old/immigration-plugs-44m-budget-gap/story-e6frgamf-1111115499954.

Sharp, D. and Atherton, S. (2007) 'To serve and protect? The experience of policing in the community of young people from black and other ethnic minority groups', *British Journal of Criminology*, 47: 746–63.

Shearing, C. and Wood, J. (2003) 'Nodal governance, democracy, and the new "denizens"', *Journal of Law and Society*, 30: 400–19.

Sheptycki, J. (1998) 'The global cops cometh: reflections on transnationalization, knowledge work and policing subculture', *The British Journal of Sociology*, 49: 57–74.

—— (2002) 'Accountability across the policing field: towards a general cartography of accountability for post-modern policing', *Policing and Society*, 12: 323–38.

Shiner, M. (2010) 'Post-Lawrence policing in England and Wales: guilt, innocence and the defence of organizational ego', *British Journal of Criminology*, 50: 935–53.

Shopfront Youth Legal Centre (2008) 'Police powers and your rights', Sydney: The Shopfront Youth Legal Centre.

Simon, J. (2007) *Governing through Crime: How the War on Crime Transformed American Democracy and Created a Culture of Fear*, New York: Oxford University Press.

Skogan, W. (2005) 'Citizen satisfaction with police encounters', *Police Quarterly*, 8: 298–321.

—— (2006) 'Asymmetry in the impact of encounters with police', *Policing and Society*, 16: 99–126.

Stumpf, J. (2006) 'The crimmigration crisis: immigrants, crime, and sovereign power', *bepress Legal Series*, Working Paper 1635.

—— (2013) 'Social control and justice: crimmigration in the age of fear', in M. J. Guia, M. van der Woude, and J. Van der Leun (eds) *Social Control and Justice: Crimmigration in the Age of Fear*, The Hague: Eleven International Publishing.

Tyler, T. R. and Wakslak, C. J. (2004) 'Profiling and police legitimacy: procedural justice, attributions of motive, and acceptance of police authority', *Criminology*, 42: 253–82.

US Department of Justice Civil Rights Division (2011) *United States' Investigation of the Maricopa County Sheriffs Office*, Washington DC: US Department of Justice.

Van der Leun, J. (2003) *Looking for Loopholes: Processes of Incorporation of Illegal Immigrants in the Netherlands*, Amsterdam: Amsterdam University Press.

Van der Leun, J. and van der Woude, M. (2013) 'A reflection on crimmigration in the Netherlands', in M. J. Guia, M. van der Woude, and J. Van der Leun (eds) *Social Control and Justice: Crimmigration in the Age of Fear*, The Hague: Eleven International Publishing.

Vasagar, J. (2012) 'Student visa row damages image of UK higher education, warns LSE chief', *The Guardian*, 5 October, retrieved from: http://www.guardian.co.uk/education/2012/oct/05/student-visa-row-image-overseas-lse.

Victoria Police (1990) 'Theme 5: implications of immigration policies', National Conference on Police Services in a Multicultural Australia, 28–31 August, Melbourne.

Waddington, P. A. J. (1999) *Policing Citizens: Authority and Rights*, London: Routledge.

Walsh, T. and Taylor, M. (2007) '"You're not welcome here": police move-on powers and discrimination law', *UNSW Law Journal*, 30: 151–73.

Walters, W. (2002) 'Deportation, expulsion and the international police of aliens', *Citizenship Studies*, 6: 265–92.

Waterford, J. (2008) 'From Ruddock to new rudders: has the culture of the immigration department really changed', *The Canberra Times*, 30 July, retrieved from: http://apo.org.au/commentary/ruddock-new-rudders.

Watson, R. and Saurine, A. (2008) 'Samoan mother and son from hell', *The Daily Telegraph*, Sydney, 15 November, retrieved from: http://www.dailytelegraph.com.au/news/samoan-mother-and-son-from-hell/story-e6freuy9-1111118040815.

Watson, S. (2009) *The Securitization of Humanitarian Migration: Digging Moats and Sinking Boats*, London: Routledge.

Webber, F. (2004) 'The war on migration', in P. Hillyard, C. Pantazis, S. Tombs and D. Gordon (eds) *Beyond Criminology: Taking Harm Seriously*, London: Pluto Press.

Weber, L. (2002a) 'The detention of asylum seekers: 20 reasons why criminologists should care', *Current Issues in Criminal Justice: Special Issue – Refugee issues and criminology*, 14(1): 9–30.

—— (2002b) 'Decisions to detain asylum seekers: routine, duty or individual choice?' in L. Gelsthorpe and N. Padfield (eds) *Exercising Discretion: Decision-making in the Criminal Justice System and Beyond*, Uffculme, Devon: Willan Publishing.

—— (2003) 'Down that wrong road: discretion in decisions to detain asylum seekers arriving at UK ports', *The Howard Journal of Criminal Justice*, 42: 248–62.

—— (2005) 'The detention of asylum seekers as a crime of obedience', *Critical Criminology*, 13: 89–109.

—— (2007) 'Policing the virtual border: punitive preemption in Australian offshore migration controls', *Social Justice: Special Issue on Transnational Criminology*, 34.

—— (2011) '"It sounds like they shouldn't be here": immigration checks on the streets of Sydney', *Policing and Society*, 21(4): 456–67.

Weber, L. and Bowling, B. (2004) 'Policing migration: a framework for investigating the regulation of global mobility', *Policing and Society*, 14: 195–212.

—— (2008) 'Valiant beggars and global vagabonds: select, eject, immobilise', *Theoretical Criminology*, 12: 355–75.

—— (eds) (2012) *Stop and Search: Police Power in Global Context*, London: Routledge Special Issue Into Book (SPIB) series.

Weber, L. and Landman, T. (2002) 'Deciding to detain: the organisational context for decisions to detain asylum seekers at UK ports', Colchester: Human Rights Centre, University of Essex.

Weber, L. and Pickering, S. (forthcoming) 'Constructing voluntarism: technologies of "intent management" in Australian border controls', in H. Schwenken and S. Russ (eds) *New Border and Citizenship Politics*, Basingstoke: Palgrave Macmillan.

Williams, G. (2008) 'New refugee solution needs legal help', *The Canberra Times*, 2 August, retrieved from: http://www.gtcentre.unsw.edu.au/sites/gtcentre.unsw.edu.au/files/mdocs/Mandatory_Detention.pdf.

Wilson, D. (2012) 'Bringing the border back home: local immigration policing in the UK', Paper presented at CEPS Policing and Security Conference, 5 October 2012, Melbourne.

Wood, J. and Shearing, C. (2007) *Imagining Security*, Uffculme, Devon: Willan Publishing.

Yin, R. (2009) *Case Study Research: Design and Methods*, Thousand Oaks, CA: Sage.

Young, J. (2003) 'To these wet and windy shores: recent immigration policy in the UK', *Punishment and Society*, 5: 449–62.

Zedner, L. (2007) 'Pre-crime and post-criminology?' *Theoretical Criminology*, 11: 261–81.

—— (2009) *Security*, London: Routledge.

—— (2010) 'Security, the state, and the citizen: the changing architecture of crime control', *New Criminal Law Review*, 13: 379–403.

INDEX